Money Changes Everything

A BEDFORD SPOTLIGHT READER

Money Changes Everything

A BEDFORD SPOTLIGHT READER

Lawrence Weinstein
Bentley University

Bedford/St. Martin's

Boston | New York

For Bedford/St. Martin's

Publisher for Composition: Leasa Burton
Executive Editor: John E. Sullivan III
Developmental Editor: Sophia Snyder
Publishing Services Manager: Andrea Cava
Production Supervisor: Lisa McDowell
Marketing Manager: Emily Rowin
Project Management: Westchester Publishing Services
Senior Art Director: Anna Palchik
Text Design: Castle Design
Cover Design: Billy Boardman
Cover Photo: *Cash register drawer* © Steven Puetzer/Getty Images
Composition: Westchester Publishing Services
Printing and Binding: RR Donnelley and Sons

President, Bedford/St. Martin's: Denise B. Wydra
Editor in Chief: Karen S. Henry
Director of Marketing: Karen R. Soeltz
Production Director: Susan W. Brown
Director of Rights and Permissions: Hilary Newman

Manufactured in the United States of America.

8 7 6 5
f e d c

For information, write: Bedford/St. Martin's, 75 Arlington Street, Boston, MA 02116 (617-399-4000)

ISBN 978-1-4576-2855-9

Acknowledgments

Acknowledgments and copyrights are continued at the back of the book on pages 317–20, which constitute an extension of the copyright page. It is a violation of the law to reproduce these selections by any means whatsoever without the written permission of the copyright holder.

The Bedford Spotlight Reader Series is a new line of single-theme readers, each featuring Bedford's trademark care and quality. The readers in the series collect thoughtfully chosen readings sufficient for an entire writing course — about thirty-five selections — to allow instructors to provide carefully developed, high-quality instruction at an affordable price. Bedford Spotlight Readers are designed to help students make inquiries from multiple perspectives, opening up topics such as money, food, sustainability, and gender to critical analysis. An Editorial Board, made up of a dozen compositionists at schools focusing on specific themes, has assisted in the development of the series.

Spotlight Readers offer plenty of material for a composition course while keeping the price low. Combine a Spotlight Reader with a handbook or rhetoric and save 20 percent off the combined price. Or package your Spotlight Reader with *Critical Reading and Writing: A Bedford Spotlight Rhetoric,* a brief rhetoric covering the essentials of critical reading, the writing process, and research, for free (a $10 value).

Each volume in the series offers multiple perspectives on the topic and its effects on individuals and society. Chapters are built around central questions such as "What Determines What We Eat?" and "What Rituals Shape Our Gender?" and so offer numerous entry points for inquiry and discussion. High-interest readings, chosen for their suitability in the classroom, provide a mix of genres and disciplines, as well as accessible and challenging selections to allow instructors to tailor their approach to each classroom. Each chapter thus brings to light related — even surprising — questions and ideas.

A rich editorial apparatus provides a sound pedagogical foundation. A general introduction, chapter introductions, and headnotes provide context. Following each selection, writing prompts provide avenues of inquiry tuned to different levels of engagement, from reading comprehension ("Understanding the Text"), to critical analysis ("Reflection and Response"), to the kind of integrative analysis appropriate to the research paper ("Making Connections"). A Web site for the series offers support for teaching: **bedfordstmartins.com/spotlight**.

Preface for Instructors

Give college students half a chance to mull the ways they are affected by money, and they'll shortly have an overwhelming number of things to say on the subject — far more than enough to energize their work on the several papers we assign to them in a semester-long writing course. That's what I learned in piloting materials for this book.

I was pleased but not surprised. As nationwide surveys of our students have revealed, the percentage who identify the benefits of college in financial terms is nearly double what it was in 1967 — now, approximately 75%.[1] They have come to college largely on a mission to match or surpass their parents' standard of living.

Even were that not the case, they would find "money issues" inescapable:

- Growing up, they've witnessed countless hard or celebrative family moments that *concern* money.

- Once they arrive on campus, most of them take charge of their budgets for living expenses.

- A great many of them now incur onerous levels of debt to attend college.

- Those who leave their home neighborhoods when they matriculate come face-to-face with peers who are not of their own social class.

- In addition, they're aware that soon they'll be expected to declare majors, an initial step toward low- or high-paying careers. Consequently, they engage in many late-night conversations in which salary looms large.

- Through it all, they are subjected to a media barrage of images associating money with pleasure and status.

- Some of them have started following stories in the news, a very large fraction of which deal with either greed or economic duress.

---

[1] Pryor, J. H., Eagan, K., Palucki Blake, L., Hurtado, S., Berdan, J., and Case, M. H. *The American Freshman: National Norms, Fall 2012.* Los Angeles: UCLA Higher Education Research Institute, 2013.

Money Changes Everything is not an economics text. It's an anthology compiled with first-year college students in mind, much less about technical matters like the GNP and the multiplier effect than about the effects, positive and negative, that the pursuit of money — and the possession of it or lack of it — have on quality of life and the human spirit. It combines thoughtful, mostly nontechnical analysis with memoir, fiction, and art. It takes up a broad range of questions about money that engage students: In what sense, if any, can money buy happiness? How does money alter friendships and family dynamics? Is money to blame for unethical behavior? Does the income gap square with our ideal of being "born equal"? Has money blinded us to higher life-values?

Over the past five years, I have read several hundred book chapters, articles, short stories, and other texts on money, with an eye to finding those likeliest to capture students' interest and to spur them to write in a course devoted to their growth as writers. *Money Changes Everything* is the result. In Chapter 1 — where the mix of types of reading is representative of the book as a whole — selections run the gamut from an affecting short story (Rebecca Curtis's "Twenty Grand") to a much-cited scholarly article (David G. Myers's "The Funds, Friends, and Faith of Happy People") and a famously successful TV ad campaign (the Master-Card "Priceless" ads). Ideologically, they range from a liberal's account of hardships endured by the lower classes in America (a chapter from Barbara Ehrenreich's *Nickel and Dimed*) to a conservative pundit's closely reasoned effort to cast doubt on the usual connections made between money and life-satisfaction (Charles Murray's "What's So Bad about Being Poor?").

Every item in this reader can be made the basis of a course paper. As you will see from the prompts that follow each selection, it leads naturally to questions of all three major types assigned at the college level: questions of comprehension, which appear in this book under the heading "Understanding the Text"; questions of judgment, indicated by the heading "Reflection and Response"; and questions that involve *juxtaposing* different texts (often with research entailed), corresponding to the heading "Making Connections." In addition, a good third of the items in this anthology are short enough to be both read and discussed during class time. This latter category, suitable to be deployed in *or* out of class, includes charts, art, and a few prose readings of only two or three pages in length.

I have piloted most of the selections in this book in classes of my own in Expository Writing on the theme of money. In my thirty-seven years of teaching at the college level, I have never seen students happier to read what they were handed or more willing to grapple with it in serious ways.

At term's end, a few have volunteered that the course was "life-changing." For a much larger number, it was definitely "writing-changing."

Finally, with that reference to real students echoing in my own ear, I am reminded of one more point about this book: Apart from theme and the array of genres, its most distinguishing feature is probably the student presence in it. For example:

- the first assignment in the book, **Your Subconscious World of Money** (page 3), is not about readings at all: it's a preliminary inventory, in which students surface and reflect on the long experience with money they've already had in life

- my section of advice on critical reading, **Finding More to Say about What You Read** (page 6), is stocked largely with comments students themselves have written in the margins of their books

- even some of the writing prompts that accompany items in the book contain quotes from students.

I — like you, I suspect — want all of our students to know that, with time and effort, they, too, will be capable of generating thought in writing worthy to be published.

Acknowledgments

I owe an outsized debt of gratitude to the many people who contributed to this book. Since its theme is money, perhaps I'll be forgiven for expressing my thanks thus:

I wish I had a dollar for

. . . each colleague, student, friend, and brother (literal brother of mine) who pointed me the way to readings worth considering — Joan Atlas, Ethan Bolker, Chris Boucher, John Case, Kathy Daly, Samir Dayal, Karen Delorey, Evelyn Farbman, Liz Galoozis, Bruce Herzberg, Diane Kellogg, Dale Kuntz, Rob Mills, Will Pang, Lowry Pei, Martha Singer, Duncan Spelman, Gerry Stenerson, Scott Sumner, Jonathan Tetrault, Warren Weinstein, and Edward Zlotkowski.[2]

. . . each experienced teacher at a U.S. college who reviewed my book proposal at the request of Bedford/St. Martin's — Craig Bartholomaus, Metropolitan Community College, Penn Valley; Robert Cummings,

---

[2] Six of these supportive, well-read human beings belonged to Bentley University's Class Book Committee, chaired by Duncan Spelman, where the idea for an anthology dwelling at the intersection of money and well-being had its birth.

University of Mississippi; Lynée Lewis Gaillet, Georgia State University; Karen Gardiner, University of Alabama; Chris Geyer, Cazenovia College; Christine Howell, Metropolitan Community College, Penn Valley; Samantha Looker, University of Wisconsin, Oshkosh; Derek Malone-France, George Washington University; Stephanie Odom, University of Texas at Austin; Megan O'Neill, Stetson University; Sara Raley, McDaniel College; Casey Rothschild, Wellesley College; Michelle Sidler, Auburn University; and Anne Trubek, Oberlin College.

. . . each senior member of the Bedford/St. Martin's team who believed in the project and committed their company's venerable imprint to it — in particular, Leasa Burton and John Sullivan.

. . . each former student who allowed me to quote him or her in this book, especially those who allowed me to quote them at length — Kelly Brown, Justin Lawlor, Alicia Maillet, and Brian Tobia.

. . . each reader who provided me invaluable feedback on the almost 30,000 words here that are mine — my wife Diane; my honest neighbor (and fellow writer) Nick Kilmer; and my gifted (not to mention admirably tactful) editor at Bedford/St. Martin's, Sophia Snyder.

. . . each person who was involved in production of the book — most notably, Debbie Masi, who never seemed to let ten minutes elapse between my transmission of a query or request and her response.

Of all those named above, however, one needs to be singled out a second time. Beyond always serving as the first reader of my prose, Diane Weinstein frequently searched libraries for me, read the same published items I was considering and offered me astute reactions to them, and supported me with love through a largish number of reversals until the project was completed.

Lawrence Weinstein

You Get More Choices

Bedford/St. Martin's offers resources and format choices that help you and your students get even more out of the book and your course. To learn more about or order any of the following products, contact your Bedford/St. Martin's sales representative, e-mail sales support (sales_support@bfwpub.com), or visit the Web site at **bedfordstmartins.com/spotlight/catalog**.

Choose the Flexible *Bedford e-Portfolio*

Students can collect, select, and reflect on their coursework and personalize and share their *e-Portfolio* for any audience. Instructors can provide as much or as little structure as they see fit. Rubrics and learning outcomes can be aligned to student work, so instructors and programs can gather reliable and useful assessment data. Every *Bedford e-Portfolio* comes pre-loaded with *Portfolio Keeping* and *Portfolio Teaching*, by Nedra Reynolds and Elizabeth Davis. *Bedford e-Portfolio* can be purchased separately or packaged with the book at a significant discount. An activation code is required. To order *e-Portfolio* with the print book, use ISBN 978-1-4576-8037-3. Visit **bedfordstmartins.com/eportfolio**.

Watch Peer Review Work

Eli Review lets instructors scaffold their assignments in a clearer, more effective way for students—making peer review more visible and teachable. *Eli* can be purchased separately or packaged with the book at a significant discount. An activation code is required. To order *Eli Review* with the print book, use ISBN 978-1-4576-8040-3. Visit **bedfordstmartins.com/eli**.

Select Value Packages

Add value to your course by packaging one of the following resources with *Money Changes Everything* at a significant discount. To learn more about package options, contact your Bedford/St. Martin's sales representative or visit **bedfordstmartins.com/spotlight/catalog**.

- ***Critical Reading and Writing: A Bedford Spotlight Rhetoric,* by Jeff Ousborne**, provides a brief overview of the critical reading, writing, and research process — for free when packaged (a $10 value). To order *Critical Reading and Writing* packaged with *Money Changes Everything*, use ISBN 978-1-4576-8299-5.

- *EasyWriter,* **Fifth Edition, by Andrea Lunsford,** distills Andrea Lunsford's teaching and research into the essentials that today's writers need to make good choices in any rhetorical situation. To order *EasyWriter* packaged with *Money Changes Everything,* use ISBN 978-1-4576-8387-9.

- *A Pocket Style Manual,* **Sixth Edition, by Diana Hacker and Nancy Sommers,** is a straightforward, inexpensive quick reference, with content flexible enough to suit the needs of writers in the humanities, social sciences, sciences, health professions, business, fine arts, education, and beyond. To order *A Pocket Style Manual* with *Money Changes Everything,* use ISBN 978-1-4576-8386-2.

- *LearningCurve for Readers and Writers,* Bedford/St. Martin's adaptive quizzing program, quickly learns what students already know and helps them practice what they don't yet understand. Game-like quizzing motivates students to engage with their course, and reporting tools help teachers discern their students' needs. An activation code is required. To order *LearningCurve* packaged with *Money Changes Everything,* use ISBN 978-1-4576-8041-0. For details, visit **bedfordstmartins.com /englishlearningcurve**.

- *Portfolio Keeping,* **Third Edition, by Nedra Reynolds and Elizabeth Davis,** provides all the information students need to use the portfolio method successfully in a writing course. *Portfolio Teaching,* a companion guide for instructors, provides the practical information instructors and writing program administrators need to use the portfolio method successfully in a writing course. To order *Portfolio Keeping* packaged with *Money Changes Everything,* use ISBN 978-1-4576-8044-1.

Try *Re:Writing 2* for Fun

What's the fun of teaching writing if you can't try something new? The best collection of free writing resources on the Web, *Re:Writing 2* gives you and your students even more ways to think, watch, practice, and learn about writing concepts. Listen to Nancy Sommers on using a teacher's comments to revise. Try a logic puzzle. Consult our resources for writing centers. All free for the fun of trying it. Visit **bedfordstmartins .com/rewriting**.

Instructor Resources

You have a lot to do in your course. Bedford/St. Martin's wants to make it easy for you to find the support you need — and to get it quickly.

- **Teaching Central** (bedfordstmartins.com/teachingcentral) offers the entire list of Bedford/St. Martin's print and online professional resources in one place. You'll find landmark reference works, sourcebooks on pedagogical issues, award-winning collections, and practical advice for the classroom — all free for instructors.

- *Bits* (bedfordbits.com) collects creative ideas for teaching a range of composition topics in an easily searchable blog format. A community of teachers — leading scholars, authors, and editors — discuss revision, research, grammar and style, technology, peer review, and much more.

- **Bedford Coursepacks** (bedfordstmartins.com/coursepacks) allow you to easily download digital materials from Bedford/St. Martin's for your course for the most common course management systems — Blackboard, Angel, Desire2Learn, Web CT, Moodle, or Sakai.

Contents

Introduction for Students

Is there a day of your life not punctuated by thoughts about money?
Pleasant thoughts about the large income you might earn in future years?
Oppressive thoughts about making ends meet in the meantime — or about
the future burden of repaying loans? Big thoughts about whether it is fair
that some inhabitants of Earth live far more comfortably than others do?
Little thoughts about whether a jacket on sale at the mall is worth the price
on its tag? As a student of mine once wrote, "A world without the issue of
money is as hard to imagine as one in which the sun does not come up in
the morning."

Americans especially have long been thought to be money-oriented.
A fictional American created by Nobel Prize-winning novelist Saul Bellow
describes money as "a vital substance like the blood or fluids that bathe the
brain's tissues" — which is a way of saying that it's always on our minds, at
some level.

But why, you ask, have I chosen money as the theme of an anthology for
first-year college students taking writing classes? I'll answer in one sentence:
Becoming someone who can read and write at a high level in college takes
practice, and students are quite understandably more willing to throw
themselves into that effort when the pieces they're assigned to read and write
about deal with subjects that already matter to them . . . like money.

That said, this is not an economics book. It won't teach you what determines wages and the pricing of goods, or even what factors led to our
society's recent devastating Great Recession. Nor will you find economics
jargon in this book. On the contrary, this book of readings deals only with
fundamental questions of how needing money, having it, and pursuing more
of it affect our quality of life and sense of well-being.

Commentators claim that money looms even larger in the consciousness
of recent generations than it did in that of past ones. They often cite a yearly
survey of more than 200,000 U.S. undergraduates, which shows that
between 1967 and 2004 the number of students who viewed college as a

place to "develop a meaningful philosophy of life" went down from 86 percent to under 40 percent, while the number who considered college a means to become "very well off financially" almost doubled to 73.8 percent.[1]

Maybe that's a good thing. The object of this book is not to turn you against money, just as it is not to make you money-mad. It's to give you a head start on deciding what you will be willing to do in life for the sake of money — even as you hone crucial reading and writing skills in the *course* of that inquiry. By the time you finish with this book, you may conclude that you've assigned wealth (or even just affluence) too high a priority in life — but you may well conclude the opposite, too: you may come to feel that you have *underestimated* how important money will be to your future happiness.

And, of course, your decision may not take a simple form, either way. It may get complicated.

Whatever you decide, a lot rides on your decision, as the readings here will demonstrate. Those readings are divided up according to the questions they address:

- **In what sense, if any, can money buy happiness?** Does it increase contentment regardless of what social class one belongs to? Does fear of death have anything to do with the pursuit of money?

- **How does money alter friendships and family dynamics?** Can dramatic changes in income level bring people together? Tear them apart? Even contribute to domestic violence?

- **Is money to blame for unethical conduct?** In what circumstances does the desire for profit induce people in business to serve the general public's true best interests? Under what conditions does it have the reverse effect?

- **Does the income gap square with our ideal of being "born equal"?** Is America's once-touted "level playing field" the world in which we live today? If not, does the situation call for action on our part?

---

[1] Pryor, J. H., Eagan, K., Palucki Blake, L., Hurtado, S., Berdan, J., and Case, M. H. *The American Freshman: National Norms, Fall 2012.* Los Angeles: UCLA Higher Education Research Institute, 2013.

- **Has money blinded us to higher life-values?** Have we let money supersede things we claim to care more about, such as good parenting, love of country, and sportsmanship? Where does the pursuit of money fit in with the tenets of various religions? Is it becoming a religion in its own right?

In sum, I have two big hopes for this book of readings. First, as a longtime teacher of expository writing at the college level, I hope the material included here provides you grist for the process of learning both to think critically and to express yourself clearly. It should do just that, if the experience of my own students is any indication. (For more along these lines, see "Finding More to Say about What You Read," beginning page 7, as well as the approximately 300 prompts for written response that follow individual readings.)

Second, I hope the pieces you encounter in this book will help you chart your own course in a world preoccupied with money.

Your Subconscious World of Money: A Preliminary Writing Assignment

You go through life with a slew of sense impressions, stories, and attitudes attached to money. After all, you have now lived 18 years or more in a world that revolves in large part around money. You have been "swimming in money" — not in the sense that you're fabulously rich, but in the sense that most of your tens of thousands of interactions on Earth have been influenced by money. You've been affected by how much of it your family has, by what all the adults in your life needed to do to earn it, by whether it was saved or freely spent, by what things were said about it in your presence, in addition to what things were said about it in books you've read and in movies and commercials you've seen. In all likelihood, your choice of college was partly determined by considerations of money. Your choice of mate, your choice of career, and a great many other future choices of yours are likely to reflect the financial side of your life history.

However, our beliefs and feelings about money are largely subterranean. We can't simply rattle them off on request (not all the real ones, anyway), because we are not usually aware of them. To surface our true attitudes — to lure them into the plain light of day and get a good look at them — we need to resort to some indirect maneuvers.

This first assignment is an opportunity to conduct a private inventory of the opinions and feelings you already have about money, so that when the current term ends, you can assess how, if at all, the readings in this book have affected you.

- In a notebook, electronic file, or blog, keep a journal for the next seven days titled "Money in My Life" or "Money Confessions." Think of it as an exhaustive collection of your memories involving money and your diverse feelings about money. Let the memories come first; once *they've* begun to flow, then your attitudes, beliefs, and nagging questions about money will come naturally — almost automatically.

- You might start with the memory of an event from yesterday:

  I had to go to the Financial Aid Office to see if I could get my scholarship increased. The worst part of it was the look of annoyance on the face of the receptionist there — how she didn't smile or even make eye contact with me, but just told me in a cold, perfunctory way to take a seat and wait my turn.

  Such a memory might lead to reflections like this one:

  Now that I relive that exchange in slow motion, I'm almost sure it was one of those times when I said to myself, "I'll bet the guys who drive BMWs to campus and order gourmet take-outs when the dining hall is closed never have to go through indignities like this." I think maybe one of my interests in money is to be treated well by others!

- Or, you might start way back — maybe with the first time you remember *making* money:

  [the memory]
  I was only seven and my teenage cousin down the street paid me a whole dollar to "pet-sit" her cat for a week. When she got back from vacation and gave me the dollar, everyone in my house asked me how I planned to spend it. I said, "No, I'm keeping it." I wanted it around just to look at.

  [the reflection]
  It's possible that even now the money that I earn is more a matter of pride than anything else. I'd have to think about that to be more sure, but it goes along with something else I just remembered . . .

It doesn't matter where you start; you'll be pulled back and forth across time by associations that arise as you write. Your lemonade stand will remind you of your admiration for someone in your family who has managed to make a living just from commission on sales. That, in turn, will set you pondering the stress involved in many jobs.

Keep your mind moving — both horizontally, from one episode to another, and vertically, going deep for better *explanations* of events. Don't be concerned if you start to contradict yourself: that's a sign your mind is on the move, encountering mistakes and complications. Don't be concerned if you are unsure about something and have to resort to speculative language ("maybe," "my impression is," etc.) — on the contrary, be concerned if you *do* feel sure all the time. That could be a sign of close-mindedness.

- Add to your journal of memories and thoughts for at least half an hour every day for the next week. Start each entry with the date. If, at the end of half an hour, you find you're on a roll, go straight on, ride it out; see how much *more* you have in you to say. Mental momentum is a terrible thing to waste.
- As you add to your journal, check that you haven't neglected areas like these:
  - mistakes that you have made with money (or have seen people make with money)
  - persons in your life — or in the world at large — whom you admire for reasons connected to money: how they made it, how they distribute it, or how they live good lives *without* much of it
  - news stories about money
  - daydreams or fantasies about money
  - actual dreams about money
  - things about money that have puzzled or fascinated you
  - the extent to which money may influence your choices in the future.
- Before you turn your journal in to your instructor, write a brief (two- or three-paragraph), informal cover note to him or her. Has this assignment led to surprises? Has it raised new questions in your mind or cast new light on old questions?

Finding More to Say about What You Read: Things I've Discovered by Looking at Notes Made by Students in the Margins of Their Books

This anthology consists mainly of articles, essays, and stories. What, exactly, do you do when you read such pieces? As you finish one, do you feel confident that you could write a three- or five-page paper about it without padding?

Here are some reading habits of successful student writers, for you to keep in mind as you read. I learned about them by being nosey — by getting a few of those successful students to let me see what comments they were making in the margins of their books. Whether consciously or not, these students were following two unspoken rules, each of which involves several powerful specific reading practices:

1. Make sense of what you read.
2. Decide whether to believe it.

1. Make Sense of What You Read

When you encounter keys terms that are new to you, make them yours. Try to surmise their meanings from context or consult a dictionary.

Say you hit the word "fungible" in a sentence reading, "Of all the manmade things on earth, money is the most fungible" — and suppose the sentences before and after that one don't make clear what "fungible" must mean. Look the word up. Add it to your vocabulary. In the margin near the sentence that includes "fungible," write,

> fungible: having the ability to be exchanged for like things.
> A car can't be assumed to have the same value as just any other car — and the same goes for houses, items of jewelry, books, living room rugs, etc. However, any dollar bill, being "fungible," can be exchanged for any other dollar bill without the slightest change in value.

By making such a marginal note, you'll (a) stand a better chance of comprehending what you're reading and (b) eventually become a more articulate writer, since having at your fingertips a larger active stock of words will increase the number of ideas you can express.

Recap important points in your own language.

One student used a margin to paraphrase ideas that he encountered in Andrew Carnegie's essay "How I Served My Apprenticeship." His way of distilling the point in a passage about how Carnegie's father, a hand-loom weaver, was put out of work by the factory system reads,

> Some people benefit from new technology, but others suffer and every-thing changes for them.

By putting Carnegie's thought into his own words, this student was consoli-dating his comprehension of the reading. He acquired more mastery of it — and later, probably remembered it better — than students who just read it passively, letting the text "wash over them," as the saying goes.

Notice tone.

Meaning is affected by voice, and tone of voice, in turn, is affected by elements like word choice and grammar — even punctuation. One student, reading Milton Friedman's essay on page 157, was convinced that she could hear Friedman *sneering* at the idea that businesses have duties to society. What she noticed — and noted in the margin — was how Friedman puts quota-tion marks around the phrase "social responsibility" in order to cast doubt on it, "as if," in this student's words, such responsibility "doesn't even exist."

Spot connections to your own experience.

As you read Barbara Ehrenreich's "Serving in Florida" (p. 36), an account of waiting on tables in Florida, it may sound to you all too similar to demeaning jobs that *you* have had. Retrieve such memories and call them into play as you make sense of Ehrenreich.

One student, in reading "Lethal Consumption: Death-Denying Materialism" (p. 75), retrieved corroborating memories about his own grandparents. In the margin of that piece, which discusses how human beings subconsciously rely on money to allay their fears of death, he wrote of how his grandparents dispense

> money and gifts to grandkids so they will be remembered as generous and will be thought of positively when they are gone.

Synthesize one reading with another.

I once laughed out loud to see the word "moocher" — just the word "moocher," without explanation — in the margin of a student's copy of a Tobias Wolff short story. The word had stood out to me and my students in a piece by libertarian Ayn Rand, who had used it to mean someone who lived off the hard work and talent of others, and the student who wrote it in the margin of Tobias Wolff's story not only remembered it but immediately saw that it applied to one of Wolff's characters. In effect, what she was saying with that single word was, "This character created by Wolff bears a notable relation to Ayn Rand's concept: he is an example of it."

An important way to get a fix on an author's idea is to situate it in relation to material by other authors:

- One author might be providing *a concrete example of the generalization* made by another author, as in the "moocher" instance above.
- One author might be setting forth *a cause or effect* of the thing described by another author.
- One author might be either *agreeing or disagreeing* with another author — or, very commonly, partly agreeing, partly disagreeing.

2. Decide Whether to Believe What You Read

Ask yourself, "Is the author credible?"

Next to the title of an article, you might insert,

> This appeared where? In *Parade* magazine–that light throwaway that gets inserted with a lot of ads in the Sunday paper? If so, these sample salaries for different jobs might have been selected just to be sensational, not typical.

As an aid in judging the trustworthiness of authors represented in this book, every headnote that accompanies a reading includes a biographical blurb about the author of the reading.

Take note of whether the author has supported his/her claims with concrete specifics.

For example, sociologist Max Weber asserts that Benjamin Franklin didn't believe in honesty as a virtue in its own right, but only as a practical necessity in money transactions. On encountering his claim, you might insist (as if you were addressing the author directly),

> Show me some hard evidence of this, Max — like some times when Franklin felt free to lie because no money was at stake.

Register the author's errors in logic.

In the margins of a reading, you might complain,

> No — you can't jump from one case (Ford Motor Company's Pinto debacle) to "all corporate America." [pointing out the fallacy of over-generalization]

or,

> The author's shifting ground now. This is not the definition of wealth she started out with in her first paragraph. [pointing out the fallacy of slippery terms]

or,

> I don't buy the either/or mentality in this article. Are my only choices (a) "to live the simple life" or (b) to be a money-grubbing workaholic? I don't think so. [pointing out the fallacy of a forced choice]

or,

> How can this guy be so sure that marital fights about money lead to divorce? Couldn't the cause of divorce be falling out of love? That is, couldn't money fights be just an early *sign* of what's to come, rather than the *reason* for it? [pointing out the fallacy called *post hoc ergo propter hoc* — meaning "*after* this, therefore *because* of this"]

Test an author's claims against firsthand knowledge you possess.

I found *this* reaction in the margin next to a reported salary that didn't jibe with what one student knew of wages in the real world:

> Tammy is a dog walker and gets paid $100,000 a year?!

My student wasn't buying it.

Sometimes, when a reader doesn't have reliable firsthand knowledge to compare an author's claim with, he or she attempts to test the claim by means of an experiment or simpler form of research. In an article on the long-term yield of compound interest, one student saw an amount that was as surprising to him as the wages of a dog walker were to the student mentioned above. He decided to pursue the matter. His note in the margin reads,

> This seems like a really high number, but I did the math and it's right.

Compare an author's thoughts with thoughts and information gleaned from other sources.

A student of mine read in a book that countries with McDonald's hamburger franchises never go to war with each other, since they have economic ties. Being skeptical, my student drew on knowledge he'd obtained from another source to lodge an objection in the margin. "Not true," he wrote — and proceeded to discuss a recent war involving Israel and Lebanon, both of which countries have McDonald's.

Generate new questions.

Use the margin of a reading to wonder,

> How come our federal government wasn't *regulating* credit default swaps?

or to wonder,

> What *explains* why some gamblers get addicted, others don't? Does it have to do with being financially desperate? Can it be traced to having had the bad luck to win a jackpot early in one's gambling experience, creating false expectations of wealth?

In Sum . . .

If you read actively — *making sense of what you read,* through practices under Rule 1 above, and *deciding whether to believe what you read,* through practices under Rule 2 above — you are likely always to have an abundance of worthwhile content for a paper. Bear it all in mind.

Keeping Track of Your More Extensive Reactions

Is it important that your reactions to a reading be written out literally within the margins? No. Margins are just handy.

Other good places to record a running commentary on your reading include index cards and a reading journal.

At times, in fact, margins won't be big enough to hold all of your thinking on a piece you read; you'll definitely need other, larger surfaces. Take, for example, the train of thought below, in which someone reacts to a proposal that, in order to reduce littering, state legislators pass a law requiring a five-cent deposit on bottles and cans. Notice how the writer ventures an initial position on the issue, then quickly sees a flaw in it and replaces it — and does the same with his next position and the one after that, driving ultimately toward a position that's a better fit with first- and secondhand experience. This is what engaged student inquiry sounds like at its best. It's too messy to submit to an instructor without revision, but it forms the basis of a strong paper.

> The law [would seek to get] people to return the bottles for five cents, instead of littering them. But I don't think five cents is enough nowadays to get people to bother. — But wait, it isn't just five cents at a blow, because people can accumulate cases of bottles or bags of cans in their basements and take them back all at once, so probably they would do that. — Still, those probably aren't the bottles and cans that get littered anyway; it's the people out on picnics or kids hanging around the streets and parks that litter bottles and cans, and they sure wouldn't bother to return them for a nickel . . . .[2]

Obviously, very few margins fit that much thinking.

Lawrence Weinstein

---

[2] Perkins, D. N., Allen, R., & Hafner, J. (1983). "Difficulties in Everyday Reasoning." In W. Maxwell (Ed.), *Thinking: The Frontier Expands* (p. 178). Philadelphia: Franklin Institute Press.

1

Can We Buy
Happiness?

n the century when America's Declaration of Independence was written, some philosophers believed a person's rights within society ought to include "life, liberty, and property." Thomas Jefferson's committee decided that a better ideal was "life, liberty, and the pursuit of happiness." America became the nation that made personal contentment a valid life-objective, not just for some people, but for all.

Why did the committee's members decide to replace "property" — meaning wealth in all its forms — with "happiness"? We don't have a transcript of their proceedings. Could one or more of them have felt that wealth was important only as a *means* to satisfaction in life — or even that it wasn't necessarily the *best* means?

Think of section 1 of this book as a chance for you to reach your own conclusions about money's role in living happily.

Two readings in the section, the firsthand account of near-poverty, "Serving in Florida," and the short story "Twenty Grand," strongly imply that money is required for happiness, and that life grows bleak and burdensome without enough of it. Other readings here complicate the picture, however. In this section, you will encounter:

- two analyses of the complex relationship between happiness and money: "The Funds, Friends, and Faith of Happy People" and "What's So Bad about Being Poor?"
- numbers that call into question whether a standard of living that was sufficient in years past would be deemed sufficient today: the Roper Survey "The Good Life"
- media images of forms of happiness that can be bought: MasterCard's "Priceless" advertisements
- an inventory of the questionable things a typical American spends money on: "When Spending Becomes You"
- a defense of current middle-class spending habits: "The Vanishing Middle Class"
- and the theory that people use money to allay their fear of death: "Lethal Consumption: Death-Denying Materialism."

The Funds, Friends, and Faith of Happy People

David G. Myers

If all you had to judge by was the endless stream of ads you see for designer jeans, well-equipped new sports cars, and bookings on cruise ships, you would probably conclude that a strong correlation exists between the size of a person's disposable income and the number of minutes he or she can be found smiling every day. But what is it that actually makes a human being happy? Money and the things that money buys? Friendships? Deep religious faith?

In his much-cited survey of the research on this question, David Myers sets forth an involved answer. The excerpt below is a section just on happiness and money.

A professor of psychology at Hope College in Michigan, Myers has authored 17 books, including the textbooks *Psychology, Exploring Psychology,* and *Social Psychology.*

Wealth and Well-Being

Could money buy you happiness? Most deny it. However, ask a different question — "Would a *little* more money make you a *little* happier?" — and many will smirk and nod yes. There is, we believe, some connection between wealth and well-being. Asked how satisfied they were with 13 aspects of their lives, including friends, house, and schooling, Americans expressed least satisfaction with "the amount of money you have to live on" (Roper Organization, 1984). What would improve their quality of life? "More money," was the most frequent response to a University of Michigan national survey (Campbell, 1981, p. 41), and the more the better. In one Gallup Poll (Gallup & Newport, 1990), one in two women, two in three men, and four in five people earning more than $75,000 reported they would like to be rich. Thus, the modern American dream seems to have become life, liberty, and the purchase of happiness. Although most realize that the seemingly happy lifestyle of the rich and famous is beyond their reach, they do imagine "the good life" that might become possible when they achieve greater wealth.

The clearest evidence of this "greening of America" comes from the annual UCLA and American Council on Education survey of nearly a quarter million students entering college. Those agreeing that a "very important" reason for their going to college was "to make more money" rose from one in two in 1971 to three in four in 1998 (Astin,

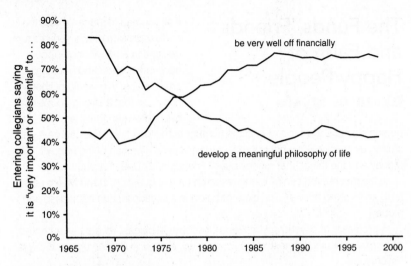

Figure 1.1 **Changing Materialism**

Note: From annual surveys of more than 200,000 U.S. students entering college (total sample approximately 6.5 million students). Data from Dey, Astin, and Korn, 1991, and subsequent annual reports, including Sax et al., 1998.

Green, & Korn, 1987; Sax, Astin, Korn, & Mahoney, 1998). The proportion who consider it "very important or essential" that they become "very well off financially" rose from 39% in 1970 to 74% in 1998 (Figure 1.1). Among 19 listed objectives, this was number one, outranking "developing a meaningful philosophy of life," "becoming an authority in my field," "helping others in difficulty," and "raising a family." For today's young Americans, money matters.

Does being well off indeed produce — or at least correlate with — psychological well-being? Would people be happier if they could exchange a middle-class lifestyle for one with palatial surroundings, Aspen ski vacations, and executive class travel? Would they be happier if they won a publishers' sweepstakes and could choose from its suggested indulgences: a 40-foot yacht, deluxe motorhome, designer wardrobe, luxury car, and private housekeeper? "Whoever said money can't buy happiness isn't spending it right," proclaimed a Lexus ad.

As Diener (2000) reported, there is some tendency for wealthy nations to have more satisfied people. The Swiss and Scandinavians, for instance, are generally prosperous and satisfied. When people in poorer nations compare their lifestyles with the abundance of those in rich nations, they may become more aware of their relative poverty. However, among nations with a gross national product of more than

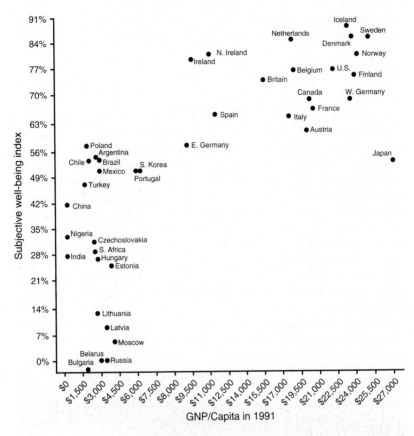

Figure 1.2 **National Wealth and Well-Being**

Note: From World Bank data and the 1990–1991 World Values Survey. The subjective well-being index combines happiness and life satisfaction (average of percentage describing themselves as [a] "very happy" or "happy" minus percentage "not very happy" or "unhappy," and as [b] 7 or above minus 4 or below on a 10-point life satisfaction scale). Figure from *Culture Shift in Advanced Industrial Society* (p. 62), by R. Inglehart, 1997, Princeton, NJ, Princeton University Press. Copyright 1997 by R. Inglehart. Reprinted with permission.

$8,000 per person, the correlation between national wealth and well-being evaporates (Figure 1.2). Better (so far as happiness and life satisfaction go) to be Irish than Bulgarian. But whether one is Irish, Belgian, Norwegian, or American hardly matters. Indeed, the Irish during the 1980s reported consistently greater life satisfaction than did the doubly wealthy but less satisfied West Germans (Inglehart, 1990). Moreover, noted Diener, Diener, and Diener (1995), national wealth is entangled with civil rights, literacy, and the number of continuous years of democracy. For a clearer look at money and happiness, researchers have therefore asked whether, across individuals and over time, people's well-being rises with their wealth.

Are Rich People Happier?

In poor countries such as India, where low income threatens basic 5 human needs more often, being relatively well off does predict greater well-being (Argyle, 1999). Psychologically as well as materially, it is better to be high caste than low. However, in affluent countries, where most can afford life's necessities, affluence matters surprisingly little. In the United States, Canada, and Europe, the correlation between income and personal happiness, noted Ronald Inglehart (1990), "is surprisingly weak (indeed, virtually negligible)" (p. 242). Happiness tends to be lower among the very poor. Once comfortable, however, more money provides diminishing returns° on happiness. Summarizing his own studies of happiness, David Lykken (1999) observed that "People who go to work in their overalls and on the bus are just as happy, on the average, as those in suits who drive to work in their own Mercedes" (p. 17).

Even very rich people — the *Forbes* 100 wealthiest Americans surveyed by Diener, Horwitz, and Emmons (1985) — are only slightly happier than the average American. Although they have more than enough money to buy many things they don't need and hardly care about, 4 in 5 of the 49 super-rich people responding to the survey agreed that "Money can increase OR decrease happiness, depending on how it is used." Some were indeed unhappy. One fabulously wealthy man could never remember being happy. One woman reported that money could not undo misery caused by her children's problems. When sailing on the *Titanic,* even first class cannot get you where you want to go.

Our human capacity for adaptation (Diener, 2000) helps explain a major conclusion of subjective well-being research, as expressed by the late Richard Kammann (1983): "Objective life circumstances have a negligible role to play in a theory of happiness." Good and bad events (e.g., a pay hike, being rejected for tenure) do temporarily influence our moods, and people will often seize on such short-run influences to explain their happiness. Yet, in less time than most people suppose, the emotional impact of significant events and circumstances dissipates (Gilbert, Pinel, Wilson, Blumberg, & Wheatley, 1998). In a

diminishing returns: a reference to the point at which continued effort ceases to produce the same results that the effort produced before.

society where everyone lived in 4,000-square-foot houses, people would likely be no happier than in a society in which everyone lived in 2,000-square-foot houses. Thanks to our capacity to adapt to ever greater fame and fortune, yesterday's luxuries can soon become today's necessities and tomorrow's relics.

Does Economic Growth Improve Human Morale?

Over time, does happiness rise with affluence? Will Frank and Shirley Mae Capaci be enduringly happier for having in 1998 won the $195 million Powerball lottery? Likely they will not be as happy as they initially supposed. Lottery winners typically gain only a temporary jolt of joy from their winnings (Argyle, 1986; Brickman, Coates, & Janoff-Bulman, 1978). Although they are delighted to have won, the euphoria eventually fades. Likewise, those whose incomes have increased over the previous decade are not happier than those whose income has not increased (Diener, Sandvik, Seidlitz, & Diener, 1993). As Richard Ryan (quoted by Kohn, 1999) noted, such satisfactions have "a short half-life."

If not surrounded by wealth, the pain of simplification may also be short-lived. Economist Robert Frank (1996) experienced this:

As a young man fresh out of college, I served as a Peace Corps Volunteer in rural Nepal. My one-room house had no electricity, no heat, no indoor toilet, no running water. The local diet offered little variety and virtually no meat. . . . Yet, although my living conditions in Nepal were a bit startling at first, the most salient feature of my experience was how quickly they came to seem normal. Within a matter of weeks, I lost all sense of impoverishment. Indeed, my $40 monthly stipend was more than most others had in my village, and with it I experienced a feeling of prosperity that I have recaptured only in recent years.

If enduring personal happiness generally does not rise with personal affluence, does collective happiness float upward with a rising economic tide? Are Americans happier today than in 1940, when two out of five homes lacked a shower or bathtub, heat often meant feeding a furnace wood or coal, and 35% of homes had no toilet ("Tracking the American Dream," 1994)? Consider 1957, when economist John Galbraith was about to describe the United States as *The Affluent Society*. Americans' per person income, expressed in today's dollars, was about $9,000. Today, it is $20,000, thanks to increased real wages into the 1970s, increased nonwage income, and the doubling of married

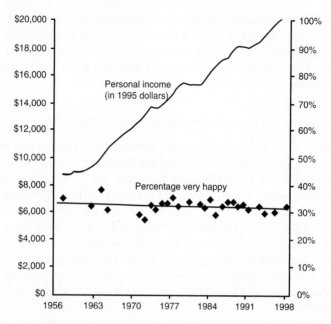

Figure 1.3 **Has Economic Growth Advanced Human Morale?**

Note: While inflation-adjusted income has risen, self-reported happiness has not. Income data from the U.S. Commerce Department, Bureau of the Census (1975), and *Economic Indicators*. Happiness data from General Social Surveys, National Opinion Research Center, University of Chicago.

women's employment. Compared with 1957, today's Americans are therefore part of "the doubly affluent society," with double what money buys. Although income disparity has increased between rich and poor, the rising tide has lifted most boats. Americans today own twice as many cars per person, eat out more than twice as often, and often enjoy microwave ovens, big-screen color TVs, and home computers. From 1960 to 1997, the percentage of homes with dishwashers increased from 7% to 50%, clothes dryers increased from 20% to 71%, and air conditioning increased from 15% to 73% (U.S. Commerce Department, Bureau of the Census, 1979, Table 1383; 1998, Table 1223). So, believing that it is "very important" to be very well-off financially and having seen their affluence ratchet upward little by little over four decades, are Americans now happier?

They are not. As Figure 1.3 indicates, the number of people reporting themselves "very happy" has, if anything, declined slightly between 1957 and 1998, from 35% to 33%: We are twice as rich and no happier. Meanwhile, the divorce rate doubled. Teen suicide tripled.

Reported violent crime nearly quadrupled. Depression rates have soared, especially among teens and young adults (Seligman, 1989; Klerman & Weissman, 1989; Cross-National Collaborative Group, 1992). Compared with their grandparents, today's young adults have grown up with much more affluence, slightly less happiness, and much greater risk of depression and assorted social pathologies. I call this conjunction of material prosperity and social recession *the American paradox* (Myers, in press). The more people strive for extrinsic goals such as money, the more numerous their problems and the less robust their well-being (Kasser & Ryan, 1996).

It is hard to avoid a startling conclusion: Our becoming much better off over the last four decades has not been accompanied by one iota of increased subjective well-being. The same is true of European countries and Japan, according to Richard Easterlin (1995). In Britain, for example, sharp increases in the percentages of households with cars, central heating, and telephones have not been accompanied by increased happiness. The conclusion is startling because it challenges modern materialism. So far as happiness goes, it is not "the economy, stupid.°" Economic growth in affluent countries has provided no apparent boost to human morale.

> It is hard to avoid a startling conclusion: Our becoming much better off over the last four decades has not been accompanied by one iota of increased subjective well-being.

References

Argyle, M. (1986). *The psychology of happiness.* London: Methuen.

Argyle, M. (1999). Causes and correlates of happiness. In D. Kahneman, E. Diener, & N. Schwartz (Eds.), *Well-being: The foundations of hedonic psychology.* New York: Russell Sage Foundation.

Astin, A. W., Green, K. C., & Korn, W. S. (1987). *The American freshman: Twenty year trends.* Los Angeles: Higher Education Research Institute, Graduate School of Education, University of California, Los Angeles.

Brickman, P., Coates, D., & Janoff-Bulman, R. J. (1978). Lottery winners and accident victims: Is happiness relative? *Journal of Personality and Social Psychology, 36,* 917–927.

Campbell, A. (1981). *The sense of well-being in America.* New York: McGraw-Hill.

Cross-National Collaborative Group. (1992). The changing rate of major depression. *Journal of the American Medical Association, 268,* 3098–3105.

"the economy, stupid": a catch phrase used by advisers to Bill Clinton in the presidential campaign of 1992, to remind themselves of what was foremost on voters' minds.

Dey, E. L., Astin, A. W., & Korn, W. S. (1991). *The American freshman: Twenty-five year trends.* Los Angeles: Higher Education Research Institute, University of California, Los Angeles.

Diener, E. (2000). Subjective well-being: The science of happiness and a proposal for a national index. *American Psychologist, 55,* 34–43.

Diener, E., Diener, M., & Diener, C. (1995). Factors predicting the subjective well-being of nations. *Journal of Personality and Social Psychology, 69,* 653–663.

Diener, E., Horwitz, J., & Emmons, R. A. (1985). Happiness of the very wealthy. *Social Indicators, 16,* 263–274.

Diener, E., Sandvik, E., Seidlitz, L., & Diener, M. (1993). The relationship between income and subjective well-being: Relative or absolute? *Social Indicators Research, 28,* 195–223.

Easterlin, R. (1995). Will raising the incomes of all increase the happiness of all? *Journal of Economic Behavior and Organization, 27,* 35–47.

Frank, R. H. (1996). *The empty wealth of nations.* Unpublished manuscript, Johnson Graduate School of Management, Cornell University, Ithaca, New York.

Gallup, G. G., Jr., & Newport, F. (1990, July). Americans widely disagree on what constitutes rich. *Gallup Poll Monthly,* pp. 28–36.

Gilbert, D. T., Pinel, E. C., Wilson, T. D., Blumberg, S. J., & Wheatley, T. P. (1998). Immune neglect: A source of durability bias in affective forecasting. *Journal of Personality and Social Psychology, 75,* 617–638.

Inglehart, R. (1990). *Culture shift in advanced industrial society.* Princeton, NJ: Princeton University Press.

Kammann, R. (1983). Objective circumstances, life satisfactions, and sense of well-being: Consistencies across time and place. *New Zealand Journal of Psychology, 12,* 14–22.

Kasser, T., & Ryan, R. (1996). Further examining the American dream: Differential correlates of intrinsic and extrinsic goals. *Personality and Social Psychology Bulletin, 22,* 280–287.

Klerman, G. L., & Weissman, M. M. (1989). Increasing rates of depression. *Journal of the American Medical Association, 261,* 2229–2235.

Kohn, A. (1999, February 2). In pursuit of affluence, at a high price. *The New York Times.* (Retrieved February 2, 1999, from the World Wide Web: http://www.nytimes.com).

Lykken, D. (1999). *Happiness.* New York: Golden Books.

Myers, D. G. (in press). *The American paradox: Spiritual hunger in an age of plenty.* New Haven, CT: Yale University Press.

Roper Organization. (1984, August/September). [Untitled survey]. *Public Opinion,* p. 25.

Sax, L. J., Astin, A. W., Korn, W. S., & Mahoney, K. M. (1998). *The American freshman: National norms for fall 1998.* Los Angeles: Higher Education Research Institute, University of California, Los Angeles.

Seligman, M. E. P. (1989). Explanatory style: Predicting depression, achievement, and health. In M. D. Yapko (Ed.), *Brief therapy approaches to treating anxiety and depression.* New York: Brunner/Mazel.

Tracking the American dream. (1994, September 13). *Grand Rapids Press*, p. A4.

U.S. Department of Commerce, Bureau of the Census. (1975). *Historical abstract of the United States: Colonial times to 1970.* Washington, DC: Superintendent of Documents.

U.S. Department of Commerce, Bureau of the Census. (1979). *Statistical abstract of the United States 1978.* Washington, DC: Superintendent of Documents.

U.S. Department of Commerce, Bureau of the Census. (1998). *Statistical abstract of the United States 1996* (116th ed.). Washington, DC: Superintendent of Documents.

Understanding the Text

1. In paragraph 2, Myers uses the popular phrase "greening of America," but puts quotation marks around it to indicate he's using it in a new way. What does he mean by it?

2. What, according to Myers, seems to be the true relationship between happiness and money? Would Myers say that the relationship is the same for people living in abject poverty as for people living above the poverty line? Are the short-term effects of having more money the same as the long-term effects?

Reflection and Response

3. In paragraph 2, Myers cites statistics that suggest a dramatic change between 1970 and 1998 in college students' prioritization of wealth in life. How do such statistics square with your own attitudes? Do you find yourself in Myers' numbers?

4. According to Myers, do people's predictions of the happiness that money will bring them correspond to reality? What is his evidence? Does it satisfy you?

Making Connections

5. What would Charles Murray ("What's So Bad about Being Poor?" page 26) make of Myers's argument? Where do Myers's and Murray's arguments overlap, and where do they diverge?

6. If, for most Americans, money turns out not to be a key to happiness, what, then, *does* bring happiness? The rest of Myers's article deals with factors other than money. Look it up using a database like EBSCOhost at your school library, and write a response that begins,

   David Myers's article "The Funds, Friends, and Faith of Happy People" leads me to believe that how much money one has is a [you fill in the blank: close second/poor second/close third/distant third] among factors that determine personal happiness in life.

The Good Life

Roper Center

Happiness seems to be a moving target, as evidenced by these results of a survey of Americans conducted by the Roper Center at the University of Connecticut, a leading source of data on public opinion in the United States since the 1930s.

Percentage Identifying Item as a Part of "The Good Life"

	1975	1991
Vacation home	19	35
Swimming pool	14	29
Color TV	46	55
Second color TV	10	28
Travel abroad	30	39
Really nice clothes	36	44
Car	71	75
Second car	30	41
Home you own	85	87
A lot of money	38	55
A job that pays much more than average	45	60
Happy marriage	84	77
One or more children	74	73
Interesting job	69	63
Job that contributes to the welfare of society	38	38
Percentage who think they have a very good chance of achieving the "good life"	35	23

Understanding the Text

1. What does this chart suggest has changed in Americans' concept of "The Good Life"? (In answering, don't go simply item by item: try to group items into meaningful categories, such as "basics" and "luxuries.")
2. How, according to this chart, has Americans' optimism about their personal wealth changed over time?
3. Is the chart laid out in such a way as to imply a causal connection between the answer to question no. 1 and the answer to question no. 2?

Reflection and Response

4. Do you lament the changes reflected in this chart? Why or why not?

5. Read over the statistics in this chart until at least two questions of genuine interest to you emerge. Write these questions out, explaining what in the data raises each one.

6. Use the Roper survey as part of a response to the student who wrote the paragraph below:

> Generally speaking, I am a pleasant and happy person. I hold broad interests, maintain great friends, and have a supportive family that allow me to experience temporary times of contentment. But at the end of the day, I recognize that I am caught up in a never-ending hunt for wealth, success, and perfection. Five years down the road when I earn $50,000 per year, I know that I will crave $100,000. If I should reach an annual income of $150,000, my heart will surely long for $200,000. Imperfection and dissatisfaction are components of life that must be accepted, and as individuals we can only ask for the freedom, from our [families and] governments, to embark on the "*pursuit* of happiness." . . . I will undoubtedly one day provide my children with the same freedom, and I can only pray that they will . . . take time out from their lifelong pursuits and recognize the rare moments of provisional bliss.

Making Connections

7. Does this chart tend to corroborate the findings of David Myers ("The Funds, Friends, and Faith of Happy People," page 15), or does it undermine them? Explain your response.

8. Shortly after the terrorist attacks of September 11, 2001, President George W. Bush was quoted as urging Americans to "go shopping," in order to keep the American economy strong. Does such an exhortation reflect a sound understanding of the workings of a capitalist system like our own? Put another way: If a person stops striving for more possessions than she already has (except for food, a new roof when the old one starts to leak, etc.) and goes from spending 100 percent of her disposable income to spending 50 percent of it — and if a great many other Americans get the same idea at the same time — does something crucial to sustaining the economy give way as a result? Does the economy collapse? If so, is our economic system in conflict with the ideal of contentment in life? Why or why not? (Your answer to this difficult question might benefit from research guided by a reference librarian.)

What's So Bad about Being Poor?

Charles Murray

Poverty, it turns out, can be defined several ways, and the different ways don't all make poverty seem equally terrible. Charles Murray brings the point home in a series of thought experiments — "what if" exercises of the mind which he asks his readers to try for themselves.

A libertarian, Murray has written several influential books, including *Losing Ground: American Social Policy 1950–1980,* which contributed significantly to the debate that resulted in reform of the U.S. welfare system in the 1990s. He has also been a fellow at the American Enterprise Institute.

One of the great barriers to a discussion of poverty and social policy in the 1980s is that so few people who talk about poverty have ever been poor. The diminishing supply of the formerly poor in policy-making and policy-influencing positions is a side effect of progress. The number of poor households dropped dramatically from the beginning of World War II through the end of the 1960s. Despite this happy cause, however, it is a troubling phenomenon. From the beginning of American history through at least the 1950s, the new generation moving into positions of influence in politics, business, journalism, and academia was bound to include a large admixture of people who had grown up dirt-poor. People who had grown up in more privileged surroundings did not have to speculate about what being poor was like; someone sitting beside them, or at the head of the table, was likely to be able to tell them. It was easy to acknowledge then, as it is not now, that there is nothing so terrible about poverty *per se.* Poverty is not equivalent to destitution. Being poor does not necessarily mean being malnourished or ill-clothed. It does not automatically mean joylessness or despair. To be poor is not necessarily to be without dignity; it is not necessarily to be unhappy. When large numbers of people who were running the country had once been poor themselves, poverty could be kept in perspective.

> To be poor is not necessarily to be without dignity; it is not necessarily to be unhappy.

Today, how many graduates of the Kennedy School of Government or of the Harvard Business School have ever been really poor? How many have ever had close friends who were? How many even have parents who were once poor? For those who have never been poor and never even known any people who were once poor, it is difficult to treat poverty as something other than a mystery. It is even more difficult to be detached about the importance of poverty, because to do so smacks of a "let them eat cake" mentality.° By the same token, however, it is important that we who have never been poor be able to think about the relationship of poverty to social policy in a much more straightforward way than the nation's intellectuals and policy-makers have done for the past few decades. To that end, I propose a thought experiment based on the premise that tomorrow you had to be poor. I do not mean "low-income" by Western standards of afflu-ence, but functioning near the subsistence level, as a very large pro-portion of the world's population still does.

In constructing this thought experiment, the first requirement is to divorce yourself from certain reflexive assumptions. Do not think what it would be like to be poor while living in a community of rich people. I do not (yet) want to commingle the notions of absolute poverty and relative poverty, so you should imagine a community in which everyone else is as poor as you are, indeed, a world in which the existence of wealth is so far removed from daily life that it is not real.

The second requirement is to avoid constructing an imaginary per-son. The point is not to try to imagine yourself in the shoes of "a poor person" but to imagine what *you*, with your particular personality, experiences, strengths, and limitations (including your middle-class upbringing and values), would do if you were suddenly thrust into this position.

To do all this in the American context is difficult. Any scenario is 5 filled with extraneous factors. So let me suggest one that I used as a way of passing the time when I was a researcher driving on the back roads of rural Thailand many years ago. What if, I would muse, I had to live for the rest of my life in the next village I came to (perhaps a nuclear war would have broken out, thereby keeping me indefinitely in Thailand; any rationalization would do)?

In some ways, the prospect was grim. I had never been charmed by sleeping under mosquito netting nor by bathing with a few buck-ets of cloudy well water. When circumstances permitted, I liked to end a day's work in a village by driving back to an air-conditioned hotel and a cold beer. But if I had no choice . . .

As it happens, Thailand has an attractive peasant culture. Survival itself is not a problem. The weather is always warm, so the requirements

"let them eat cake" mentality: a callous attitude toward poverty attributed to the French queen Marie Antoinette, who allegedly dismissed reports that peasants didn't have enough bread to eat by saying "Let them eat cake."

for clothes, fuel, and shelter are minimal. Village food is ample, if monotonous. But I would nonetheless be extremely poor, with an effective purchasing power of a few hundred dollars a year. The house I would live in would probably consist of a porch and one or two small, unlit, unfurnished rooms. The walls might be of wood, more probably of woven bamboo or leaf mats. I would have (in those years) no electricity and no running water. Perhaps I would have a bicycle or a transistor radio. Probably the nearest physician would be many kilometers away. In sum: If the criterion for measuring poverty is material goods, it would be difficult to find a community in deepest Appalachia or a neighborhood in the most depressed parts of South Chicago that even approaches the absolute material poverty of the average Thai village in which I would have to make my life.

On the other hand, as I thought about spending the next fifty years in a Thai village, I found myself wondering precisely what I would lack (compared to my present life) that would cause me great pain. The more I thought about the question, the less likely it seemed that I would be unhappy.

Since I lacked any useful trade, maybe I could swap the Jeep for a few *rai* of land and become a farmer. Learning how to farm well enough to survive would occupy my time and attention for several years. After that, I might try to become an affluent farmer. One of the assets I would bring from my Western upbringing and schooling would be a haphazardly acquired understanding of cash crops, markets, and entrepreneurial possibilities, and perhaps I could parlay that, along with hard work, into some income and more land. It also was clear to me that I probably would enjoy this "career." I am not saying I would *choose* it, but rather that I could find satisfaction in learning how to be a competent rice farmer, even though it was not for me the most desired of all possible careers.

What about my personal life? Thais are among the world's most handsome and charming people, and it was easy to imagine falling in love with a woman from the village, marrying her, and having a family with her. I could also anticipate the pleasure of watching my children grow up, probably at closer hand than I would in the United States. The children would not get the same education they would in the States, but I would have it within my power to see that they would be educated. A grade school is near every village. The priests in the local *wat* could teach them Buddhism. I could also become teacher to my children. A few basic textbooks in mathematics, science, and history; Plato and Shakespeare and the Bible; a dozen other well-chosen classics — all these could be acquired even in up-country Thailand. My children could reach adulthood literate, thoughtful, and civilized.

My children would do well in other ways too. They would grow up in a "positive peer culture," as the experts say. Their Thai friends in the village would all be raised by their parents to be considerate, hard-working, pious, and honest — that's the way Thai villagers raise their children. My children would face few of the corrupting influences to be found in an American city.

Other personal pleasures? I knew I would find it easy to make friends, and that some would become close. I would have other good times, too — celebrations on special occasions, but more often informal gatherings and jokes and conversation. If I read less, I would also read better. I would have great personal freedom as long as my behavior did not actively interfere with the lives of my neighbors (the tolerance for eccentric behavior in a Thai village is remarkably high). What about the physical condition of poverty? After a few months, I suspect that I would hardly notice.

You may conclude that this thought experiment is a transparent setup. First I ask what it would be like to be poor, then I proceed to outline a near-idyllic environment in which to be poor. I assume that I have a legacy of education experiences that would help me spend my time getting steadily less poor. And then I announce that poverty isn't so bad after all. But the point of the thought experiment is not to suggest that all kinds of poverty are tolerable, and even less that all peasant societies are pleasant places to live. When poverty means the inability to get enough food or shelter, it is every bit as bad as usually portrayed. When poverty means being forced to remain in that condition, with no way of improving one's situation, it is as bad as portrayed. When poverty is conjoined with oppression, be it a caste system or a hacienda system or a people's republic, it is as bad as portrayed. *My thought experiment is not a paean to peasant life, but a paean to communities of free people.* If poverty is defined in terms of money, everybody in the Thai village is poor. If poverty is defined as being unable to live a modest but decent existence, hardly anyone there is poor.

• • •

Does this thought experiment fail when it is transported to the United States? Imagine the same Thai village set down intact on the outskirts of Los Angeles. Surely its inhabitants must be miserable, living in their huts and watching the rest of the world live in splendor.

At this point in the argument, however, we need no longer think in 15
terms of thought experiments. This situation is one that has been faced
by hundreds of thousands of immigrants to the United States, whether
they came from Europe at the end of World War II or from Vietnam in
the mid-1970s. Lawyers found themselves working as janitors, professors found themselves working on assembly lines. Sometimes they
worked their way up and out, but many had to remain janitors and
factory workers, because they came here too late in life to retool
their foreign-trained skills. But their children did not have to remain
so, and they have not. A reading of their histories, in literature or in
the oral testimony of their children, corroborates this pattern. Was a
Latvian attorney forced to flee his country "happy" to have to work as
a janitor? No. Was he prevented by his situation — specifically, by his
poverty — from successfully pursuing happiness? Emphatically, no.

Let us continue the thought experiment nonetheless, with a slightly
different twist. This time, you are given a choice. One choice is to be
poor in rural Thailand, as I have described it, with just enough food
and shelter and a few hundred dollars a year in cash: a little beyond
bare subsistence, but not much. Or you may live in the United States,
receive a free apartment, free food, free medical care, and a cash grant,
the package coming to a total that puts you well above the poverty
line. There is, however, a catch: you are *required* to live in a particular
apartment, and this apartment is located in a public-housing project
in one of the burned-out areas of the South Bronx. A condition of
receiving the rest of the package is that you continue to live, and
raise your children, in the South Bronx (you do not have the option of
spending all of your waking hours in Manhattan, just as the village
thought experiment did not give you the option of taking vacations in
Bangkok). You still have all the assets you took to the Thai village —
once again, it is essential that you imagine not what it is like for an
Alabama sharecropper to be transplanted to the South Bronx, but
what it would be like *for you.*

In some ways, you would have much more access to distractions.
Unlike the situation in the Thai village, you would have television you
could watch all day, taking you vicariously into other worlds. And,
for that matter, it would be much easier to get books than in a Thai
village, and you would have much more money with which to buy
them. You could, over time, fix up your apartment so that within its
walls you would have an environment that looked and felt very like
an apartment you could have elsewhere.

There is only one problem: You would have a terrible time once
you opened your door to the outside world. How, for example, are you

going to raise your children in the South Bronx so that they grow up to be the adults you want them to be? (No, you don't have the option of sending them to live elsewhere.) How are you going to take a walk in the park in the evening? There are many good people in the South Bronx with whom you could become friends, just as in the village. But how are you to find them? And once they are found, how are you to create a functioning, mutually reinforcing community?

I suggest that as you think of answers to those questions, you will find that, if you are to have much chance to be happy, the South Bronx needs to be changed in a way that the village did not — that, unlike the village as it stood, the South Bronx as it stands does not "work" as an environment for pursuing happiness. Let us ignore for the moment how these changes in environment could be brought about, by what combination of government's doing things and refraining from doing things. The fact is that hardly any of those changes involve greater income for you personally, but rather changes in the surrounding environment. There is a question that crystallizes the roles of personal *v.* environmental poverty in this situation: How much money would it take to persuade you to move self and family to this public-housing project in the South Bronx?

● ● ●

The purpose of the first two versions of the thought experiment was to   20 suggest a different perspective on one's own priorities regarding the pursuit of happiness, and by extension to suggest that perhaps public policy ought to reflect a different set of priorities as well. It is easy in this case, however, to assume that what one wants for oneself is not applicable to others. Thus, for example, it could be said that the only reason the thought experiments work (if you grant even that much) is that the central character starts out with enormous advantages of knowledge and values — which in themselves reflect the advantages of having grown up with plenty of material resources.

To explore that possibility, I ask you to bear with me for one more thought experiment on this general topic, one I have found to be a touchstone. This time, the question is not what kinds of material resources you (with your fully developed set of advantages) need for your pursuit of happiness, but what a small child, without any developed assets at all, needs for his pursuit of happiness — specifically, what your own child needs.

Imagine that you are the parent of a small child, living in contemporary America, and in some way you are able to know that tomorrow you and your spouse will die and your child will be made an orphan. You do not have the option of sending the child to live with a friend or relative. You must select from among other and far-from-perfect choices. The choices, I assure you, are not veiled representations of anything else; the experiment is set up not to be realistic, but to evoke something about how you think.

Suppose first this choice: You may put your child with an extremely poor couple according to the official definition of "poor" — which is to say, poverty that is measured exclusively in money. This couple has so little money that your child's clothes will often be secondhand and there will be not even small luxuries to brighten his life. Life will be a struggle, often a painful one. But you also know that the parents work hard, will make sure your child goes to school and studies, and will teach your child that integrity and responsibility are primary values. Or you may put your child with parents who will be as affectionate to your child as the first couple but who have never worked, are indifferent to your child's education, think that integrity and responsibility (when they think of them at all) are meaningless words — but who have and will always have plenty of food and good clothes and amenities, provided by others.

Which couple do you choose? The answer is obvious to me and I imagine to most readers: the first couple, of course. But if you are among those who choose the first couple, stop and consider what the answer means. This is *your own child* you are talking about, whom you would never let go hungry even if providing for your child meant going hungry yourself. And yet you are choosing years of privation for that same child. Why?

Perhaps I set up the thought experiment too starkly. Let us repeat 25 it, adding some ambiguity. This time, the first choice is again the poor-but-virtuous couple. But the second couple is rich. They are, we shall say, the heirs to a great fortune. They will not beat your child or in any other way maltreat him. We may even assume affection on their part, as we will with the other couple. But, once again, they have never worked and never will, are indifferent to your child's education, and think that integrity and responsibility (when they think of them at all) are meaningless words. They do, however, possess millions of dollars, more than enough to last for the life of your child and of your child's children. Now, in whose care do you place your child? The poor couple or the rich one?

This time, it seems likely that some people will choose the rich couple — or more accurately, it is possible to think of ways in which the decision might be tipped in that direction. For example, a wealthy person who is indifferent to a child's education might nonetheless ship the child off to an expensive boarding school at the earliest possible age. In that case, it is conceivable that the wealthy ne'er-do-wells are preferable to the poor-but-virtuous couple, *if* they end up providing the values of the poor family through the surrogate parenting of the boarding school — dubious, but conceivable. One may imagine other ways in which the money might be used to compensate for the inadequacies of the parents. But failing those very chancy possibilities, I suggest that a great many parents on all sides of political fences would knowingly choose hunger and rags for their child rather than wealth.

Again, the question is: Why? What catastrophes are going to befall the child placed in the wealthy home? What is the awful fate? Would it be so terrible if he grew up to be thoughtlessly rich? The child will live a life of luxury and have enough money to buy himself out of almost any problem that might arise. Why not leave it at that? Or let me put the question positively: In deciding where to send the child, what is one trying to achieve by these calculations and predictions and hunches? What is the good that one is trying to achieve? What is the criterion of success?

One may attach a variety of descriptors to the answer. Perhaps you want the child to become a reflective, responsible adult. To value honesty and integrity. To be able to identify sources of lasting satisfaction. Ultimately, if I keep pushing the question (Why is honesty good? Why is being reflective good?), you will give the answer that permits no follow-up: You want your child to be happy. You are trying to choose the guardians who will best enable your child to pursue happiness. And, forced to a choice, material resources come very low on your list of priorities.

● ● ●

So far, I have limited the discussion to a narrow point: In deciding how to enhance the ability of people to pursue happiness, solutions that increase material resources beyond subsistence *independently of other considerations* are bound to fail. Money *per se* is not very important. It quickly becomes trivial. Depending on other non-monetary conditions, poor people can have a rich assortment of ways of pursuing happiness, or affluent people can have very few.

The thought experiments were stratagems intended not to con- 30 vince you of any particular policy implications, but rather to induce you to entertain this possibility: When a policy trade-off involves (for example) imposing material hardship in return for some other policy good, *it is possible* (I ask no more than that for the time being) that imposing the material hardship is the right choice. For example, regarding the "orphaned child" scenario: *If* a policy leads to a society in which there are more of the first kind of parents and fewer of the second, the sacrifices in material resources available to the children involved might conceivably be worth it.

The discussion, with its steady use of the concept of "near-subsistence" as "enough material resources to pursue happiness," has also been intended to point up how little our concept of poverty has to do with subsistence. Thus, for example, if one simply looks at the end result of how people live, a natural observation concerning contemporary America might be that we have large numbers of people who are living at a subsistence or subsubsistence level. But I have been using "subsistence" in its original sense: enough food to be adequately nourished, plus the most basic shelter and clothing. The traditional Salvation Army shelter provides subsistence, for example. In Western countries, and perhaps especially the United States, two problems tend to confuse the issue. One is that we have forgotten what subsistence means, so that an apartment with cockroaches, broken windows, and graffiti on the walls may be thought of as barely "subsistence level," even if it also has running water, electricity, heat, a television, and a pile of discarded fast-food cartons in the corner. It might be an awful place to live (for the reasons that the South Bronx can be an awful place to live), but it bears very little resemblance to what "subsistence" means to most of the world. Secondly, we tend to confuse the way in which some poor people *use* their resources (which indeed can often leave them in a near-subsistence state) with the raw purchasing power of the resources at their disposal. Take, for example, the apartment I just described and move a middle-class person with middle-class habits and knowledge into it, given exactly the same resources. Within days it would be still shabby but a different place. All of which is precisely the point of the thought experiments about Thailand and the South Bronx: Money has very little to do with living a poverty-stricken life. Similarly, "a subsistence income" has very little to do with what Americans think of as poverty.

Understanding the Text

1. Why does Murray feel it is important to undertake his thought experiments? Support your answer with direct quotations from the text or with paraphrases.

2. Find at least two points in Murray's essay where he anticipates and addresses an objection that his reader may have. Does his doing so make his argument more convincing or less convincing? Explain.

Reflection and Response

3. How convincing do you find Murray's series of thought experiments? Why? Be specific. (Don't leave out the last of them, in paragraphs 22–28.)

4. Would you describe Murray's tone as compassionate? Mine his text for evidence.

Making Connections

5. In paragraph 3, Murray writes, "I do not (yet) want to commingle the notions of absolute poverty and relative poverty, so you should imagine a community in which everyone else is as poor as you are, indeed, a world in which the existence of wealth is so far removed from daily life that it is not real." Even when he sets a thought experiment in the South Bronx, he refrains from discussing the effects of relative poverty — the effects of knowing that other members of one's society live much more comfortably than oneself, in economic terms.

   Write a paper built on a thought experiment involving *relative* poverty. In constructing it, draw on details in Melanie Scheller's "On the Meaning of Poverty and Plumbing" (page 85).

6. How does your thinking about *relative* poverty compare with that of economist John Kenneth Galbraith, below?

   People are poverty-stricken when their income, even if adequate for survival, falls markedly behind that of the community. Then they cannot have what the larger community regards as the minimum necessary for decency; and they cannot wholly escape, therefore, the judgment of the larger community that they are indecent. They are degraded [because], in the literal sense, they live outside the grades or categories which the community regards as acceptable.

Serving in Florida

Barbara Ehrenreich

Journalist Barbara Ehrenreich set out to learn firsthand what life is like for the working poor in America: Can they pay their bills? Can they live in modest comfort? To find out, she temporarily abandoned her middle-class home and hit the road, taking low-paying jobs around the country, doing stints as waitress, house cleaner, nursing-home aide, and Wal-Mart salesperson. Here is an edited version of her chapter on waitressing.

Although Ehrenreich earned her Ph.D. in cellular biology, most of her numerous books — including the *New York Times* bestseller *Nickel and Dimed: On (Not) Getting By in America* (2001), from which the excerpt below has been taken — are products of investigative reporting on contemporary social issues. Other titles by her include *Fear of Falling: The Inner Life of the Middle Class* (1989) and *The Worst Years of Our Lives: Irreverent Notes from a Decade of Greed* (1990). She was born in Butte, Montana, where members of her family worked in the mines and on the railroad.

I still flinch to think that I spent all those weeks under the surveillance of men (and later women) whose job it was to monitor my behavior for signs of sloth, theft, drug abuse, or worse. Not that managers and especially "assistant managers" in low-wage settings like this are exactly the class enemy. Mostly, in the restaurant business, they are former cooks still capable of pinch-hitting in the kitchen, just as in hotels they are likely to be former clerks, and paid a salary of only about $400 a week. But everyone knows they have crossed over to the other side, which is, crudely put, corporate as opposed to human. Cooks want to prepare tasty meals, servers want to serve them graciously, but managers are there for only one reason — to make sure that money is made for some theoretical entity, the corporation, which exists far away in Chicago or New York, if a corporation can be said to have a physical existence at all. Reflecting on her career, Gail tells me ruefully that she swore, years ago, never to work for a corporation again. "They don't cut you no slack. You give and you give and they take."

"They don't cut you no slack. You give and you give and they take."

Managers can sit — for hours at a time if they want — but it's their job to see that no one else ever does, even when there's nothing to do, and this is why, for servers, slow times can be as exhausting as rushes. You start dragging out each little chore because if the manager on duty catches you in an idle moment he will give you something far nastier to do. So I wipe, I clean, I consolidate catsup bottles and recheck the cheesecake supply, even tour the tables to make sure the customer evaluation forms are all standing perkily in their places — wondering all the time how many calories I burn in these strictly theatrical exercises. In desperation, I even take the desserts out of their glass display case and freshen them up with whipped cream and bright new maraschino cherries; anything to look busy. When, on a particularly dead afternoon, Stu finds me glancing at a *USA Today* a customer has left behind, he assigns me to vacuum the entire floor with the broken vacuum cleaner, which has a handle only two feet long, and the only way to do that without incurring orthopedic damage is to proceed from spot to spot on your knees.

On my first Friday at Hearthside there is a "mandatory meeting for all restaurant employees," which I attend, eager for insight into our overall marketing strategy and the niche (your basic Ohio cuisine with a tropical twist?) we aim to inhabit. But there is no "we" at this meeting. Phillip, our top manager except for an occasional "consultant" sent out by corporate headquarters, opens it with a sneer: "The break room — it's disgusting. Butts in the ashtrays, newspapers lying around, crumbs." This windowless little room, which also houses the time clock for the entire hotel, is where we stash our bags and civilian clothes and take our half-hour meal breaks. But a break room is not a right, he tells us, it can be taken away. We should also know that the lockers in the break room and whatever is in them can be searched at any time. Then comes gossip; there has been gossip; gossip (which seems to mean employees talking among themselves) must stop. Off-duty employees are henceforth barred from eating at the restaurant, because "other servers gather around them and gossip." When Phillip has exhausted his agenda of rebukes, Joan complains about the condition of the ladies' room and I throw in my two bits about the vacuum cleaner. But I don't see any backup coming from my fellow servers, each of whom has slipped into her own personal funk; Gail, my role model, stares sorrowfully at a point six inches from her nose. The meeting ends when Andy, one of the cooks, gets up, muttering about breaking up his day off for this almighty bullshit.

Just four days later we are suddenly summoned into the kitchen at 3:30 P.M., even though there are live tables on the floor. We all — about ten of us — stand around Phillip, who announces grimly that there has been a report of some "drug activity" on the night shift and that, as a result, we are now to be a "drug-free" workplace, meaning that all new hires will be tested and possibly also current employees on a random basis. I am glad that this part of the kitchen is so dark because I find myself blushing as hard as if I had been caught toking up in the ladies' room myself: I haven't been treated this way — lined up in the corridor, threatened with locker searches, peppered with carelessly aimed accusations — since at least junior high school. Back on the floor, Joan cracks, "Next they'll be telling us we can't have *sex* on the job." When I ask Stu what happened to inspire the crackdown, he just mutters about "management decisions" and takes the opportunity to upbraid Gail and me for being too generous with the rolls. From now on there's to be only one per customer and it goes out with the dinner, not with the salad. He's also been riding the cooks, prompting Andy to come out of the kitchen and observe — with the serenity of a man whose customary implement is a butcher knife — that "Stu has a death wish today."

Later in the evening, the gossip crystallizes around the theory that 5 Stu is himself the drug culprit, that he uses the restaurant phone to order up marijuana and sends one of the late servers out to fetch it for him. The server was caught and she may have ratted out Stu, at least enough to cast some suspicion on him, thus accounting for his pissy behavior. Who knows? Personally, I'm ready to believe anything bad about Stu, who serves no evident function and presumes too much on our common ethnicity, sidling up to me one night to engage in a little nativism directed at the Haitian immigrants: "I feel like I'm the foreigner here. They're taking over the country." Still later that evening, the drug in question escalates to crack. Lionel, the busboy, entertains us for the rest of the shift by standing just behind Stu's back and sucking deliriously on an imaginary joint or maybe a pipe.

The other problem, in addition to the less-than-nurturing management style, is that this job shows no sign of being financially viable. You might imagine, from a comfortable distance, that people who live, year in and year out, on $6 to $10 an hour have discovered some survival stratagems unknown to the middle class. But no. It's not hard to get my coworkers talking about their living situations, because housing, in almost every case, is the principal source of disruption in their lives, the first thing they fill you in on when they arrive for their shifts. After a week, I have compiled the following survey:

Gail is sharing a room in a well-known downtown flophouse for $250 a week. Her roommate, a male friend, has begun hitting on her, driving her nuts, but the rent would be impossible alone.

Claude, the Haitian cook, is desperate to get out of the two-room apartment he shares with his girlfriend and two other, unrelated people. As far as I can determine, the other Haitian men live in similarly crowded situations.

*Annette, a twenty-year-old server who is six months pregnant and aban-
doned by her boyfriend, lives with her mother, a postal clerk.*

*Marianne, who is a breakfast server, and her boyfriend are paying $170 a
week for a one-person trailer.*

*Billy, who at $10 an hour is the wealthiest of us, lives in the trailer he owns,
paying only the $400-a-month lot fee.*

*The other white cook, Andy, lives on his dry-docked boat, which, as far as
I can tell from his loving descriptions, can't be more than twenty feet long.
He offers to take me out on it once it's repaired, but the offer comes with
inquiries as to my marital status, so I do not follow up on it.*

*Tina, another server, and her husband are paying $60 a night for a room
in the Days Inn. This is because they have no car and the Days Inn is in
walking distance of the Hearthside. When Marianne is tossed out of her
trailer for subletting (which is against trailer park rules), she leaves her
boyfriend and moves in with Tina and her husband.*

*Joan, who had fooled me with her numerous and tasteful outfits (hostesses
wear their own clothes), lives in a van parked behind a shopping center at
night and showers in Tina's motel room. The clothes are from thrift shops.*[1]

It strikes me, in my middle-class solipsism,° that there is gross im-
providence in some of these arrangements. When Gail and I are wrap-
ping silverware in napkins — the only task for which we are permitted to sit — she tells me she is thinking of escaping from her roommate
by moving into the Days Inn herself. I am astounded: how she can
even think of paying $40 to $60 a day? But if I was afraid of sounding
like a social worker, I have come out just sounding like a fool. She
squints at me in disbelief: "And where am I supposed to get a month's
rent and a month's deposit for an apartment?" I'd been feeling pretty
smug about my $500 efficiency, but of course it was made possible
only by the $1,300 I had allotted myself for start-up costs when I be-
gan my low-wage life: $1,000 for the first month's rent and deposit,
$100 for initial groceries and cash in my pocket, $200 stuffed away
for emergencies. In poverty, as in certain propositions in physics,
starting conditions are everything.

solipsism: the belief that the only thing that's real (or important) is oneself.

---

[1] I could find no statistics on the number of employed people living in cars or vans, but
according to a 1997 report of the National Coalition for the Homeless, "Myths and
Facts about Homelessness," nearly one-fifth of all homeless people (in 29 cities across
the nation) are employed in full- or part-time jobs.

There are no secret economies that nourish the poor; on the contrary, there are a host of special costs. If you can't put up the two months' rent you need to secure an apartment, you end up paying through the nose for a room by the week. If you have only a room, with a hot plate at best, you can't save by cooking up huge lentil stews that can be frozen for the week ahead. You eat fast food or the hot dogs and Styrofoam cups of soup that can be microwaved in a convenience store. If you have no money for health insurance — and the Hearthside's niggardly plan kicks in only after three months — you go without routine care or prescription drugs and end up paying the price. Gail, for example, was doing fine, healthwise anyway, until she ran out of money for estrogen pills. She is supposed to be on the company health plan by now, but they claim to have lost her application form and to be beginning the paperwork all over again. So she spends $9 a pop for pills to control the migraines she wouldn't have, she insists, if her estrogen supplements were covered. Similarly, Marianne's boyfriend lost his job as a roofer because he missed so much time after getting a cut on his foot for which he couldn't afford the prescribed antibiotic.

My own situation, when I sit down to assess it after two weeks of work, would not be much better if this were my actual life. The seductive thing about waitressing is that you don't have to wait for payday to feel a few bills in your pocket, and my tips usually cover meals and gas, plus something left over to stuff into the kitchen drawer I use as a bank. But as the tourist business slows in the summer heat, I sometimes leave work with only $20 in tips (the gross is higher, but servers share about 15 percent of their tips with the busboys and bartenders). With wages included, this amounts to about the minimum wage of $5.15 an hour. The sum in the drawer is piling up but at the present rate of accumulation will be more than $100 short of my rent when the end of the month comes around. Nor can I see any expenses to cut. True, I haven't gone the lentil stew route yet, but that's because I don't have a large cooking pot, potholders, or a ladle to stir with (which would cost a total of about $30 at Kmart, somewhat less at a thrift store), not to mention onions, carrots, and the indispensable bay leaf. I do make my lunch almost every day — usually some slow-burning, high-protein combo like frozen chicken patties with melted cheese on top and canned pinto beans on the side. Dinner is at the Hearthside, which offers its employees a choice of BLT, fish sandwich, or hamburger for only $2. The burger lasts longest, especially if it's heaped with gut-puckering jalapeños, but by midnight my stomach is growling again.

So unless I want to start using my car as a residence, I have to find a second or an alternative job. I call all the hotels I'd filled out house- 10 keeping applications at weeks ago — the Hyatt, Holiday Inn, Econo Lodge, Hojo's, Best Western, plus a half dozen locally run guest houses. Nothing. Then I start making the rounds again.

Understanding the Text

1. What are the reasons for the author's unhappiness in her job? Which of these reasons involve money? Which don't? (Take special care not to miss the "money dimension" to things that, on the surface, seem to have nothing to do with money.)

2. One student of this anthology's editor wrote that she could hear a pun — a double meaning — in the title "Serving in Florida." To her mind, it meant both "serving tables" in Florida and "serving time" there. Are both meanings apt, given the content of Ehrenreich's piece?

Reflection and Response

3. Does Ehrenreich's unhappiness stem from the contrast between waiting tables and her normal, professional working life? Do her co-workers — who are people more used to such jobs — feel happier than she does at the restaurant? In answering, provide specifics from the text.

4. How does Ehrenreich's account compare with experiences you have had — or know about — in the workplace?

Making Connections

5. Does Ehrenreich's account square with the argument made by Charles Murray in "What's So Bad about Being Poor?" (p. 26)? Why or why not?

6. Some readers say that Ehrenreich provided a public service with her book, by pointing out conditions widespread throughout the United States. Others contend that she was "slumming it" — having a contrived, inauthentic taste of "how the other half lives" — and that she was using the experience not to come to new, objective conclusions, but rather to advance a political agenda.

   Does this excerpt seem to you to be less worthy to be taken seriously than other firsthand accounts of hard times included in this reader, such as "On the Meaning of Plumbing and Poverty" (p. 85) or "Should Working-Class People Get B.A.'s and Ph.D.'s?" (p. 206)? Please explain.

7. *Nickel and Dimed* is not the first book by someone leading a comfortable life who deliberately assumes a false identity to learn what life at the low end of the economy is like. Two notable examples are listed below. Read one and compare it with *Nickel and Dimed*. (The first is by a famous author of fiction and non-fiction. The second is by a man who, at the time, was president of Haverford College; it includes some references to campus life.)

   Down and Out in Paris and London, by George Orwell, 1933

   Blue Collar Journal: A College President's Sabbatical, by John Royston Coleman, 1974.

Twenty Grand

Rebecca Curtis

As the title of this short story suggests, money is at the heart of it. It's a page-turner.

Author Rebecca Curtis teaches in Columbia University's graduate writing program. Her work has appeared in *Harper's*, *McSweeney's*, *n+1*, and *The O. Henry Prize Stories*, as well as other publications. In 2005 she received a Rona Jaffe Foundation Writers' Award. "Twenty Grand" originally appeared in *The New Yorker* and is collected with some of her other short stories in *Twenty Grand: And Other Tales of Love and Money*, published in 2007.

On December 13, 1979, when my mother was thirty years old, she lost an old Armenian coin. That winter was cold, and she had been sleeping with my sister and me on a foldout couch in the living room to save on heat. We lived on a cleared ledge, a natural shelf on a mountain high above a lake. The wind on the shelf was amazing. At night it leaped up to the blinking red light at the tip of the peak behind our house, then skidded back down across the pines and whistled past our windows, somehow inserting, through tiny cracks between the window and the frame, snow that piled, sloped and sparkling, on the sills.

Our driveway was a dirt road that wound through a field. It was often lined by eight-foot banks — which I climbed on my way home from school — with teetering, sand-specked bucket-lumps at their tops. Sporadically, a kid came with a tractor. When he left, the lane was clear. But overnight the wind swept snow across the shelf, up over the banks, and into the road. By morning the drifts were as deep as if the driveway hadn't been plowed at all. Every day, my mother called the kid, who was slow and did the easy jobs in town first, to try to get him to come. Then she shoveled a path to the woodpile and one to the car.

She barely ever looked at the coin. It was silver and heavy. On one side was a man with a craggy profile, a square crown, and one sleepy, thick-lidded eye, and on the other was a woman. The woman was voluptuous, wore a gown, and held something in her outstretched hand — maybe wheat. The coin wasn't a perfect circle, and its surface was pocked. But it had been my mother's mother's, and she kept it in her purse.

On that day she was in a foul mood. My sister was one and a half, and I was six. For weeks, the sky had been a chalky gray that darkened to charcoal in the afternoon. Snowflakes were wafting onto the car. We were going to visit my father. Before we left, my mother glanced in the kitchen mirror, tucked her hair behind her ears, and said, "We're out of groceries. If we don't get some cash from your father, I don't know what we'll eat tonight."

We often drove to visit him. He was a Guard bum for the Air National Guard, and lived sixty miles south, at the base in Portsmouth, where he was on alert. Occasionally, he flew to England to pilot refuelers for the looking-glass planes that swung along the Russian coast, but mostly he was on alert. This was temporary. He and my mother had married young, hastily, out of excitement, and spent five years moving around the country, to wherever my father was posted. But when my mother got pregnant they'd decided they needed a house. He'd switched from active duty to the Guard, and was stationed in New Hampshire. My mother liked Portsmouth. The sea kept the air mild, the streets in the downtown were cobblestoned and lined by brass lanterns, and the university, where she could get a job or take classes, was close by. But the houses there were expensive, and my father's mother, who lived an hour north, offered my parents an acre of land for free. They drove up to the mountain. They walked across the shelf. It was summer. The hay was high, gold and flecked with Queen Anne's lace. My father asked what she thought. He said, "It's just for now"; and she said, "All right." They moved all their things into his mother's house. A week later, my father began to build a bungalow with a steep roof, gingerbread trim, and a small wooden deck, like the ones he'd seen built into hills nearby.

While on alert, my father lived with several hundred other men and wore a pea-green jumpsuit that, aside from the gold-zippered pockets on his calves and hips and the blue patch on his left shoulder, looked not unlike the pajamas that my sister and I wore to bed. The other men also wore the jumpsuits — except for the ones who wore navy polyester suits with stars — and they bunked alongside my father, in a vast facility that, much like a high-tech rabbit warren, existed largely under the earth. The complex was surrounded by two barbed-wire fences. To get inside, we had to stop at an electric gate and be "checked" by friendly black men wearing rifles. Then we walked — I always looked over my shoulder — down a long, dark, sloping concrete tunnel.

In the bunker, we were allowed to go to the library. The room was small, gingery, and hot, with shelves of leather-bound books. On the scratchy red chairs in the narrow aisles lay magazines, their articles about naked women or cars. Brown stuffing sprang out from the seats of the chairs, and cigarettes burned in tins on their arms.

The other place we could go was the rec center, which contained a Foosball table, a pool table (one ball missing, two cues with broken tips), a Parcheesi board, and a soda machine. The cafeteria down the hall smelled foreign and delicious — at its far end were vats of spaghetti and of soupy brown sauce, inside which, I guessed, was steak. Best of all, the food was free. But my mother and my sister and I were not allowed to eat it. We were not supposed to be in the warren, in fact, for more than an hour at a time. But my father sometimes sneaked us into the theater, a room with a few benches and a slide screen, to watch a movie; and when I got hungry, as I always did, he'd carry me into the cafeteria, just far enough so that I could see the vats, then take me back out and ask me what I wanted, so that he could order it himself and slip it to me in the library. Usually I wanted lime Jell-O and garlic bread.

My father was on base five or six days at a stretch, four times a month. He was often on duty at Christmas, and was never sick. He was short and pale. But he had excellent posture. He admired Elvis's style, and Henry Ford's business sense. When my mother burned toast, he told her not to throw it out. He ate it himself and washed it down with burnt coffee from the bottom of the pot. He was cheerful, deeply in love with my mother, and quick to get mad.

However much money he left for us while he was on alert, we 10 were careful with it, spending it until it was gone. Then, on the third or fourth day of his absence, we'd drive to visit him and ask for more.

He'd tried to get a job in town. He'd taken a position at a cement plant, but it had gone bankrupt. Next, he'd signed on with a stationery company. But he didn't love his boss or selling pencils, and soon he rejoined the Guard. The work, he said, was steady. We were all healthy, so could do without benefits. He missed us. But it was neat when he got to fly the jets. The economy would swing up soon. And when it did we'd look at our options.

• • •

My mother zipped us into our snowsuits and dragged us to her Rabbit hatchback. We waited while she started it, swept the snow off, and scraped the ice from the windows. Then we wobbled down our long driveway, the engine ululating through drifts. Once we reached the bottom of the mountain, we drove on sharply twisting two-lane roads, under fifty-foot pines. In the distance were striped mountains, dots of skiers, lifts. After coming down from the Belknap Range, we wound along the last miles of Winnipesaukee. Passing the lake took time, and it was entertaining to imagine the elegant houses that sprawled upon its white edge as our own, and to count the trucks and the bright-colored ice shacks on its surface and predict how soon they'd fall in.

After the lake was a long highway bordered by forest, and then the tolls, and beyond them our father.

Each trip was thrilling, because in winter we never left the house, except to go to Tillman's Discount World. We bought nothing, unless my mother saw something we needed. She'd study the item, then touch it and say, "It's all cotton, no polyester. We could use a new comforter. The old one's worn." She'd turn it, see the price, and put it back. Later she'd say, "It's a good deal. It's seventy percent off. It might not be here tomorrow." I'd nod. She'd add, "We don't need it. Your father would be upset." We'd walk the aisles. An hour would pass. She'd buy me a pair of jeans for school. Just as we were about to leave the store, the cart would swerve, go back to home furnishings, and she'd lift the heavy package and say firmly, "The old one has holes."

At home we had great days. She was good at cooking, sewing, and folding laundry. She could wash my sister's diapers then bleach the tub and wash my sister in an hour flat. She did our taxes without a calculator. Sometimes she seemed quiet and marked off days on the calendar. But she also said that our life would be perfect if my father's mother didn't live next door.

My grandmother lived in the only other house on the shelf, a tall 15 white Colonial, and she called often, to tell my mother that once again wind or raccoons had knocked our trash cans over, or to ask when my father would be home. She'd given us land and loved my father, so she also gave advice. If his car was gone for a week, she'd tell my mother that he should work less hard or he'd get sick. If his car was in our driveway for more than two days, she'd call to say that he'd better go back to the base, lest his superiors realize that he wasn't necessary and fire him. In his absence, she sometimes appeared at our door with a gift: raspberry jam she'd canned herself. And, while she drank the coffee my mother had brewed, her eyes would light on whatever was new in our house — a set of dishtowels, a plastic tablecloth — and she would praise the object's beauty and ask how much the object had cost.

That morning, she'd installed a snow fence in our field. My mother thought snow fences were ugly. Also, she had a theory that they caused more drift than they prevented. But three men and two trucks had been in our road at six a.m. By the time my mother heard the drills and ran outside to ask the men what they were doing, her black hair flying in the wind, the fence was already installed. When my mother called my grandmother to say, politely, that she didn't want a snow fence, my grandmother said, "I know you don't, Annah. It's for him." And hung up.

My mother looked at the phone. Put it back on the hook. Looked in the fridge and saw that, except for some leftover meat loaf, we were

out of food. She turned to me and said, "She should have asked." I nodded. "Your grandmother," she said, "does not respect our privacy." I
nodded again.

But secretly I admired my grandmother, because she read me the
books I liked five times in a row upon demand and kept crystal bowls
of foil-wrapped chocolates all around her den. She also hugged me a
lot, and at times she sat me down for serious talks:

"Your mother spends all your father's money."

"I know." 20

"I myself waited twenty years to buy a dishwasher."

"I know."

"People should only spend what they have."

"I agree."

"I didn't even think about a washer or a dryer." 25

"We don't have a dryer."

"Your mother has ruined your father's life."

"I know."

"Want to play Rack-O?"

"Okay." 30

And later:

"Take this coffee cake to your mother."

"She won't want it."

"Do you want it?"

"Yes." 35

"Then say it's for you."

"Okay."

• • •

We drove the long stretch before the tolls. At the first tollbooth, my
mother used the last token in the roll between the seats. She
hummed; my sister fell asleep. The snow was falling straight down
so that the air seemed both white and light purple and the firs
peeked through it from along the side of the road. When the second
tollbooth appeared in the distance, my mother's hand moved
through her purse. But she kept looking ahead. Then she passed the
purse back to me. "Look in here," she said. "See if you can find some
quarters."

I looked. I found safety pins, a tissue, and a dinner mint. "No quarters," I said.

She slowed and peered at the tollbooth. "Do me a favor," she said. 40
"Check and see if you find any under the seats."

I climbed past my sister. Her head was on her shoulder, and she had thrush-blobs at the edges of her mouth. I pushed my belly to the hump, and reached into the dark space above each mat. Eventually, I touched a cracker with a soft mauled edge.

"It's okay," my mother said. "It's all right. Come up."

We'd pulled into the toll. My mother looked through the purse herself. Then she told the woman in the booth that she was out of money. That she was sorry, but she could pay the woman on her way back.

"I'm sorry, too," the woman said. "But you can't do that."

The woman was older — sixty, perhaps — her hair gray and short. 45 Above the trim of her parka, her large face was grim, or maybe just red from the cold.

My mother took a picture from her wallet and handed it up. "I'm going to see my husband," she said. "This is him. He's at the base down the road. I can get cash from him as soon as I get there, and I'll come right back." She hesitated. "You can keep the I.D. if you need something to hold," she said.

The woman pointed toward the empty lot to the right of the tolls.

My mother pleaded with the woman, to the extent that she was capable of it, saying we were an hour from home, the roads were bad, she couldn't turn around now, had two kids, in tow — but her pleading, more insistent than humble, just made the woman mad. The woman said that if my mother did not pull over she would sound an alarm.

My mother looked down at her lap. Her lips pressed together; she seemed nonplussed. She reached into her purse, unzipped a small pocket, and removed the old coin.

"Here," she said. "It's the same as a dollar." 50

The woman stuck out her arm, took it, and grunted.

For the rest of the ride, my mother did not speak, and when we arrived at the bunker we did not go in. Instead, we stood outside the fence. I was cold, and I could see Derek, the chief guard inside the gate, waiting to check me. I mentioned this.

"You don't need to be checked," my mother said.

"Yes, I do," I said. "I need to be checked."

Derek smiled at me. His smile said, We have serious business to 55 do. I know we might not be able to do it now. But later, I will check you.

At last my father came out. He was grinning. The electric gate lifted. He ducked under and swung out his arms.

My mother walked into them.

Derek looked away, in order to preserve our dignity — mine and his.

"What's wrong?" my father said.

She shook her head. 60

We got back into the car and drove past a frozen marsh and some acres of trailers to the guesthouse: a yellow one-story building with a flat tar roof. Its entry consisted of a dining room — a room with a table long enough for several families to eat at — and a kitchenette with a fridge that was always empty except for the perpetually abandoned Chinese food in deteriorating, grease-soaked brown bags. Above the stove were cupboards containing sugar packets, mouse turds, and instant coffee. Down a hall were three bedrooms, each equipped with bed, nightstand, ashtray, dock radio. Typically two or three families made use of the guesthouse at any one time, and the sounds of radio static floated through the hall. In the living room, two brown couches sat atop an orange rug. Behind them was a bin of toys I knew well: plastic rabbits with foolish, ink-smeared faces and stuffed bears with crusty patches on their bodies.

I was dumped in the living room. My mother pulled my father into a bedroom. I turned on the TV and set my sister in front of it. Then I slipped down the hall and sat by the bedroom door.

At first I heard the usual sounds: low voices, metal legs scraping the floor, the radio. Then there was fiscal talk. My mother asked for money. He gave her a ten. She asked for a twenty. He told her ten was all he had, save for a five he'd set aside for himself. She said we needed groceries.

"You got groceries last week," he said.

"We need groceries for this week," she said.   65

"Here," he said. He gave her the five.

"I don't want it," she said. "What will you use?"

"The food here is free." He paused. "If I want a beer," he added, "I'll borrow a few bucks from the guys."

"You have tokens?"

"Yeah. I have a roll in my car."   70

A sound escaped her: a sigh.

My knees had fallen asleep. Intriguing Chinese-food smells were coming from the kitchen: another couple had finished their nap and heated some up. I wanted food, and thought they might give me some if I asked, but was too intrigued to leave the door.

"I can't do it," my mother said. "I can't do it anymore."

"Come on, Annah."

"I'm by myself with the girls for a week. Your mother calls every day. 75 I go crazy."

"Why don't you just tell her when I'll be home?"

"It's not her business."

"I don't know what you want me to do."

"You need to get another job."

"We tried that already."   80

"I need to see you at night. I want you to come home at night like other men."

"I'll apply for shorter shifts."

"That's not enough."

They went back and forth for a while. Truly, I think, he liked his job. He'd never been in a war. Or only twice, and only to fly refuelers for the bombers, which meant he'd hovered beyond missile range and hardly seemed to count. Finally, she said, "I spent my coin."

"Your coin?"   85

"My mother's coin."

"You spent that coin?"

"Yes."

He said, "I wish you hadn't spent that coin."

"Well, I did."   90

Nothing. Then, "Why did you do that?"

"I needed money for the toll."

"You said you'd never spend it."

"I told you, I was out of money. I needed money for the toll."

Silence.   95

"It was my coin," she said.

I knew the coin. I knew that my mother's mother had given it to her just before she died, and that she'd died when my mother was a child. During her life, she'd worked as the superintendent of two apartment buildings in Watertown, Massachusetts, and had owned a corner store. She was heavy-set, kept her hair in a bun, and wore a gray wool dress and single strand of pearls, even when collecting rent from tenants or loading coal into a furnace. She had not been home much. But she'd had a lot of friends and had loved her life. In the hospital, she gave my mother the coin and said that it was a dollar, and that if my mother kept it, she would always have a dollar in her purse.

"That coin was very valuable," my father said.

"I know," my mother said. "It was money."

"No, Annah, that coin was worth a lot."   100

"What do you mean?"

"I mean it was worth a lot."

"How come you didn't tell me?"

"You would have spent it."

Silence. He was right. She would have spent it. Then, "How do you 105
know?"

A long pause. "I got it evaluated."

"How much?"

"Twenty grand," he said.

A cave opened its mouth in my heart. I knew what twenty grand was. I knew what a googol, the largest number in the world, was, too — a hundred zeroes — but twenty grand seemed better. I saw a lifetime of unshared Happy Meals and always getting a soda with dinner at Ye Olde Tavern restaurant. I knew that with twenty grand we couldn't have bought the ocean but it seemed to me that we could have bought Wallace Sands, the beach we went to, and perhaps its section of ocean, and the Isles of Shoals, which my mother was always pointing out and which appeared from the shore as a long humpy gray shadow on the horizon, like a whale.

"You tricked me," she said. I'd heard her sound indignant before, 110 but I'd never heard her sound indignant and justified. "You tricked me," she said again.

"I didn't trick you," my father said. "I just didn't tell you."

She said nothing.

He cleared his throat. "We'll get it back."

"What?"

"We'll get it back." 115

"How?"

His plan unfolded. It was simple and obvious: The lady would still be at the tollbooth. They'd give her a dollar, or a ten if need be, and get the coin back. A discussion followed. They'd get it back. Then they'd sell it. They would? They really would. Were they partners? They were. Was my father willing to quit the military, sell the house, and move us someplace warmer and more exciting, like Portsmouth? No, he wasn't sure about selling the house. But he thought we could rent it out — maybe some skiers might want it — and use the money to rent a small place in Portsmouth. As for the Guard, he said, he wouldn't mind getting out. The Guard had been good to him. But he didn't want to be a Guard bum forever. He knew guys who'd opened franchises — Kentucky Fried Chickens — and done well. "You just need" — his voice deepened — "seed money and a loan." The bed creaked. If she still wanted to go to school, he said, he was willing to help her look into it.

She said, "I want to decorate it myself. The house."

He said, "I'd like a garage."

"We have to be careful. We don't want to spend it all at once." 120

He cleared his throat.

"I'd like a new couch," she said.

"You can have that," he said. "I'd like a garage."

"First the move," she said. "Then see what's left."

● ● ●

My father checked out on a one-hour emergency pass. We all got into 125
my mother's car. We drove to the exit of the base, stopping at the gate-
house so that my father could show the pass to the guard. The guard
was young, with blond eyebrows and fat hands. He saw us, read the
pass, and stopped smiling. He said, "Don't be late, Bill." The gate rose.
We headed back the way we'd come.

On the way, I saw a McDonald's. It was in a valley that we could see
from the highway, a big gold "M" in the distance. I requested a stop. I
mentioned my desire for a Happy Meal.

"We don't have any money," my mother said.

"Yes, you do," I said. "You have ten dollars."

"The ten dollars is not for Happy Meals," she said. "It's for groceries."

I made what I felt was a tragic sound. 130

"Just wait," she said. "There's crackers in the glove compartment."

"No crackers," I wailed.

She reached back and slapped me.

The slap was weak and barely touched my skin. But I was humili-
ated, because she was my great love. I vowed that I would never care
for her again.

We pulled over just before the tollbooths. We parked in the shame- 135
ful turnaround lot. My mother and father got out and spoke together
near the car. Then they opened my door and studied my sister and me.

"What about them?" my mother said.

My father shrugged. "We'll just be a minute."

She glanced at the tollbooths. Hers was fifth, in a row of ten. Snow-
laden trucks were sliding up to the booths at thirty miles an hour,
floating on ice and sometimes missing the stop. She held out her palm,
and in an instant the flakes falling on it became water.

She said, "We could carry them."

He checked his watch. "Leave them here." 140

She looked at me, said, "Stay in the car," and shut the door.

I watched them walk to the edge of the highway and grab hands.
They stood and waited for several minutes while trucks passed. Then
they ran across the first lane, paused on the first toll island, and dashed
across again.

● ● ●

Later that night, I asked my mother what had happened and she said
it wasn't my business. But after I asked her a fourth time, she told me.

• • •

The woman was still there.

"Sure, I remember you," she said. "You gave me this." She held it up.   145

Just then a blue sedan slid into the stall. My parents hurried up onto the platform behind the booth, a raised nub, and squished themselves against the booth's metal side. "I have a dollar now," my mother said, when the sedan was gone. "This is my husband." My father said, "Hello, I'm Bill," in his most charming, glad-to-meet-you voice. The woman nodded.

"I came to get my coin back," my mother said. She held out a token. The woman shook her head. "This coin belongs to me," she said.

"It's my coin," my mother said.

"You gave it to me," the woman said, "and now it's mine. I took it out   150 of the box" — she pointed to a cardboard box on a metal counter — "and I replaced it with my own dollar."

A car veered into the stall. My parents climbed back onto the nub. More cars followed. When they stepped down, my mother had to shout to be heard above the traffic. "I didn't give it to you," she said. "I left it with you for safekeeping."

The woman told my parents to leave. She said she wasn't a fool. She knew the coin was worth money. She could tell, because it looked old. She'd called a friend who knew about coins, and the friend had said it sounded valuable, perhaps very. My mother nodded. Then she begged. The coin was the only thing she had of her mother's, she said, and her mother had died when she was nine. It was why she'd kept it all these years. Yes, it was worth something. But it was sentimental to her. It was her memory, really, of her mother.

My father rubbed his nose. "It's not worth much," he said.

The woman gestured my parents back onto the nub. Then she opened a panel in the booth, and spoke to them through it while she serviced cars. Her own mother was not alive, of course, she said. Her own mother had died years ago. She herself was sixty-two and worked in a tollbooth. She had arthritis and shingles, not to mention other things. She shrugged, and said she was getting it appraised by a dealer, and selling it.

They had been at the booth for half an hour. The sky was dark.   155

If they didn't leave now, the woman said, she'd call the police.

My mother leaned forward. "It's worth twenty grand," she said.

The woman blinked, and waved my mother away.

• • •

When they got back to the lot, they found that we were gone. My father was enraged — he was overdue on his emergency pass — but he proposed a plan.

My mother agreed to his plan. She started walking north along the shoulder, looking for us. But then she turned into the woods. She felt sure that wandering into them was something I might have done. It was, but it was equally something she herself might have done. There were an infinite number of places to enter the forest, which stretched darkly, politely, on both sides of the road. It was overwhelming, but also irresistible. My mother was compelled, perhaps, by the hopelessness of the task. Of course, footprints would have been the thing to look for; but the snow was falling thickly and had already left two inches on top of the Rabbit, and she decided that it had covered our tracks. She walked into the forest until she could no longer hear the cars on the highway, and sat down. A tree, a handsome green pine, immediately dropped a load of snow on her head. She brushed it off. Her jeans grew wet. The forest said shuh, shuh, and the pines leaned to and fro in the wind. Thirty more minutes passed; my father strode back and forth by the tollbooths, looking for my mother. He was unable to find her tracks in the dark. He shouted her name and swore a lot. When he finally saw her footprints, he followed them a quarter mile into the woods and found her sitting, covered in snow, under the spruce.

"Get up," he said.

"I can't."

"Get up."

"It's too late," she said. "They're gone. We've lost them, and it's my fault. I never should have left them in the car."

He was a fool, but he was not a fool. He saw that she was pining for the coin.

He slapped her.

"We're looking for the girls," he said.

They trudged back to the car. They opened the choke, pumped the gas, and turned the car on. Then they got out the brush and the scraper and brushed off the snow and scraped off the ice, and got in.

● ● ●

After my parents had left, I'd unbuckled my sister and pulled her from the car. I'd walked us south along the shoulder toward McDonald's. We'd gone about thirty feet when a white sedan pulled over. The door opened, and a woman in a burgundy coat stepped out. She asked me where our parents were. My sister began to cry. I said they'd gone on an errand, and saw, in the woman's face, that she thought we'd been abandoned. She asked me where my parents' vehicle was; I walked her to it. When she saw the Rabbit — with its mismatched fenders (one orange, one blue) and rusty frame — I saw that she thought they'd left the car behind, too. She squatted down, there in the lot, and brought her large white face close to mine. She asked if I was hungry. I nodded. Her brow wrinkled. She asked if my sister and I had eaten that day at all. We'd had meat loaf right before leaving home. But for some reason when I looked at her long burgundy coat my mouth twitched and I said, "Just crackers."

At McDonald's I ate two boxes of Chicken McNuggets and six con- 170
tainers of sweet-and-sour sauce and drank two orange drinks. My sister was too senseless with sorrow to eat her own, and the woman's husband, Mr. Swendseid, had to walk around the restaurant, bouncing her up and down in his arms. Mrs. Swendseid watched me eat. Then she told me to put on my coat.

By the time my parents reached the police station, Mrs. Swendseid had played three sets of Connect Four with me and was going for a fourth. She'd let me win twice and had won once herself. She'd also described her house on the sea, where, she'd suggested, we might stay temporarily.

I don't know what my parents said when they arrived. Eventually, a sergeant must have shoved a thumb toward the lounge in back.

My father made some stiff gestures toward gratitude at first: "Glad you found them, thanks for bringing them here — "

Which were answered by the Swendseids: "The least we could do . . . on a day like this . . . twenty degrees. That's without the wind-chill, dear, with the windchill it's twenty below — "

And interrupted by my father: "For Christ's sake!" 175

Then various accusations came out: "Stole our children . . . we were ten feet away . . . left them alone for five minutes — "

"More like twenty, I'd say. We waited by your Rabbit — "

"You were nowhere in sight. What kind of parent" — this was Mr. Swendseid, in whose arms I was being squeezed — "these babies . . . nothing but crackers for a week — "

At which point the accumulated joy of the two boxes of Chicken Mc-Nuggets, six packets of sweet-and-sour sauce, and two orange drinks overcame me, and I threw up in his lap.

"Christ," he said, and shoved me away. 180

Mrs. Swendseid extended her arms somewhat gingerly. Produced a tissue and wiped my mouth. "The poor dear," she said. "No wonder! No protein in weeks — she can't digest it anymore!"

My father looked very small next to Mr. Swendseid, and, perhaps because of this, was standing far away from him, near the door.

My mother knelt down. Her hair hung in wild curls. Her eyes were dark brown with spots of gold, like stars drowning in a muddy pond. She said, "Tell the lady you lied."

I took a look at Mrs. Swendseid. Her face expressed disappoint- 185 ment. Her white hair was coiled high on her head; in the press of her maple lips, which she'd colored in my presence, there was a tremor. I saw a snobbish pity in her eyes. I thought of the green train with working lights and three speeds that I'd admired two Christmases running in the Sears catalog, and I had felt I'd get this one from Mrs. Swendseid.

"You're stupid," I told her.

My mother made me apologize. I did. Mrs. Swendseid said that she should have known better than to pick up a strange child from the highway.

• • •

On the way back to the base, my parents laughed about the whole fiasco. They did not mention the coin. My father particularly enjoyed the fact that I'd got sick on Mr. Swendseid, and said more than once, "He was pretty surprised," as if my dinner's ejection had been a swift and patriotic strike in his defense.

But when we reached the base my mother grew quiet. My father got out of the car and walked around to the driver's side.

"Okay," he said.   190

She looked into the dark. Snow was falling thickly on the windshield, through which the lights along the barbed-wire fence twinkled, exotic and smeared.

"You can't stay here," he said.

She mentioned that she'd hoped he would come home. She said that he could say it was an emergency.

"It's not an emergency," he said.

She put the car in gear. The shift stuck, and she did it a second time.   195

"Drive slow," he said.

We did. The snow came down in gusts, like ghosts slapping themselves against the car, and I knew we would die. When we reached the bottom of our mountain, it was past midnight. Before the steep hill to our house was a flat stretch of fifty feet. My mother stopped the Rabbit, gunned the engine, and hoped the momentum would take us up. On the fifth try, it did. When she got to our driveway, she pulled hard to the right, the car swung into the drive, and its wheels spun, then spun again.

She got out and got my sister out. "Put your hat and mittens on," she said. The snow had stopped. Around us was the world I knew well: my grandmother's house at the midpoint of the mountain, the road climbing up into the woods, and the little mountain behind, all covered in white. Our driveway was a perfect slide of ice. I took a step and fell. Got up and fell again. I decided to crawl. My mother laughed at me. But after falling a few times she hooked my sister under an arm and crawled, too. When we rounded the bend, I saw our house far ahead — she'd left a lamp on — and the black vigil of trees at the field's edge. At the top of the sky was the moon.

"The moon!" I said. "Ooh!"

It was full. Or almost full, like a lumpy opal or a nice fake pearl.   200

I howled. The idea had appeal. The forest seemed dark and deadly, the house worse, as if it might be concealing something upstairs that would wait until the lights went out to strike. But as a wolf I was safe. I howled, and my mother howled obligingly, and my sister made a silly woo-woo noise. We heard a weak bark from the trees.

"Hurry up," my mother said.

The yip came again. It was a coyote, the one that skulked by the woods' edge in late afternoon. But I felt a thrill in my loins as when I had to pee. I howled.

"Shut up," my mother said.

We reached the house. She turned on more lights. I saw a maudlin   205 tear in her eye.

"You shut up," I said. I began to imagine that it wasn't too late to find Mrs. Swendseid and tell her I'd changed my mind.

But why did my mother cry? Undoubtedly, for the twenty grand. But also, perhaps, for other things, such as all the things twenty grand could have bought — the house in Portsmouth, the garage, the new job for my father. Or perhaps for her dead mother, the coin, her someday career.

● ● ●

When my father came home a few days later, he was unusually solicitous for several days. He made dinner and washed the dishes after, and when he drove to the store, he brought back a Hershey's chocolate bar and left it in the china cabinet for my mother, where it disappeared piece by piece. He told her she looked pretty in a blue dress, and in the afternoons he walked to the shed and chopped wood. Then one morning, in the middle of ironing a shirt, my mother paused and said, "I miss my mother's coin," and my father turned from the other room and said, "Then you shouldn't have spent it."

Understanding the Text

1. In the case of this family, would having more money have made the difference between unhappiness and happiness? Explain.

2. How healthy is the mother's response to trouble and loss in "Twenty Grand"? How about the father's?

3. In paragraph 11, the father is described as feeling that the economy "would swing up soon" and that, when it did, he and his family would "look at [its] options." What do you predict for this family if the father finds work at double the pay? Why?

Reflection and Response

4. Which details of this family's story will probably stick with you the longest? Why?

5. As a work of fiction, is "Twenty Grand" less persuasive than government reports or scholarly analyses would be? Why or why not?

Making Connections

6. How do the hard times described in "Twenty Grand" compare with those of Barbara Ehrenreich in "Serving in Florida" (p. 36)? How do they compare with the lives of Thai peasants described by Charles Murray in "What's So Bad about Being Poor?" (p. 26)?

7. Interview a person who is now — or was once — poor enough to know what it means to worry about money for the basics in life, like food and shelter. That person might be a friend or family member, or someone living in a nursing home or retirement community.

   Ask that person to describe his/her poverty to you:
   - What caused it?
   - What are all the challenges that came with it? (The more specific anecdotes you can elicit from your interviewee, the better.)
   - Did it end? If so, how?
   - Has it produced any benefits, such as strength of character or a heightened appreciation of certain aspects of life?
   - Would the person whom you interview recommend being poor for a while?

     Alternatively, find a good, lengthy interview with such a person in a nonfiction source. Locate in the text, or infer from it, as many answers to these five questions as you can.

"Priceless" TV Ads

MasterCard

Most Americans are familiar with the "Priceless" ads of MasterCard, which began airing on TV in 1997. They trace happiness to money in almost poetic ways. Men, women, and children are depicted doing things highly valued by our society — taking part in sports (or attending sports events), sharing warm occasions with family and friends, going on exotic vacations, etc. — and, in each case, the expenses incurred for the activity are itemized. Then, the activity's payoff is dubbed "priceless." Here are a few examples.

Ad No. 1:

What Happens

We see a woman in her twenties or thirties horseback riding, driving a sports car, scuba diving, floating in a simulated zero gravity space flight, fencing, and cliff diving. During footage of her horseback riding, one expense incurred to ride horseback is mentioned. During footage of her driving at high speed, one expense involved in doing that is mentioned . . . and so forth.

Text

Riding boots: $600.

Vintage helmet: $125.

Dive mask: $125.

Zero gravity flight: $3,700.

Fencing foil: $97.

Singing lessons: $183.

What Happens Then

At this point, we see the young woman — who, a moment earlier, had dived off a seaside cliff — emerge from the water below, smiling.

Text

Getting the most out of life:

Priceless.

Ad No. 2

What Happens

A boy and his father go to a baseball game together.

Text

Two tickets: $46.

Two hot dogs, two popcorns, two sodas: $27.

One autographed baseball: $50.

Real conversation with eleven-year-old son:

Priceless.

Ad No. 3

What Happens

Different people in an airport in the UK reunite happily with loved ones who arrive from around the world.

Text

Ticket from Toronto: 299 pounds.

Ticket from New York: 228 pounds.

Ticket from Cape Town: 449 pounds.

Ticket from Sydney: 595 pounds.

Spending Christmas together: Priceless.

Ad No. 4

What Happens

A simply dressed, cute, one-year-old girl plays with a big empty 5 box. By the end, she walks away unsteadily with the box over her head.

Text

Most popular toy for toddlers: $500.

Most popular stuffed animal for toddlers: $350.

Most popular picture book for toddlers: $60.

Watching her play with a cardboard box instead:

Priceless.

Standard Tag Line

"There are some things money can't buy.
For everything else, there's MasterCard."

Understanding the Text

1. The adjective "priceless" can mean either "having no price" or "being of value beyond any price." Which is the operative meaning in these ads — the first definition? the second? both? Elaborate.

Reflection and Response

2. Do these ads succeed with you? That is, do they incline you to make use of a credit card? Why or why not?

3. What could explain MasterCard's decision to produce Ad No. 4, which features an empty box, rather than the product that *came* in the box and might have been charged on a credit card?

4. Of the different types of experience you've had so far in life, which do *you* consider "priceless" sources of happiness? Do any of them actually come with no price tag, free?

Making Connections

5. How might David Myers (p. 15) view the MasterCard ads?

6. Would Juliet Schor (p. 61) and Elizabeth Warren (p. 64) agree with each other about the extent to which such advertising explains the financial straits middle-class Americans find themselves in? Cite examples from their texts to support your argument.

When Spending Becomes You

Juliet Schor

Juliet Schor is a prolific analyst of American consumption, but at one point in her writing she briefly puts aside her data and regression analyses to do something so simple that any reader of this anthology could have done the same: she makes a list of all the items and services a typical, middle-class American family spends its money on. Then, she simply wonders out loud whether we Americans need it all.

Schor's books include *The Overworked American: The Unexpected Decline of Leisure* (1992), *The Overspent American: Why We Want What We Don't Need* (1998), and *Plenitude: The New Economics of True Wealth* (2010).

The most striking feature of household spending in modern America is its sheer volume. The typical middle- to upper-middle-class house-hold occupies more than two thousand square feet of floor space, owns at least two cars, a couple of couches, numerous chairs, beds, and tables, a washer and dryer, more than two televisions, a VCR, and has cable. The kitchen contains a conventional oven, a microwave, a frost-free refrigerator, a blender, a coffee maker, a tea kettle, a food processor, and so many pots, pans, dishes, cups and glasses, storage containers, kitchen utensils, and pieces of flatware that they aren't even counted. Elsewhere in the house are a personal computer and printer, telephones, an answering machine, a calculator, a stereo or CD player, musical instruments, and many pieces of art — in addition to paintings and reproductions, there are decorative items such as vases, plates, and statuettes, photographs in frames, and knick-knacks. In the bathroom are a hair dryer, a scale, perhaps an electric toothbrush or shaver, and cabinets overflowing with towels, shampoos, conditioners, face creams, and other cosmetics. The closets are stuffed with clothes and shoes of all types: dresses, suits, pants, shirts, sweaters, coats, hats, boots, sneakers, flats, pumps, walking shoes, patent leathers, and loafers. And don't forget the jewelry. In addition to watches, the diamond ring, and other high-value items, there's usually a large collection of costume jewelry: bead necklaces, bracelets, and earrings, earrings, earrings. The family room is filled with books, videos, tapes, CDs, magazines, and more photos and knickknacks. The floors are covered with rugs or carpet, and throughout the house are scattered other pieces of furniture, accented perhaps with dried or silk flowers. Stored in the garage or basement is all the sports equipment, such as bicycles and skis, as well as luggage and totes, lawn and garden tools, and broken appliances. (Some developers now routinely build three-car garages — two spaces for the cars, one for the junk.) In addition to all these durable products (of which this is a very incomplete inventory), households spend heavily on services such as child care, movies, restaurants and bars, hotel stays, airplane trips, haircuts, massages, visits to Disney World, lawyer bills, insurance premiums, interest payments, and, sometimes, rental on the storage space where even more stuff resides.

> Some developers now routinely build three-car garages — two spaces for the cars, one for the junk.

If you are a typical American consumer, you did not always have so much. There was probably a time in your adult life when you could fit everything you owned into your car and drive off into the sunset. Now you need professionals to transport your possessions. You spend hundreds, perhaps thousands of dollars a year to insure or protect them. As you survey your material landscape, you may wonder how this state of affairs came to be. You certainly didn't intend to imitate those medieval armies that became sitting ducks — unable to move on account of the creature comforts they started lugging around. Each purchase made sense at the time. Many were truly necessary. Some were captivating, giving you that "I just have to have this" feeling. But added together, they raise the possibility that yours is a lifestyle of excess.

Understanding the Text

1. Schor doesn't outright say, "You don't *need* items a., b., and c.; you could live just as well without such things." Would her point have had a greater impact if she had put it more explicitly? Why or why not?

2. How do you interpret Schor's comparison of us to "medieval armies" in paragraph 2? Does it make sense to you?

Reflection and Response

3. Write a response to this piece that starts in one of these two ways:

   - Of the possessions of a typical middle-class American household today, I suspect that certain ones Juliet Schor considers dispensable are ones I consider essential.

   or

   - Juliet Schor's implicit critique of American overconsumption resonates with me.

Making Connections

4. In the book from which this reading was taken, Juliet Schor inserts the same Roper Center chart, "The Good Life," that appears in this anthology (p. 24). Is that surprising? Elaborate.

5. The reading above was taken from Juliet Schor's *The Overspent American,* but another one of Schor's books is titled *The Overworked American.* Arguably, a person should want to know more than whether a given purchase adds to happiness: he or she should want to know whether the happiness produced (if any) is sufficient to justify the amount of work required to earn enough money to cover the price of the purchase.

   Is making such a calculation feasible? How would you go about it? What problems must be overcome in doing such a calculation? (For example, would you need to factor in whether someone's paying job is *inherently* rewarding?)

The Vanishing Middle Class

Elizabeth Warren

Millions of middle-class Americans experience hardships today unknown to their parents. One analysis lays part of the blame for this situation at those Americans' own doorstep, concluding that they spend too much on services and items they don't need. Elizabeth Warren, however, rises to the defense of the middle class. The current state of affairs, she claims, is not of ordinary people's own making.

One influential event from Warren's youth was the heart attack her father suffered when she was 12. In the months that followed, she saw her family's income plunge, even as medical expenses mounted. One result was the loss of their car, on which they couldn't keep up payments.

A specialist in consumer law and bankruptcy, Elizabeth Warren has taught at the Harvard University Law School since 1992. In 2012, she was elected to the U.S. Senate from Massachusetts.

Making It to the Middle

What is the middle class? Whatever it is, most Americans believe that they are in it. When asked in an open-ended question to identify their class membership, more than 91.6 percent of the adult population of the United States volunteer an identification with "working" or "middle" class.[1] Although there are people who call themselves upper class and others who call themselves lower class, these identifications are numerically somewhat rare.

Although the U.S. government has defined the poverty level, no government agency defines the middle class. One reason is that class status is not a function merely of money or other easily counted characteristics. The running joke of *The Beverly Hillbillies* was that money did not change the social class of the Clampetts. On the other side, people from "good families" who have fallen on hard times might be described as "high class," but their status is not a matter of current income.

Careful studies of the American population show that Americans determine class identification using many variables, including education, occupational status, cultural factors, lifestyle, beliefs and feelings, income, wealth, and more.[2] Political scientists Kenneth Dolbeare and

---

[1] General Social Survey, 1976–1996, Variable 185A CLASS, http://www.ssdc.ucsd.edu.

[2] Mary R. Jackman and Robert W. Jackman, *Class Awareness in the United States* (Berkeley: University of California Press, 1983), 216–17 (reporting that only 4 percent of the population places itself in either the upper class or the lower class).

Janette Hubbell assert, "Middle-class values are by definition those of the American mainstream."[3]

This discussion is concentrated on the economic median — the numerical middle — of America. Few families hit the dead center of the economic spectrum, but there is a large group that is roughly in the middle. Even if we cannot tell precisely where the middle shifts over to the lower class or the upper class, knowing what happens to the exact middle explains a lot about what happens to America's middle class.

Higher Incomes, but at a Price

Over the past generation new economic forces have reshaped the middle 5 class. The most profound changes have taken place in family income.

As Figure 1.4 shows, today's median-earning family is making a lot more money than their parents did a generation ago. (Throughout this discussion all dollar figures will be adjusted for the effects of inflation.) Today the two-parent family right in the middle is earning about $66,000.[4]

But notice that there are two lines on the figure on page 66. The second line shows what has happened to the wages of a fully employed male over the same time period. The answer is that the typical man working full-time, after adjusting for inflation, earns about $800 less than his father earned in the early 1970s. After decades of rising incomes earlier in the twentieth century, about 30 years ago wages for middle-class men flat-lined.

How did family incomes rise? Mothers of minor children went back to work in record numbers. In the early 1970s the median family lived on one paycheck. Today the family in the middle brings home two paychecks.

The shift from one income to two has had seismic implications for families across America. It means that all the growth in family income came from adding a second earner. Among two-paycheck families median income is now $76,500, but the middle one-paycheck family now earns only $42,300.[5] This means that one-income households — whether

---

[3] Kenneth M. Dolbeare and Janette Kay Hubbell, *U.S.A. 2012: After the Middle-Class Revolution* (Chatham, N.J.: Chatham House Publishers, 1996), 3.

[4] U.S. Bureau of the Census, "2005 American Community Survey, S. 1901, Income in the Past 12 Months (in 2005 Inflation Adjusted Dollars)," http://factfinder.census.gov /servlet/STTable?_bm=y&-qr_name=ACS_2005_EST_G00_S1901&-geo_id=01000US& -context=st&-ds_name=ACS_2005_EST_G00_&-tree_id=305.

[5] U.S. Bureau of the Census, *Historical Income Tables — Families*, Table F-13, http://www .census.gov/hhes/www/income/histinc/fl3ar.html.

Figure 1.4 Median Income of Married Couples and Fully Employed Males, 1970–2004
Source: U.S. Bureau of the Census.

they are couples where one works and one stays at home or households with only one parent — have fallen sharply behind. A generation ago a one-earner family was squarely in the middle, but now that average one-earner family has slipped down the economic ladder. Over the past generation critical economic divisions within the middle class have begun to emerge.

Savings and Debt

While not every family brought home two paychecks, by the 2000s a substantial majority of families sent both parents into the workforce. For those families, it would seem that the economic picture would be rosy. Not so.

In the early 1970s the typical one-income family was putting away about 11 percent of its take-home pay in savings (Figure 1.5).[6] That family carried a mortgage, and it also carried credit cards and other

---

[6] "Table 2, Personal Income and Its Disposition," http://www.bea.gov/bea/dn/nipaweb/TableView.asp#Mid (savings rates reported by quarter).

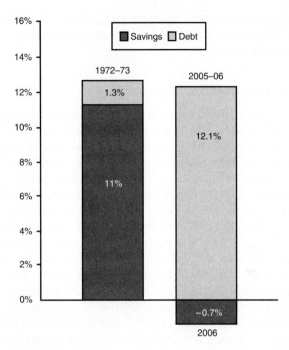

Figure 1.5   **Savings and Revolving Debt as Percentages of Annual Income, 1972–73 to 2005–06**
Sources: U.S. Census Bureau, Federal Reserve Bank.

revolving debt that, on average, equaled about 1.3 percent of its annual income.[7]

By 2004 that picture had shifted dramatically. The national savings rate dropped below zero.[8] Revolving debt — largely credit cards — ballooned, topping 12 percent of the average family's income.[9]

In a single generation the family had picked up a second earner, but it had spent every dollar of that second paycheck. Worse yet, it had

---

[7] Computed from data on debt, both revolving and total, from the Federal Reserve (available at http://www.federalreserve.gov/releases/g19/hist/cc_hist_sa.html) and number of households and data on household income from the Bureau of the Census (available at http://factfinder.census.gov/servlet/ADPTable?_bm=y&-geo _id=01000US&-ds_name and http://factfinder.census.gov/servlet/STTable?_bm=y& -qr_name=ACS_2005_EST_G00).

[8] The 2006 savings rate was −0.7 percent. Bureau of Economic Analysis, National Economic Accounts, Table 2.1, "Personal Income and Its Disposition," http://www.bea .gov/bea/dn/nipaweb/TableView.asp?SelectedTable=58&FirstYear=2004&LastYear= 2006&Freq=Qtr.

[9] See data cited in note 7.

also spent the money it once saved, and it had borrowed more besides. By the most obvious financial measures the middle-class American family has sunk financially.

Overconsumption—The Standard Story

There is no shortage of experts who are willing to explain exactly where the money went. The story is all about overconsumption, about families spending their money on things they do not really need. Economist Juliet Schor blames "the new consumerism," complete with "designer clothes, a microwave, restaurant meals, home and auto-mobile air conditioning, and, of course, Michael Jordan's ubiquitous athletic shoes, about which children and adults both display near-obsession."[10] Sociologist Robert Frank claims that America's new-found "luxury fever" forces middle-class families "to finance their consumption increases largely by reduced savings and increased debt."[11] John de Graaf and his co-authors claim that "urge to splurge" is an affliction affecting millions of Americans who simply have no willpower.[12] The distinction is critical; overconsumption is not about medical care or basic housing, and it is not about buying a few good-ies with extra income. It is about going deep into debt to finance con-sumer purchases that sensible people could do without.

The beauty of the overconsumption story is that it squares neatly   15
with many of our own intuitions. We see the malls packed with shop-pers. We receive catalogs filled with outrageously expensive gadgets. We think of that overpriced summer dress that hangs in the back of the closet or those new soccer shoes gathering dust there. The con-clusion seems indisputable: the "urge to splurge" is driving folks to spend, spend, spend like never before. But is it true? Deep in the recesses of fed-eral archives is detailed information on Americans' spending patterns go-ing back for more than a century. It is

> The conclusion seems indis-putable: the "urge to splurge" is driving folks to spend, spend, spend like never be-fore. But is it true?

---

[10] Juliet B. Schor, *The Overspent American: Upscaling, Downshifting, and the New Consumer* (New York: Basic Books, 1998), 20, 11.

[11] Robert H. Frank, *Luxury Fever: Why Money Fails to Satisfy in an Era of Excess* (New York: Free Press, 1999), 45.

[12] John de Graaf, David Waan, and Thomas H. Naylor, *Affluenza: The All-Consuming Epidemic* (San Francisco: Berrett-Koehler, 2001), 13.

possible to analyze data about typical families from the early 1970s, carefully sorting spending categories and family size.[13] If today's families really are blowing their paychecks on designer clothes and restaurant meals, then the expenditure data should show that they are spending more on these frivolous items than their parents did a generation earlier. But the numbers point in a very different direction.

Start with clothing. Everyone talks about expensive sneakers, designer outfits, and the latest fashions. But how much more is today's typical family of four spending on clothing than the same family spent in the early 1970s? They are spending less, a whopping 32 percent less today than they spent a generation ago.[14] The differences have to do with how people dress (fewer suits and leather shoes, more T-shirts and shorts), where they shop (more discount stores), and where the clothes are manufactured (overseas). Compared with families a generation ago, today's median earners are downright thrifty.

How about food? People eat out now more than ever before, and bottled water turns something that was once free into a $2 purchase. So how much more is today's family of four spending on food (including eating out) than the same family in the early 1970s? Once again, they are spending less, about 18 percent less.[15] The reasons are that people eat differently (less meat, more pasta) and shop differently (big discount supercenters instead of corner grocery stores), and agribusiness has improved the efficiency of food production.

What about appliances? Families today have microwave ovens, espresso machines, and fancy washers and dryers. But those appliances are not putting a big dent in their pocketbooks. Today's family spends about 52 percent less each year on appliances than their counterparts

---

[13] The Bureau of Labor Statistics maintains the Consumer Expenditure Survey (CES), a periodic set of interviews and diary entries, to analyze the spending behavior of over 20,000 consumer units. Much of the analysis compares the results of the 1972–1973 CES with those of the 2004 CES. In some instances prepublished tables from the 1980 or the 2000 survey are used in order to use the most comparable data available. In both time periods the data used are for four-person families. Available online at www .bls.gov/cex/.

[14] 1972–1973 CES, Table 5, "Selected Family Characteristics, Annual Expenditures, and Sources of Income Classified by Family Income before Taxes for Four Person Families"; 2004 CES, Table 4, "Size of Consumer Unit: Average Annual Expenditures and Characteristics," See also Mark Lino, "USDA's Expenditures on Children by Families Project: Uses and Changes over Time," *Family Economics and Nutrition Review* 13, no. 1 (2001): 81–86.

[15] 1972–1973 CES, Table 5; 2004 CES, Table 4. See also Eva Jacobs and Stephanie Shipps, "How Family Spending Has Changed in the U.S.," *Monthly Labor Review* 113 (March 1990): 20–27.

of a generation ago.[16] Today's appliances are better made and last longer, and they cost less to buy.

Cars? Surely luxury vehicles are making a difference. Not for the median family. The per car cost of owning a car (purchase, repairs, insurance, gas) was on average about 24 percent lower in 2004 than in the early 1970s.[17]

That is not to say that middle-class families never fritter away any money. A generation ago no one had cable, big-screen televisions were a novelty reserved for the very rich, and DVD and TiVo were meaningless strings of letters. Families are spending about 23 percent more on electronics, an extra $225 annually. Computers add another $300 to the annual family budget.[18] But the extra money spent on cable, electronics, and computers is more than offset by families' savings on major appliances and household furnishings alone. 20

The same balancing act holds true in other areas. The average family spends more on airline travel than it did a generation ago, but it spends less on dry cleaning; more on telephone services, but less on tobacco; more on pets, but less on carpets.[19] And, when it is all added up, increases in one category are pretty much offset by decreases in another. In other words, there seems to be about as much frivolous spending today as there was a generation ago.

Where Did the Money Go?

Consumer expenses are down, but the big fixed expenses are up — way up. Start at home. It is fun to think about McMansions, granite countertops, and media rooms. But today's median family buys a three-bedroom, one-bath home — statistically speaking, about 6.1 rooms altogether.[20] This is a little bigger than the 5.8 rooms the median family lived in during the early 1970s. But the price tag and the resulting

---

[16] 1972–1973 CES, Table 5; 2004 CES, Table 4.

[17] 1972–1973 CES, Table 5; 2004 CES, Table 4.

[18] 1972–1973 CES, Table 5; 2004 CES, Table 1400. Electronics comparison includes expenditures on televisions, radios, musical instruments, and sound equipment. Computer calculation includes computer hardware and software.

[19] For example, in 2000 the average family of four spent an extra $290 on telephone services. On the other hand, the average family spent nearly $200 less on floor coverings, $210 less on dry cleaning and laundry supplies, and $240 less on tobacco products and smoking supplies. 1972–1973 CES, Table 5; 2004 CES, Table 1400.

[20] U.S. Bureau of the Census, *American Housing Survey, 1975: General Housing Characteristics,* Current Housing Reports, H-150-75A, Table A1; *American Housing Survey, 1997,* Current Housing Reports, H150/97 (October 2000), Table 3-3, "Size of Unit and Lot — Owner Occupied Units."

mortgage payment are much bigger. In 2004 the median homeowner was forking over a mortgage payment that was 76 percent larger than a generation earlier.[21] The family's single biggest expense — the home mortgage — had ballooned from $485 a month to $854. (Remember that all the numbers have already been adjusted for inflation.)

Increases in the cost of health insurance have also hit families hard. Today's family spends 74 percent more on health insurance than its earlier counterparts — if it is lucky enough to get it at all.[22] Costs are so high that 48 million working-age Americans simply went without coverage in 2005.[23]

The per car cost of transportation is down, but the total number of cars is up. Today's family has two people in the workforce, and that means two cars to get to work. Besides, with more families living in the suburbs, even a one-earner family needs a second car for the stay-at-home parent to get to the grocery store and doctor appointments. Overall transportation costs for the family of four have increased by 52 percent.[24]

Another consequence of sending two people into the workforce is the need for child care. Because the median 1970s family had someone at home full-time, there were no child-care expenses for comparison. But today's family with one preschooler and one child in elementary school lays out an average of $1,048 a month for care for the children.[25]

25

---

[21] 1984 CES, Table 5; 2004 CES, Table 4.

[22] 1972–1973 CES, Table 5; 2004 CES, Table 4.

[23] Commonwealth Fund, "Gaps in Health Insurance: An All-American Problem" (2006).

[24] Transportation costs, 1972 data: Bureau of Labor Statistics, *Consumer Expenditure Survey: Interview Survey,* 1972–73 (1997) Table 5, Selected Family Characteristics, Annual Expenditures, and Sources of Income Classified by Family Income before Taxes for Four Person Families.

1985–2004 data: Bureau of Labour Statistics, Consumer Expenditure Survey, Customized Tables, Series CXUTR000405, Four Person in Consumer Unit, Transportation. Available at http://data.bls.gov/PDQ/outside.jsp?survey=cx.

To estimate 2006 numbers, I used the 2004 CES data as described above, inflated to 2006 dollars using the CPI seasonally adjusted average increase in transportation costs for all urban consumers.

Note: Includes all transportation costs, including privately owned vehicles, fuel, repairs, and public transportation.

[25] Day-care costs are calculated from average child-care costs for mothers employed full-time with a child aged 5 to 14, and preschool costs are calculated from average child-care costs for mothers employed full-time with a child under 5. 2004 CES, Table 1A, "Consumer Price Index for All Consumers: U.S. City Average, by Expenditure Category and Commodity and Service Group," 1999 annual and 2004 annual. Preschool and day-care cost data were adjusted using the consumer price index for "Tuition and Childcare."

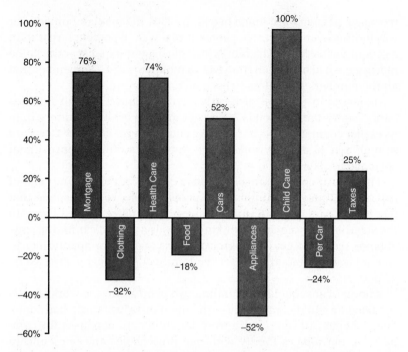

Figure 1.6 **Median Family Spending by Category, Percentage Change, 1972–2004**

Source: Updated from sources cited in Elizabeth Warren and Amelia Warren Tyagi, *The Two-Income Trap: Why Middle-Class Mothers and Fathers Are Going Broke* (New York: Basic Books, 2003).

Taxes also took a bigger bite from the two-income family of 2004. Because their second income is taxed on top of their first income, the average tax rate was 25 percent higher for a two-income family in 2004 than it was for a one-income family in 1972.[26]

The ups and downs in family spending over the past generation are summarized in Figure 1.6. Notice that the biggest items in the family budget — the mortgage, taxes, health insurance, child care — are on the up side. The down side — food, clothing, and appliances — represents relatively smaller purchases.

---

[26] Claire M. Hintz, *The Tax Burden of the Median American Family*, Tax Foundation Special Report 96 (Washington, DC: Tax Foundation, March 2000), Table 1, "Taxes and the Median One-Income American Family." For more details on the complex tax calculations, see Elizabeth Warren and Amelia Warren Tyagi, *The Two-Income Trap: Why Middle-Class Mothers and Fathers Are Going Broke* (New York: Basic Books, 2003), chap. 2, pp. 206–7 n. 115.

Also notice that the items that went down were more flexible, the sorts of things that families could spend a little less on one month and a little more the next. If someone lost a job or if the family got hit with a big medical bill, they might squeeze back on these expenses for a while. But the items that increased were all fixed. It is not possible to sell off a bedroom or skip the health insurance payment for a couple of months. If both parents are looking for work, child-care costs will go on even during a job search.

When it is all added up, the family at the beginning of the twenty-first century has a budget that looks very different from that of its early 1970s counterpart. As Figure 1.7 shows, there is more income, but the relationship between income and fixed expenses has altered dramatically.

The family of the 1970s had about half its income committed to big 30 fixed expenses. Moreover, it had a stay-at-home parent, someone who

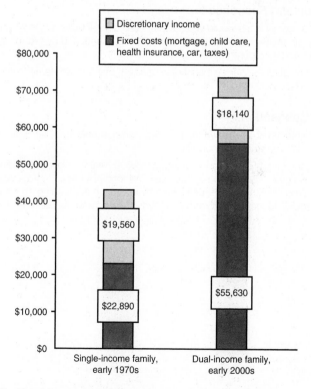

Figure 1.7 **Fixed Costs as a Share of Family Income, 1972–2005**
Source: Updated from sources cited in *The Two-Income Trap* (adjusted for inflation).

could go to work to earn extra income if something went wrong. By contrast, the family of 2004 has already put everyone to work, so there is no extra income to draw on if trouble hits. Worse yet, even with two people in the workforce, after they pay their basic expenses, today's two-income family has less cash left over than its one-income parents had a generation ago.

Understanding the Text

1. Why does Elizabeth Warren despair of formulating a precise definition of the middle class? Which group of people does she use to represent the middle class in this article, and why?

2. For what reasons, according to Warren, has the increase in income for median-earning families over the past generation not resulted in improved quality of life?

Reflection and Response

3. To which social class would you say that you yourself belong? On what do you base your answer? Money alone? Other factors mentioned by Warren in her second and third paragraphs?

4. How, if at all, does Warren's analysis shed light on your own family's circumstances?

Making Connections

5. Warren mentions another writer included in this anthology: Juliet Schor (p. 61). Where do Warren and Schor differ?

6. During the Great Recession that began in 2008, Warren played a leading role in creating the U.S. Consumer Financial Protection Bureau. Find out what its mandate is. Which of the issues raised by Warren in the reading above will this new federal agency seek to address? Which are beyond its purview? Explain.

Lethal Consumption: Death-Denying Materialism

**Sheldon Solomon,
Jeff Greenberg, and
Thomas A. Pyszczynski**

This piece argues that amassing wealth contributes to our happiness in a problematic way not often discussed: it lets us believe our lives have no endpoint. All three authors are pioneers of terror management theory, which attempts to explain a host of human behaviors as ways to deal with the reality that we don't "last forever" — we die. Sheldon Solomon teaches at Skidmore College; Jeff Greenberg, at the University of Arizona; Thomas A. Pyszczynski, at the University of Colorado, Colorado Springs.

> Modern man is drinking and drugging himself out of awareness, or he spends his time shopping, which is the same thing.
>
> —ERNEST BECKER, *THE DENIAL OF DEATH*

A Terror Management Account of Conspicuous Consumption

How does terror management theory help us to understand humankind's insatiable lust for money and conspicuous consumption of goods and services? For Becker and terror management theory, conspicuous possession and consumption are thinly veiled efforts to assert that one is special and therefore more than just an animal fated to die and decay. Spending eternity in a heavenly afterlife is a quaint and attractive prospect (e.g., Islamic Jihad's Sheik Abdulla Shamni's 1995 [reported by Abu-Nasr, 1995, p. 1A] description of heaven as "a world of castles, flowing rivers, and lush fields" where the blessed "can eat the most delicious food, the most luscious fruits and the tenderist cuts of meat"), but ultimately intangible and empirically uncertain, whereas large piles of gold, enormous mounds of possessions, and lavish consumption are ineluctably° real and symbolically indicative of immortal power. The notion that the urge to splurge is fundamentally defensive death denial above and beyond the quite legitimate pursuit of material comfort and aesthetic° pleasure is supported by both the historical record and contemporary empirical research.

ineluctably: inevitably.
aesthetic: related to the appreciation of beauty.

Historical Record

Money and Possessions in Indigenous° Cultures

Psychoanalytic anthropologist Geza Roheim studied the economic behavior of indigenous peoples in New Guinea and Melanesia in the early 1900s to understand the psychological underpinnings of money and avaricious° possessiveness. Roheim (1934) found that the primary motive for acquiring money and possessions in virtually all known tribal cultures is ultimately symbolic and ceremonial, in the service of gaining and maintaining prestige, and has little to do with money as a rational medium of exchange of goods and services:

> *In the life of the people of Duau whom I know, and also in the lives of other New Guinea and Melanesian people, money . . . plays a conspicuous role. The shell-money in question signifies wealth, but even more than wealth it means social prestige . . . the great aim in life for everybody in Duau is . . . in piling up and distributing yams. But however "rich" anybody may be this makes no difference in practical life, it does not mean less work and more pleasure. . . . In societies of this kind wealth means magic power and magic power means wealth. (p. 401)*

The underlying motive for accumulating money is thus to acquire magic power through social prestige.

However, *prestige* means to assume a commanding position in people's minds, and the word *prestige* is derived from words meaning conjuror's tricks, illusions, deceptions, or enchantment. People lust for money to quench their thirst for power, and all power is ultimately bound to issues surrounding sustaining life and forestalling death, ideally permanently. Again following Roheim (1934): "originally people do not desire money because you can buy things for it, but you can buy things for money because people desire it (sic)" (p. 402). Long ago, people began to measure themselves, not by actual achievement, but by garnering prestige (a conjurer's trick, recall) through the ceremonial acquisition of more symbols than one's neighbors:

> *The beautiful skins or head-dresses or obsidians displayed at a dance by one rich man excite the interest and envy of visitors of wealth. . . . Such wealthy spectators return home determined to exhibit an even greater value of property the next year. Their effort in turn excites the first man to outdo*

---

indigenous: native to the area.
avaricious: greedy.

all his competitors. (A. L. Kroeber, Handbook of Indians of California, as cited in Roheim, 1934, p. 402)

Here there is no hint of the rational exchange of goods and services 5 (the typical definition of economic behavior); rather, what we see is the beginnings of a frenzied effort to use deception and illusion to acquire magic power over death through the pursuit of unbridled wealth, a frenzy that continues to this day.

Money and Possessions in Western Civilization

Norman O. Brown (1959) built explicitly on Roheim's work in his examination of the history of money in Western civilization in a chapter entitled "Filthy Lucre"° in *Life against Death*. Brown started by noting that it is very difficult for people today to recognize the true nature of money, because in contemporary societies we make a sharp distinction between the secular and the sacred. Money is now viewed as the rational medium by which we transact our affairs in the material (i.e., secular) world, completely independent of our admittedly non-rational relationship with the spiritual world in the sacred domain. Brown argued that the distinction between secular and sacred is a false and relatively recent one, in that all cultural contrivances are ultimately sacred in nature; all serve the same death-denying function, whether we are aware of it or not.

Money has always been used to buy and sell spiritual absolution° (e.g., medieval indulgences) and has always been first and foremost a sacred value, and only secondarily a secular medium of exchange; as Big Daddy knew so well in Tennessee Williams's (1955) *Cat on a Hot Tin Roof*, what we really want to buy with it is everlasting life.

The human animal is a beast that dies and if he's got money he buys and buys and buys and I think the reason he buys everything he can buy is that in the back of his mind he has the crazy hope that one of his purchases will be life ever-lasting. (p. 73)

Three examples point to this connection between money and the world of the spirit (and of death).

First, gold's value developed partly through its connection to life-giving myths. Becker (1975) observed that "the great economist Keynes noted that the special attraction of gold . . . was due to [its] symbolic

---

lucre: money (a word with negative associations, often used — as it is in this article — as part of the phrase *filthy lucre*).
absolution: forgiveness.

identification with the sun . . ." (p. 78) or that which gives life. In Egypt, gold was relatively ignored until it became a popular means of making replicas of a cowrie shell that was "prized as a token of life-giving powers as an amulet° to ward off the danger of death and to prolong the existence of the souls that were already dead" (Becker, 1975, p. 77). According to Smith (1929, as quoted in Coblentz, 1965), "the gold models soon became more popular than the original shells, and the reputation for life-giving was then in large measure transferred from the mere form of the amulet to the metal itself" (p. 24).

A second example pertains to the connections between the priesthood and money. The first mints were in temples and churches; the first minters were the priests: 10

With the ascendancy of priestcraft it became the priests themselves who monopolized the official trade in sacred charms and in the exchange of favors for gold. The first mints were set up in the temples of the gods, whence our word "money" — from the mint in the temple of Juno Moneta, Juno the admonisher, on the Capitoline hill in Rome. In India the gold fee was the proper one to pay to a god, whose essence was gold. Whence the tradition of the earliest coins being imprinted with the images of the gods, then divine kings, down to presidents in our time. (Becker, 1975, p. 79)

As can be seen, the very roots of the word *money* have ties to the spirit, and thus to death.

A final example concerns the contemporary world's dominant currency, the dollar bill of the United States. Look at the back of a dollar bill. Try to find anything about the use of the dollar as a rational medium of exchange between honest traders, but you cannot. Instead, see the real power behind money: God! *In God We Trust!* Now gaze to the left at the pyramid. There are no pyramids in the United States, so clearly they are not depicted on the dollar as cultural artifacts per se. Why else would there be pyramids on the backs of dollars, except as the ultimate symbol of death-denial and the royal gateway to immortality? Now keep looking up toward the top of the pyramid, broken off and hovering above a bit, apparently levitating,° the enlightened (literally) disembodied eyeball. According to Joseph Campbell (1988), this reflects the eye of God opening to us when we reach the top of the pyramid and attain immortality. Even the Latin phrases surrounding the pyramid and eyeball speak to immortality. Loosely translated,

amulet: an object thought to have magical power to protect the person who wears it.
levitating: being suspended in midair.

the phrase *annuit coeptis* above the floating eyeball means "He favors new undertakings," seemingly giving God's blessing to the nation (and its currency), whereas *novus ordo seclorum* on the banner at the base underlying the pyramid refers to "a new order of the ages," or something that lasts into posterity (B. Fineberg, February 22, 2002, personal communication).

Money: The New Ideology of Immortality

In the past, people's zeal for money and stuff in pursuit of prestige as magic power to ward off death was tempered somewhat by the edicts of the church against the desire for wealth as an end in itself and in support of the proposition that people are responsible for the well-being of those around them. Now that "God is dead," however, in the sense that the Judeo-Christian tradition has waned in power in the last century, the pursuit of money has become the primary immortality ideology for the average American; but now people are unencumbered by a sense of responsibility to the community and unrestricted by moral edicts against massive wealth:

Money . . . buys bodyguards, bullet-proof glass, and better medical care. Most of all it can be accumulated and passed on, and so radiates its powers even after one's death, giving one a semblance of immortality as he lives in the vicarious enjoyments of his heirs that his money continues to buy, or in the magnificence of the art works that he commissioned, or in the statues of himself and the majesty of his own mausoleum. In short, money is the human mode par excellence of coolly denying animal boundness, the determinism of nature. (Becker, 1975, pp. 81–82)

So God isn't dead after all: God has metamorphosized into money and materialism in contemporary society. We may not trust God anymore, but we do trust cash.

In accord with the notion that money, avaricious possession, and conspicuous consumption are essentially aspects of a secular religion — the dominant immortality ideology of the Western world — at a press conference one month after the September 11, 2001, terrorist attacks on the World Trade Center and the Pentagon, President George W. Bush responded (in part) to the question "is there anything you can say to Americans who feel helpless to protect themselves?" by stating "the American people have got to go about their business. We cannot let the terrorists achieve the objective of frightening our nation to the point where we don't conduct business, where people don't shop" ("Excerpts from the President's Remarks," October 12, 2001, p. B4). Bush reiterated this advice a few days later (reported in Carney & Dickerson,

2001, p. 4): "Well, Mrs. Bush and I want to encourage Americans to go out shopping." Beyond the egregious loss of life, one of the most disturbing aspects of September 11 was the destruction of what were central immortality symbols for most Americans, one economic, the other military. As Becker (1971) observed:

> *Modern man is denying his finitude° with the same dedication as the ancient Egyptian pharaohs, but now whole masses are playing the game, and with a far richer armamentarium° of techniques. The skyscraper buildings . . . the houses with their imposing facades and immaculate lawns — what are these if not the modern equivalent of pyramids: a face to the world that announces: "I am not ephemeral,° look what went into me, what represents me, what justifies me." The hushed hope is that someone who can do this will not die. (pp. 149–150)*

Empirical Evidence of the Role of Death Denial in Conspicuous Consumption

Could the American Dream actually be just another psychopathological form of death denial raised to the level of civic virtue by cultural ideology? Is there any empirical evidence that bears directly on these claims? Yes. Kasser and Sheldon (2000) asked people to think either about their own death or about listening to music; they then answered questions about their expected financial status 15 years in the future. The results showed inflated fiscal expectations after thinking about death (relative to listening to music), both in terms of overall worth, and especially in the amount participants expected to spend on luxury items such as clothing and entertainment. This suggests that concerns about mortality play a strong, albeit generally unconscious, role in economic aspirations and behavior.

> Concerns about mortality play a strong, albeit generally unconscious, role in economic aspirations and behavior.

In a second study, Kasser and Sheldon (2000) wondered whether fear of death disposed people to become greedy over-consumers of scarce natural resources. Following either a mortality salience or music control induction, participants engaged in a forest-management simulation. The results were striking. First, people asked to ponder their own mortality reported intending to harvest sig-

---

finitude: limitedness.
armamentarium: the whole range of tools and materials available to complete a certain task.
ephemeral: not lasting.

nificantly more of the available acres of forest than their counterparts in the music control condition (62 vs. 49 acres, respectively). Second, mortality salience significantly increased the desire for profit, leading Kasser and Sheldon to conclude: "Interestingly, the results suggested that mortality salience particularly enhanced feelings of greed, or the desire to acquire more than other people" (p. 350). For many in our culture, out-competing others, out-earning them, may be central to feeling of special value. Indeed, in a currency-based culture, how much money you earn and have is an indication of how much you are valued in the culture, and this is spiritual currency as much as, if not more than, it is financial currency. This finding suggests that greedy plundering of natural resources is at least partially engendered by concerns about death.

Another way in which mortality concerns may contribute to consumption is suggested by two studies by Koole and van den Berg (2001) demonstrating that mortality salience increases people's preferences for scenes of cultivated nature over wild nature. Cultivated scenery provides the illusion of order and control over nature and thus may also serve to manage our fears about the realities of existence. By compulsively controlling nature, we create the illusion that we can avoid death. In Becker's (1971) words:

Life in contemporary society is like an open air lunatic asylum with people cutting and spraying their grass (to deny untidyness, hence lack of order, hence lack of control, hence their death), beating trails to the bank with little books of figures that worry them around the clock (for the same reason) . . . filling shopping carts, emptying shopping carts . . . and all this dedicated activity takes place within a din of noise that tries to defy eternity: motorized lawn mowers, power saws, giant jets, motorized toothbrushes, . . . (p. 150)

In summary, the historical record and empirical research provide convergent support for the proposition that the denial of our mortality is at the root of humankind's feverish pursuit of wealth.

References

Abu-Nasr, D. (1995, January 30). Devout human bombs die in Allah's name. *Charleston Gazette*, p. 1A.

Becker, E. (1971). *The birth and death of meaning.* New York: Free Press.

Becker, E. (1975). *Escape from evil.* New York: Free Press.

Brown, N. O. (1959). *Life against death: The psychoanalytical meaning of history.* Middletown, CT: Wesleyan University Press.

Campbell, J. (1988). *The power of myth* (with Bill Moyers; B. S. Flowers, Ed.). New York: Doubleday.

Carney, J., & Dickerson, J. F. (2001, October 22). A work in progress. *Time*, p. 4.

Coblentz, S. A. (1965). *Avarice: A history.* Washington, DC: Public Affairs Press.

Excerpts from the President's remarks on war on terrorism. (2001, October 12). *New York Times,* p. B4.

Kasser, T., & Sheldon, K. M. (2000). Of wealth and death: Materialism, mortality salience, and consumption behavior. *Psychological Science, 11,* 348–351.

Koole, S., & van den Berg, A. (2001, July). *Lost in the wilderness: Terror management and the experience of nature.* Paper presented at the First International Conference on Experimental Existential Psychology: Finding Meaning in the Human Condition. Free University Amsterdam, Amsterdam, The Netherlands.

Roheim, G. (1934). The evolution of culture. *International Journal of Psycho-Analysis, 15,* 387–418.

Williams, T. (1955). *Cat on a hot tin roof.* New York: New Directions.

Understanding the Text

1. Which effects of human greed do the authors of this piece consider problematic? Why?

2. What do the authors identify as greed's root cause? Reconstruct as much of their reasoning as you can.

Reflection and Response

3. Which examples offered in this excerpt do you find convincing? Which, not? Why?

4. Some might argue that there is a simpler connection between compulsive moneymaking and the fear of death than the one advanced in "Lethal Consumption": Conveniently, making money keeps us too *busy* to worry about death. What do you think?

Making Connections

5. The authors of "Lethal Consumption" dissect the pictorial elements of a U.S. dollar bill to press their case that our thinking (and *subconscious* thinking) about money has a magical aspect to it. Scrutinize both sides of a dollar bill. Do the elements of it cited in "Lethal Consumption" have the effect on you that the article claims for them? Why or why not? Does a dollar have visuals or words in its design that the authors of "Lethal Consumption" don't mention but which call their ideas into question, or complicate them?

6. Research the history of the design of the U.S. dollar bill. What thinking actually went into it? How does your research square with the authors' claims?

7. The authors of "Lethal Consumption" refer to two writings by David G. Myers, whose piece "The Funds, Friends, and Faith of Happy People" (p. 15) is the first reading in this anthology. Write a positive or negative response to the following:

> The word "happiness," as employed by such psychologists as David G. Myers, is, in the end, too vague to be of much use in determining the real effects of money. Thankfully, the authors of "Lethal Consumption" avoid the "happiness" trap.

Start your paper off with this block-indented quote, and say why you agree or disagree.

2

How Does
Money Shape
Relationships?

How many of your friendships before entering college crossed social class lines? Few, if any, probably. Has college made a difference in this regard?

This section of the book walks you through life chronologically, noting some effects that money has on personal relationships in each biographical phase.

Even with kids still too young to have bank accounts, money turns out to play a major role in friendship formation. The first items in this section — "On the Meaning of Plumbing and Poverty," an autobiographical essay, and *New Kids in the Neighborhood,* a painting — both deal with childhood.

The next selection — "What's a Little Money between Friends?," is a journalistic profile of some recent college graduates, all women, whose close bonds with one another start to fray as their incomes and standards of living begin to diverge. And the remaining four selections — "Till Debt Do Us Part," "Shaken Baby Cases on the Increase," the Mary Kay "Survey of Shelters for Women," and "My Inheritance" — all address the potential for disruption (even violence) on account of money problems faced by married couples and families.

There would seem to be no stage of life when our ties to other people can't be somehow influenced by money: either strengthened or utterly destroyed by it.

On the Meaning of Plumbing and Poverty

Melanie Scheller

In a largely affluent society like the United States, poverty can involve more than physical hardship: it can bring shame — as it has throughout the life of this author, Melanie Scheller.

Scheller is a children's book writer committed to telling the stories of Southern textile mill workers, tenant farmers, and sharecroppers living in the early 1900s. Much of her writing addresses social and economic injustices, particularly poverty and inequities in health care. Her book *My Grandfather's Hat* was published in 1992. The essay below, which won a contest of the North Carolina Writers Network in 1990, has appeared in several publications, including the *Utne Reader*.

Several years ago I spent some time as a volunteer on the geriatric ward of a psychiatric hospital. I was fascinated by the behavior of one of the patients, an elderly woman who shuffled at regular intervals to the bathroom, where she methodically flushed the toilet. Again and again she carried out her sacred mission as if summoned by some supernatural force, until the flush of the toilet became a rhythmic counterpoint for the ward's activity. If someone blocked her path or if, God forbid, the bathroom was in use when she reached it, she became agitated and confused.

Obviously, that elderly patient was a sick woman. And yet I felt a certain kinship with her, for I too have suffered from an obsession with toilets. I spent much of my childhood living in houses without indoor plumbing, and while I don't feel compelled to flush a toilet at regular intervals, I sometimes feel that toilets, or the lack thereof, have shaped my identity in ways that are painful to admit.

I'm not a child of the Depression, but I grew up in an area of the South that had changed little since the days of the New Deal. My mother was a widow with six children to support, not an easy task under any circumstances, but especially difficult in rural North Carolina during the 1960s. To her credit, we were never seriously in danger of going hungry. Our vegetable garden kept us stocked with tomatoes and string beans. We kept a few chickens and sometimes a cow. Blackberries were free for the picking in the fields nearby. Neighbors did their good Christian duty by bringing us donations of fresh fruit and candy at Christmastime. But a roof over our heads — that wasn't so easily improvised.

Like rural Southern gypsies, we moved from one dilapidated Southern farmhouse to another in a constant search for a decent place to live. Sometimes we moved when the rent increased beyond the 30 or 40 dollars my mother could afford. Or the house burned down, not an unusual occurrence in substandard housing. One year when we were gathered together for Thanksgiving dinner, a stranger walked in without knocking and announced that we were being evicted. The house had been sold without our knowledge and the new owner wanted to start remodeling immediately. We tried to finish our meal with an attitude of thanksgiving while he worked around us with his tape measure.

Usually we rented from farm families who'd moved from the old 5 home place to one of the brick boxes that are now the standard in rural Southern architecture. The old farmhouse wasn't worth fixing up with a septic tank and flush toilet, but it was good enough to rent for a few dollars a month to families like mine. The idea of tenants' rights hadn't trickled down yet from the far reaches of the liberal North. It never occurred to us to demand improvements in the facilities. The ethic of the land said we should take what we could get and be grateful for it.

Without indoor plumbing, getting clean is a tiring and time-consuming ritual. At one point I lived in a five-room house with six or more people, all of whom congregated in the one heated room to eat, do homework, watch television, dress and undress, argue, wash dishes. During cold weather we dragged mattresses from the unheated rooms and slept huddled together on the floor by the woodstove. For my bathing routine, I first pinned a sheet to a piece of twine strung across the kitchen. That gave me some degree of privacy from the six other people in the room. At that time our house had an indoor cold-water faucet, from which I filled a pot of water to heat on the kitchen stove. It took several pots of hot water to fill the metal washtub we used.

Since I was a teenager and prone to sulkiness if I didn't get special treatment, I got to take the first bath while the water was still clean. The others used the water I left behind, freshened up with hot water from the pot on the stove. Then the tub had to be dragged to the door and the bath water dumped outside. I longed to be like the woman in the Calgon bath oil commercials, luxuriating in a marble tub full of scented water with bubbles piled high and stacks of thick, clean towels nearby.

• • •

People raised in the land of the bath-and-a-half may wonder why I make such a fuss about plumbing. Maybe they spent a year in the Peace Corps, or they back-packed across India, or they worked at a summer camp and, gosh, using a latrine isn't all that bad. And of course it's *not* that bad. Not when you can catch the next plane out of the country, or pick up your duffel bag and head for home, or call mom and dad to come and get you when things get too tedious. A sojourn in a Third World country, where everyone shares the same primitive facilities, may cause some temporary discomfort, but the experience is soon converted into amusing anecdotes for cocktail-party conversation. It doesn't corrode your self-esteem with a sense of shame the way a childhood spent in chronic, unrelenting poverty can.

In the South of my childhood, not having indoor plumbing was the indelible mark of poor white trash. The phrase "so poor they didn't have a pot to piss in" said it all. Poor white trash were viciously stereotyped, and never more viciously than on the playground. White-trash children had cooties — everybody knew that. They had ringworm and pink-eye — don't get near them or you might catch it. They picked their noses. They messed in their pants. If a white-trash child made the mistake of catching a softball during recess, the other children made an elaborate show of wiping it clean before they would touch it.

> I knew if I expressed delight in having a bathroom I would immediately be labeled a hick.

Once a story circulated at school about a family whose infant 10 daughter had fallen into the "slop jar" and drowned. When I saw the smirks and heard the laughter with which the story was told, I felt sick and afraid in the pit of my stomach. A little girl had died, but people were laughing. What had she done to deserve that laughter? I could only assume that using a chamber pot was something so disgusting, so shameful, that it made a person less than human.

My family was visibly and undeniably poor. My clothes were obviously hand-me-downs. I got free lunches at school. I went to the health department for immunizations. Surely it was equally obvious that we didn't have a flush toilet. But like an alcoholic who believes no one will know he has a problem as long as he doesn't drink in public, I convinced myself that no one knew my family's little secret. It was a form of denial that would color my relationships with the outside world for years to come.

Having a friend from school spend the night at my house was out of the question. Better to be friendless than to have my classmates know my shameful secret. Home visits from teachers or ministers left me in a dither of anticipatory anxiety. As they chattered on and on with Southern small talk about tomato plants and relish recipes, I sat on the edge of my seat, tensed against the dreaded words, "May I use your bathroom, please?" When I began dating in high school, I'd lie in wait behind the front door, ready to dash out as soon as my date pulled in the driveway, never giving him a chance to hear the call of nature while on our property.

With the help of a scholarship I was able to go away to college, where I could choose from dozens of dormitory toilets and take as many hot showers as I wanted, but I could never openly express my joy in using the facilities. My roommates, each a pampered only child from a well-to-do family, whined and complained about having to share a bathroom. I knew that if I expressed delight in simply having a bathroom, I would immediately be labeled as a hick. The need to conceal my real self by stifling my emotions created a barrier around me and I spent my college years in a vacuum of isolation.

Almost 20 years have passed since I first tried to leave my family's chamber pot behind. For many of those years it followed behind me — the ghost of chamber pots past — clanging and banging and threatening to spill its humiliating contents at any moment. I was convinced that everyone could see it, could smell it even. No college degree or job title seemed capable of banishing it.

If finances had permitted, I might have become an Elvis Presley or a Tammy Faye Bakker, easing the pain of remembered poverty with gold-plated bathtub fixtures and leopard-skinned toilet seats. I feel blessed that gradually, ever so gradually, the shame of poverty has begun to fade. The pleasures of the present now take priority over where a long-ago bowel movement did or did not take place. But for many Southerners, chamber pots and outhouses are more than just memories. 15

In North Carolina alone, 200,000 people still live without indoor plumbing. People who haul their drinking water home from a neighbor's house or catch rainwater in barrels. People who can't wash their hands before handling food, the way restaurant employees are required by state law to do. People who sneak into public restrooms every day to wash, shave, and brush their teeth before going to work or to school. People who sacrifice their dignity and self-respect when forced to choose between going homeless and going to an outhouse. People whose children think they deserve the conditions in which they live and hold their heads low to hide the shame. But they're not the ones who should feel ashamed. No, they're not the ones who should feel ashamed.

Understanding the Text

1. In her second paragraph, Melanie Scheller writes that ". . . toilets, or the lack thereof, [may] have shaped my identity in ways that are painful to admit." What is she referring to?

2. How do you construe Scheller's closing line? Who, in the end, should "feel ashamed," in her view? What details of Scheller's text inform your answer?

Reflection and Response

3. Are Scheller's feelings ones you can readily imagine having yourself, in her circumstances, or do you find it difficult to empathize with her? Why?

4. Does Scheller's phrase "less than human," in paragraph 10, seem overstated to you? Please explain.

Making Connections

5. What light, if any, does Charles Murray's essay "What's So Bad about Being Poor?" (p. 26) shed on the feelings expressed in this memoir? Would Scheller have experienced poverty in the same way if she had lived in the kind of Thai village Murray describes?

6. Whose experience of poverty does Scheller's more nearly resemble, that of Barbara Ehrenreich (p. 36) or that of the mother in Rebecca Curtis's story "Twenty Grand" (p. 42)? How does it differ even from the case it most resembles?

New Kids in the Neighborhood
Norman Rockwell

This painting by Norman Rockwell (1967) first appeared on the cover of a magazine containing an article about racial integration. But is race the only factor involved in Rockwell's scene? What about money? Do you see its hand at work here, too, boding well or ill for the prospects that these kids will get along with each other?

One of the best known artists of the twentieth century, Norman Rockwell created many still-familiar images of life in America, ranging from his somber *Four Freedoms* series of paintings (based on principles set forth by President Franklin Delano Roosevelt during World War II) to his humorous cover illustrations for the *Saturday Evening Post,* which spanned more than four decades.

Understanding the Text

1. What do you predict for these pre-teens and teenagers? Will they become friends? What specific details of the painting — such as skin, clothing, haircuts, and demeanor — lead you to your answer?

2. Do a Web search for a color version of this painting. How is its meaning affected by Rockwell's use of color? (Notice, for example, how much of the coloration of clothes and other possessions on the right side of the canvas echoes that of clothing and possessions on the left side. Also, for example, notice which kids have a pet that's white; which, a pet that's black.)

Reflection and Response

3. Of the details you have listed in response to question 1 above, how many are features of race? How many are features of social class?

4. Rockwell's art is sometimes criticized for being too upbeat or complacent. Would you describe this painting in such terms?

Making Connections

5. As a white child, would Melanie Scheller (p. 85) have had less difficulty assimilating into Rockwell's neighborhood than these particular African-American children would? Would she have had just as much difficulty? More difficulty? Why?

6. Does class matter more than race in America?

   Write a paper on the relative importance (or unimportance) of socioeconomic status in relations between people of different races or ethnicities. In your paper, be sure to discuss the Rockwell painting, but don't confine yourself to it: also draw on personal experience, other readings in this book, and/or research.

What's a Little Money between Friends?

David Amsden

Can friends remain friends after they begin to earn starkly different incomes, and the ones who earn more begin to exercise options in life unavailable to those who earn less? Journalist David Amsden explores this question by profiling several young women who have known each other for years.

Amsden started writing for *New York Magazine* at age 19, while in college. At age 21, he wrote his first novel, *Important Things That Don't Matter.*

I'm feeling very uncomfortable about your apartment," said Liz. She was talking to her best friend, Sara, who at the age of 24 had just purchased a cozy one-bedroom (price: $675,000) on the Upper East Side. They were on their way to dinner, two carefully groomed, impeccably dressed young women trying to hail a cab, when Liz's remark just kind of . . . slipped out. Sara was startled — "I guess it had just been in her head for so long," she later told me — though she knew something had been brewing. Until she bought the apartment, it had been easy — and convenient — to overlook how different their lives were becoming. They had known each other since their freshman year at Stuyvesant and had attended the University of Pennsylvania together; they recognized each other immediately as similar products of middle-class Jewish households (Liz grew up on East 18th Street, Sara in Brooklyn) in which a great deal of pressure was put on them to succeed. They spent practically every other day together, talking about books or politics or going out and buying each other rounds of overpriced cocktails and feeling the particular bond of being young in New York City. But now there was this apartment, this doorman building with decent views, starkly highlighting certain developments in their lives. Namely, that Sara was making money and Liz was not.

This was just over a year ago. As they told me the story recently over dinner — gourmet takeout and red wine — at, yes, Sara's apartment, they laughed about it, emphasizing the whole ordeal as a purely past-tense affair.

Liz: "It was just growing pains."

Sara: "A dissociation of our lives."

Liz: "It's hard. You have these feelings you don't want to have. It 5 helped just being able to say, 'I'm envious. I'm proud of you, but I'm jealous.'"

The dinner was one of several conversations I had with them as a means of dissecting a pernicious, rarely discussed drama among friends: the way money bores into the dynamic and disrupts fragile equilibriums. I met them after sending out an e-mail to friends and acquaintances asking if anyone knew a group with the "sense of humor" required to talk openly about money. The responses ranged from the anxious ("I wouldn't know where to start") to the vaguely accusatory ("Are you insane?"), but a few were willing to go along with it. In addition to Liz and Sara (who asked to be called by her Hebrew name), I also spent time with their close friends Alex and Michelle (who asked to go by her middle name) and met another member of the group whom I'll refer to as Miss X (she both comes from serious money and makes serious money and elected not to participate in an article on the subject). Like many friends in New York, they're bound by a paradox: living similar lifestyles on massively diverging budgets. As a Ph.D. candidate in neuroscience at Rockefeller University, Liz receives a $23,000 annual stipend; Sara works in finance, in a job where she can expect a significant raise every year or so, and now earns what she describes as a "low to mid" six-figure salary. Both Alex and Michelle work in advertising, earning "mid to upper" five-figure salaries, though Alex, a fellow Penn alum, has years of loans to pay off.

Genuine friendships are a connection, of course, not a transaction. But in a city where money has a way of becoming the subtext of every exchange — where just choosing a restaurant can carry relationship-straining implications — certain snags and fissures are inevitable. Take Sara and Liz. It's one thing for Liz to have admitted jealousy, another to eradicate it. Ever since the apartment became an issue, Liz has developed a habit of turning almost any topic into a conversation about money — specifically, about everyone in New York having more than her — which wears thin on Sara. ("Liz has the least of any of us," Sara told me privately, "but is by far the most obsessed.") They both admit that they no longer see each other as often, that they are not quite as open as they used to be, and that, for better or worse, they understand why. Though they grew up in the same city, they have come to inhabit entirely different New Yorks.

As if to illustrate this, Liz invited me to see her apartment after dinner at Sara's. "Just so you can compare and contrast," she said as we walked down East End Avenue and through the gates of Rockefeller University — only a few blocks but many psychic miles away from Sara's. Liz lives in student housing, which she sublets when she's out of town to help pay for vacations like the trip to Spain she took with Sara and Alex a couple of years ago. The fluorescent-lit, linoleum-floored one-bedroom, furnished in Classic American Dorm Room style, is spacious by New York standards, 500 square feet or so, but it's a space in which it is almost physically impossible to feel like an adult. For Liz, who is 26, I can imagine this getting old.

"Oh, wait, you gotta see this," she said as I was leaving. She opened the freezer, which was packed with frozen meats and cheeses purchased by her mother at BJ's, the bulk-discount store. "We go shopping there every six months. That's how I can afford to go out with my friends."

Imagine the four of them at dinner — Liz, Sara, Alex, and Michelle — talking about work, about men, about what the Democrats need to do to get their act together. What they don't bring up, ever, is money. A somewhat subconscious omission, it's also a function of necessity: the maintenance of an illusion, a way for them to believe that they are the same. But even among friends — especially among friends — the illusion has a shelf life. The check comes. Handbags — some newer than others — are reached for. The bill is split. For Sara, it's a splurge with no lasting reverberations. For Liz, it's something she is able to do — occasionally — because she is a "very clever budgeter" who supplements her income by babysitting, dog-walking, coat-checking, and selling things like old cell phones on eBay. For Michelle and Alex, it's something in between: a reminder of why neither has any savings.

Alex and Michelle, both 27, are in almost identical financial situations — similar salaries, similar spending habits — and are seemingly all the closer for it. When they go shopping together, they try on everything, pretending they can afford it all but purchasing just one or two items. Both guessed they spend about $500 a month on clothes and beauty products. Alex jokes about how her savings account isn't really for putting money away, "it's just sort of like delayed spending." Michelle — who's single and happy to live in her Soho studio for many more years — doesn't think twice about this lifestyle. "Unfortunately, I have good taste" is how she put it, as serious as she was sarcastic. She wouldn't mind having an apartment big enough to entertain in, but she has friends with money, like Miss X, and when she feels the urge to throw a dinner party, she calls them up and asks if she can cook them dinner.

Alex, on the other hand, has started to question the sustainability of an adult life that feels like an extension of adolescence. She's been living with her boyfriend for two years, and wants to start a family sometime soon(ish). Raised in Virginia, she's thinking that one day she'll leave New York for a place where you don't have to think so much

10

about money. "In Manhattan, you can't help but have an attitude of consumption," she said. "You walk down the street — all those ads are for you. Even going to meet friends is about consuming. You don't meet at a park bench — you get coffee, you get a drink, you have to buy something. Every time I walk outside, I just feel like I'm losing money."

The idea of Alex leaving remains too much of an abstraction for Michelle to really worry about. When I asked her about where she noticed money affecting her friendships the most, she brought up Miss X, who operates on a seemingly limitless budget. "I try to avoid going to Barneys with her," Michelle told me half-jokingly. "Like, maybe just once a month. Otherwise, I'll get in trouble." During a recent outing, Miss X bought a $600 sweater. "I would never do that," Michelle said. "If I really 'needed' a $600 sweater, I would maybe, like, get it in double discount or mention to my parents that I need really nice sweaters for Christmas because I'm so cold."

Then there is the matter of vacations. When New Year's plans were recently discussed, Miss X brought up the idea of spending a long weekend in Croatia, or maybe the Maldives, which Michelle and Alex took to mean the group wouldn't be spending the holiday together. "Last year, she wanted to go to the Dominican Republic and was like, 'If you can't afford it, just ask your parents for Christmas,'" said Michelle. "I can't have the same dismissing quality that she can — oh, a weekend in the Dominican Republic!" Both Michelle and Alex stressed that this doesn't stir any animosity or envy on their part. In fact, they point out, Miss X can be quite generous, loaning Michelle money when she moved into a new apartment. But there is some distance where before there was none. "Three years ago, we would spend every single weekend together," Michelle said. "Now there are some weekends where I don't see her. But I think that's also, like, healthy for us."

• • •

Bring up Miss X's wealth around Liz, on the other hand, and within 15 five minutes she'll run the gamut from aggravated to embittered to confounded to repelled to even more aggravated. Back at our takeout dinner at Sara's, not long after assuring me that she no longer felt any resentment over Sara's apartment, Liz turned the conversation back to real estate. This time, the object of understandable envy was Miss X's recent apartment purchase for an amount that not one of the other girls could even conceive of touching: $1.5 million, rumored to have been paid in cash.

"Every time that apartment comes up, I just have to leave the room," Liz huffed, her cheeks flushed, her arms gesticulating wildly. "What drives me nuts is that she does not credit Mommy and Daddy! I cannot handle it! When someone I am 'friends' with spends $1.5 million on something, and I can't ask her where she got the dough? She's under 30! There's no way I can be down with that. I will just lose my shit!"

For Liz, Miss X's apartment — the price of it, the casual attitude toward it — has taken on a symbolic, somewhat perverse meaning: proof that the New York of Liz's childhood no longer exists. The sale of Stuyvesant Town devastated her, and she often complains about how the city is being overrun by "bankers and banker spawn." And when she confronts the fact that some of the wealthy people making the city less affordable are her own friends, the issue becomes even more loaded and distressing. "We're not talking about some shack!" Liz continued. "We're talking about some nice apartment that my parents could never afford. Give some respect to the purchase. Otherwise, I'm sort of like, you're an asshole!"

Sara, who recently quit smoking, stood up and searched out an emergency pack of cigarettes. As Liz went on about Miss X (*She thinks the average salary is $1 million! She lives in a different fucking universe than I do!*), I watched the expression on Sara's face change. The easy smile had morphed into a tense glower. It turned out that what bothered her wasn't just the way Liz was talking about a friend — Sara could sympathize with Liz's struggles — it was that Liz had a way of being more forgiving when it came to men with money.

"I think you make snap judgments about people if you don't have romantic intentions," Sara said, opening up a second bottle of wine.

"That is not true!"   20

Sara turned to me. "Liz will let herself get manipulated and hurt by people she gets involved with because they're rich and they're Jewish."

"I don't want to get into this," Liz declared. "The degree of psychosis that I have when I'm dating is pretty severe. It's not linked to money. Well, it is, maybe." She shook her head, as if trying to purge the thought from her mind. (But days earlier, she had admitted as much to me: "It's like this," she had explained. "I want to live in New York and I want to be a scientist, which means I'll probably never make very much money. If I meet someone with money, I could do this. If not, I don't know. Is that such a terrible way to think?") Over dinner, Liz eventually said to Sara, "Who I date and who I am friends with are very different things. It's not consistent, but . . ." She waited for the thought to gel. "My approach to all relationships is different and retarded."

Sara seemed satisfied with this, put in a better mood. I asked her how she felt about Miss X, if she was bothered by her wealth and nonchalance.

"It's hard. You have these feelings you don't want to have. It helps being able to say, 'I'm envious. I'm proud of you, but I'm jealous.'"

"I don't react that way to money," she replied. "I'm much more 25 stoic. More than that, I know the world that she travels in. I've studied with them, I've worked with them. To them, it's not a big fucking deal."

"*Exactly*," said Liz.

This conversation — not particularly pleasant as it happened — took on a vengeful life of its own in the days that followed. Sara was clearly more bothered than she had let on, and related every nuance (what Liz said, how Liz said it) to Alex and Michelle, who related it back to Miss X, who then sent me a caustic e-mail for starting the whole thing. Over the next day or so, I became something of an inadvertent (and ineffectual) moderator in a nasty four-way argument. Liz was on the outs. Michelle was siding with Miss X. Sara, her loyalties torn, decided it was all too stressful and didn't want to talk to me anymore. "As you can see, it's just raised too much shit," she said before hanging up.

The whole affair made a twisted kind of sense. You go to write a story about how money can come between friends, and suddenly you're watching money come between a group of friends because of a story you're trying to write. To encourage friends to discuss their relationships in terms of money is perhaps inevitably to hasten the end of those friendships.

Everyone stressed that money wasn't the "real" problem here, just a catalyst making other long-festering "issues" impossible to ignore. And maybe that's true: Friendships are complicated, and an outsider can never have the full story. They're also wonderfully resilient and — who knows? — it's possible that Liz, Sara, Michelle, Alex, and even Miss X will make peace and agree to never again talk about average salaries and shopping sprees, to tiptoe around the subjects of expensive apartments and vacations.

Then again, maybe not. As Liz told me, "I'm closer now with my 30 friends who live in Brooklyn and don't have any money. We come from a similar background, and that's who you want to be friends with — the people you relate to."

Understanding the Text

1. Amsden could have opened his article with a general statement of the problem, like "Friends become estranged from each other when their material standards of living diverge too much" — but, instead, he opens with a comment blurted out by one friend to another as the two were hailing a cab on the street. Was this writing decision a good one? Why?

2. How would you describe:
   - the attitudes of Liz and Sara toward each other?
   - the attitudes of Alex and Michelle toward each other?
   - the attitudes of Liz, Sara, Alex, and Michelle toward Miss X?

Reflection and Response

3. Liz and Sara grow apart. Alex and Michelle remain close. Do you have any trouble believing that money is the decisive factor in these two trajectories of friendship? Why or why not? (Feel free here to draw on your own first- or secondhand experience, changing people's names as needed.)

4. After all of Liz's complaints about *friends* with money, are you surprised by her interest (paragraphs 18–22) in finding a *spouse* who has money? Does such an interest on her part seem hypocritical?

5. At several points in Amsden's article, the city of New York is singled out for being money-conscious. Would a story like Liz and Sara's turn out differently where you live? Why or why not?

Making Connections

6. In fields ranging from physics to psychology, the phrase "the observer effect" refers to the way an observer's presence can unintentionally alter the behavior (or phenomenon) being observed. For example, many TV critics point out "the observer effect" on reality TV shows, where some participants play to the camera. Can you detect that effect in Amsden's article, where Amsden is the observer?

7. Do money's effects on us *change* from one stage of life to the next? In your answer, draw on Amsden's account of young adults and the depictions of childhood by Melanie Scheller (p. 85) and Norman Rockwell (p. 90).

Till Debt Do Us Part

Mary Loftus

Money is often a factor in one's attractiveness to prospective mates, but its biggest effect on relationships may occur after one has found one's life-partner, and, in fact, the wedding bells have stopped ringing. The piece excerpted below catalogues a number of the ways in which problems with money strain marital relations.

In addition to being associate editor of Emory University's alumni publication, *Emory Magazine*, Mary Loftus has reported for the *New York Times* and freelanced for other periodicals, covering such stories as the Israeli-Palestinian conflict.

Most adults — 67 percent of women, 74 percent of men — enter marriage with at least some debt. Of those with debt, about half owe more than $5,000, primarily from auto loans, credit cards, student loans and medical bills, research associate David Schramm of Utah State University found in a study of 1,010 newlyweds. This "negative dowry" places a tremendous strain on new marriages at a time when couples would rather be focusing on future financial goals. "It's pretty common to find out that the person you married has more debt and less income than you realized," says Scott Stanley, professor of psychology at the University of Denver and coauthor of *You Paid How Much for That? How to Win at Money without Losing at Love.* "Essentially they had other relationships with money going on that you didn't know about. The opportunity to feel betrayed is huge."

Yet the way a couple deals with money disagreements and disappointments can predict the long-term success, or failure, of the relationship. "Money is the intersecting point where couples make most of their decisions," says Stanley, who with colleague Howard Markman conducted a survey of nearly a thousand committed couples across the country. "Money arguments have added potency because they allow for power and control dynamics to be triggered. It's an area of conflict where one partner can make unilateral decisions that affect both partners, sometimes for the rest of their lives."

Take the case of Donald, a farmer who got a loan from the bank to purchase seed in the spring. The whole economy of his farm and family depended on his planting. While he was accruing $35,000 for repayment in their joint bank account, his wife, Susann, was discovering Internet gambling. Soon the account balance was zero. Donald, in turn, lost all possibility of profit from the family farm's production and was burdened with debt for years to come.

"If your spouse makes a bad decision, even if you had no knowledge of that decision, when you're married you're treated as one financial entity," Stanley says. Even after a divorce, debt acquired by either party during the marriage is often considered communal responsibility.

Spouses—But Not Partners

Hidden financial dealings not only have legal and long-lasting conse-   5
quences, they also take a high emotional toll on couples as well. Like all secrets, energy is required to maintain the deception, undermining the most important aspect of a good relationship — the intimacy that comes from letting down one's guard.

There are three important elements of safety in relationships: the ability to talk freely, safety from physical harm and a sense of security about the future, says Stanley. "The last thing in the world you want in a marriage is to feel that you have to protect yourself against your partner, or that you have to wall off a portion of your life. Money is a very potent context in which these forces get acted out."

By hiding information about expensive purchases, risky invest-ments or debts that have accumulated to the point of crisis, he says, relationship land mines are planted that can explode with great force when triggered by outside events (when, say, creditors come calling or the Lexus is repossessed).

Even income secrets are not unusual, observes Barry McCarthy, a psychologist in Washington, D.C., and coauthor — with his wife, Emily — of *Getting It Right the First Time: How to Build a Healthy Marriage*. People may withhold information about their wages, assets and bonuses.

One husband, for example, claims he makes $120,000, and he and his wife live a fairly modest life. But the man actually makes $400,000 and keeps a separate bank account. He doesn't trust his wife. That's a typical pattern in financial dishonesty, says McCarthy — one spouse commits the "infidelity" but blames the other as the cause.

Should the hidden account be discovered, the partner who was for-   10
merly kept in the dark will think the other is hedging his bets and safeguarding individual interests over the couple's interests. "There's a sense that 'maybe you have this separate account in case you want to leave me,'" points out Scott Stanley. "The symbol becomes the prob-lem itself."

. . . Not all financial infidelity is intentional. "People just fall into it — they don't think deeply about it," says Natalie Jenkins, coauthor of *You Paid How Much for That?* A lot of people soothe themselves by buy-ing. Perhaps they feel "It's my turn, I deserve this. I'm not getting any younger," or "Rather than resent my partner over not buying this, I'm just going to charge it." Little dishonesties start growing, debts start mounting — and an avenue of intimacy is closed off.

. . . Rarely does an American go through a day without earning, spending or dealing with money in some form. Even when people sleep, their money gains interest, loses value and restlessly resides in wallets, IRAs, money markets and bank accounts. Money can be a magnet for all of the highly charged emotions hovering around the space between two people.

And fiscal self-control is more difficult today than in the past, when sidewalk barkers didn't boast "six months same as cash" and "no money down, no payments for a year." Consumption has been elevated to an art form, complete with megamalls, personal shoppers and stores that sell containers to hold more stuff.

Shopping is an act of affirmation and affiliation, a communal sport, a weekend pastime, an addiction and a designation in *DSM-IV*, psychiatry's diagnostic directory. In a media-saturated era, money buys both self-fulfillment and social acceptance — a lifestyle in which wants are transformed into needs. We come to believe that we are entitled to what those around us seem to have, and somehow spending $20,000 for a sofa appears perfectly normal.

"Some people are committing financial infidelity by hiding financial 15 misbehavior," says Denver's Stanley. "Others are having an open affair with material wealth. That represents an alternative relationship that is undermining the quality of the marital relationship." The pressure on people to produce and to make money has become enormous. "Those who can do it are so busy doing it that they don't have much time to be in relationships," observes New York psychiatrist John Jacobs.

Seductive as materialism is, it's having a devastating effect on couples. It's creating an epidemic of people who are never satisfied. "Once you're married, if you feel you don't have enough, it's very easy to blame your spouse," says Jacobs, author of *All You Need Is Love and Other Lies about Marriage*. It's a logical consequence of the romantic belief that a spouse is supposed to complete us.

"Women complain that their husband has failed to provide the kind of support they expected, or that they have to work and don't want to," Jacobs reports. "Men complain that women demand too much of them and aren't carrying their fair share in the relationship. The disappointment drives a wedge between them." . . .

Bait and Switch?

More than 60 percent of wives work outside the home, and both men and women are accommodating to this fact. Surveys show that men are taking on more of the household and parenting chores (although not yet half) and that couples are enjoying the higher standard of living that dual salaries provide. The majority of husbands, in fact, say they wouldn't mind if their wives earned more than they earn (nearly a third of working wives already make more, with another third earning around the same). Some men even admit to evaluating earnings potential in a prospective spouse, a sentiment unthinkable a few generations ago, when a working wife was an aberration, not a value-added proposition.

Outright economic gender reversal, in which a wife outearns her spouse substantially, can feel like a very subtle form of fiscal betrayal. Modern couples are the products of thousands of years of socialization that teaches us that it's the man's job to provide and the woman's job to stay home and be cared for and protected. "No matter how much we acknowledge that we want the world to change," Jacobs says, "it's still inside all of us." . . .

Full Partnership

Marriage is as much a promise of fiscal partnership as of sexual mo-   20
nogamy. Despite the natural inclination to let money issues remain dormant, dealt with largely through avoidance and denial, the more proactive couples can be about creating a strategic plan and a shared vision of their financial lives, the better.

Understanding the Text

1. What effect does Loftus produce on her reader by using words that normally refer to *sexual* cheating, such as "infidelity"?

2. Name at least two issues Loftus addresses *beyond* "infidelity."

Reflection and Response

3. How do you react to the Loftus article? Is it an eye-opener for you? Does it, on the contrary, seem overblown to you? Elaborate.

4. Loftus cites several forms of financial betrayal by a spouse. Put them into rank order, starting with the one you think of as most serious. Use a paragraph to justify your ranking of each one.

Making Connections

5. Which marital dynamics described by Loftus are at play in Rebecca Curtis's story "Twenty Grand" (p. 42)? Elaborate.

6. Research pre-nuptial agreements, the documents some couples sign before marrying to protect their assets from action by each other or to keep their assets from being divided in a future divorce settlement. Make a case for or against them.

7. With the Loftus article in mind, write a short story that opens:

   When Clara pulled the day's mail from the mailbox, one letter instantly caught her attention.

Shaken Baby Cases on the Increase

Carey Goldberg

Economic hard times produce a spate of newspaper articles on how people under financial stress act out against those closest to them. Carey Goldberg's article below appeared in the *Boston Globe* in the middle of the great economic "meltdown" of 2008 and 2009.

Goldberg has had stints as Boston bureau chief for the *New York Times*, Moscow correspondent for the *Los Angeles Times*, and health/science reporter for the *Boston Globe*.

Cases of the potentially devastating brain injury known as shaken baby syndrome have at least doubled in the last few months, a jump that Massachusetts child abuse specialists say is apparently influenced by families' economic stress.

Child protection teams at Children's Hospital Boston and Massachusetts General Hospital, which consult on many of the state's cases of maltreatment, have seen nine infants with shaken baby syndrome in the last three months, compared with four in the same period last year.

The number of cases of brain trauma has increased statewide, officials say, amid an overall rise in child abuse and neglect reports of 8 percent in the 2008 fiscal year, compared with the previous year.

Research has linked increased family stress, economic crunches in particular, to increased child abuse. Among recent shaken baby cases at Children's, several involved parents who had recently been laid off or faced other stresses such as the utilities being turned off, said Dr. Alice Newton, medical director of the hospital's Child Protection Team.

> Research has linked increased family stress, economic crunches in particular, to increased child abuse.

"This is a tragedy that we need to 5 pay attention to, especially during these really difficult, stressful economic times," said Suzin Bartley, executive director of the Massachusetts Children's Trust Fund, which was created by the Legislature in 2006 to run programs to prevent shaken baby syndrome.

The organization plans to brief legislators today on the latest figures and on its prevention efforts. There is some concern, Bartley said, that the program might not continue to receive its annual $350,000 allocation because the money is no longer listed separately in the state budget.

Broader public education about how to avoid shaken baby syndrome is still badly needed, said Alison Goodwin, spokeswoman for the Department of Children and Families, because it can be very hard to predict which infants are most at risk. She said the majority of cases do not involve clients of the agency, which works with families that have been the subject of previous abuse or neglect reports.

The syndrome occurs when an adult — usually driven to distraction by crying — violently shakes a baby, whose neck muscles are too weak to hold his or her head steady, exposing the fragile brain to potentially overwhelming injury. There are no reliable national figures on how common the syndrome is, but about one in four victims die, and the rest are usually left with severe neurological problems.

The syndrome gained particular attention locally in 1997, when a British au pair, Louise Woodward, was convicted in the shaken baby syndrome death of an 8-month-old Newton boy in her charge, Matthew Eappen.

The state does not have complete data on shaken baby syndrome 10
statewide, but reports of head trauma have increased in recent months, consistent with the increase in shaken baby cases seen at the Boston hospitals, Goodwin said.

Bartley said it seems clear that economic stress is piling on to the usual stress of parenting in dangerous ways.

"You never know what the level of frustration is in an individual family that may be contributing to them feeling totally overwhelmed," she said. "And an inconsolable, incessantly crying baby can send you right over the edge. And if you've got other young children, and you're working odd hours trying to keep a family together, and you don't understand that sometimes babies just cry, then you can be more vulnerable to shaking as a reaction."

The Children's Hospital team has seen an increase of late in the number of abuse cases and in their severity, and also in the number involving very young babies, said Newton. In the last three months, there have been 16 cases of serious physical abuse, predominantly of babies under 3 months old, compared with a dozen cases last winter, Newton said.

Though she has no proof, Newton said, "I think it's a combination of the current economic situation and the deteriorating social infrastructure," such as services for poor families.

Allison Scobie, the program director for child protection at Chil- 15
dren's, said the recent cases do coincide with "the collective stress and hopelessness that I think pervades everything."

But "I can't attribute it entirely to the economic situation," she added. "It's just this intense brutality."

About half of the recent cases have been in families with no known risk factors for child abuse, such as previous suspicious child injuries, Newton said. Many of the families are socially isolated, she said, and that can contribute to abuse. Families should try to forge social connections to help support their child-rearing, she said, and anyone who sees an infant with a pattern of bruising or other injuries should report it to authorities.

Just the other night, Newton said, a 6-month-old baby came in to the hospital with multiple fractures and bruises, consistent with inflicted injury. He was "a really sweet baby, who was so easily comforted and just snuggles right into your neck," she said.

"It's just heartbreaking when you see these."

Understanding the Text

1. By what means does this author set and maintain a tone of journalistic objectivity?

2. In addition to household money problems, one person quoted in this article cites "deteriorating social infrastructure" as a factor that contributes to the increased frequency of cases of shaken baby syndrome (paragraph 14). The appearance of the word "infrastructure" is quite unusual in this context. Look up the word, and decide what it must mean to the person quoted, based on the text that follows it.

Reflection and Response

3. Do you have any difficulty believing that economic hardship leads to a higher incidence of violent behavior? Why or why not?

4. How credible do you find the people interviewed in this piece? Are there alternate ways to explain the facts they present?

Making Connections

5. Is this article in line with the Mary Kay Foundation Survey of Shelters for Women (p. 107), a more systematic look at the connection between the state of the economy and domestic violence?

6. Investigate these pieces: the fairy tale "Hansel and Gretel" and Bob Dylan's song "The Ballad of Hollis Brown." Contemplate what, if any, economic meaning they may have. Then, suppose that you are writing an article on shaken baby syndrome. Compose an engaging one- or two-paragraph introduction to that article, making use of the fairy tale, the Dylan song, or both.

Survey of Shelters for Women

Mary Kay Foundation

Responding to the same recent economic hard times that form the backdrop to several pieces in this book, these charts make a numerical statement. Staff at the Mary Kay Foundation sought to quantify the impact of the economic "meltdown" of 2008 on domestic violence.

Created through a bequest of Mary Kay Ash, the founder of Mary Kay Cosmetics, the Mary Kay Foundation has two goals: to eliminate cancers affecting women and to end domestic violence.

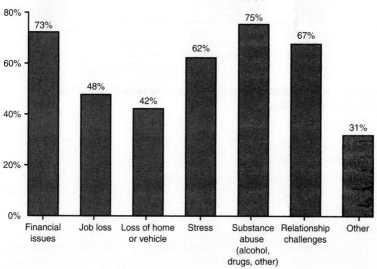

Of the women who have sought assistance as a result of domestic violence, was the abuse primarily attributed to any of the following situations? (Choose all answers that apply.)

73 Percent of Shelters Attribute Rise in Abuse to Financial Issues, 48 Percent to Job Loss

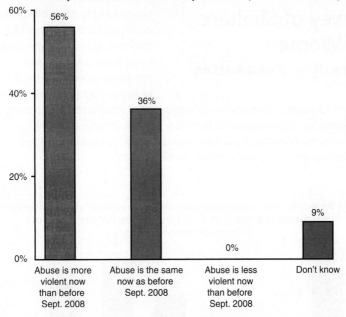

Of the women who have sought assistance as a result of domestic violence, how would you characterize the severity of abuse? (Select one answer.)

More Than Half of Shelters Report the Abuse Is More Violent Now Than before Economic Downturn

Understanding the Text

1. Translate the information presented as charts here into two paragraphs of writing, one paragraph for each chart. Aim to be so clear that a reader would have no need for the charts themselves.

Reflection and Response

2. Could the Mary Kay survey have been designed to make you more sure of what can logically be concluded from it? If so, point out its flaws and suggest improvements. If not, point out the ways in which its designers took care to make it objective and conclusive.

3. Respond to the following proposal:

   People accused of violent crimes can already plead innocent by reason of insanity. They should also be allowed to plead innocent by reason of economic duress.

Making Connections

4. If the family created by Rebecca Curtis for the story "Twenty Grand" (p. 42) were a real family, would you judge the prospect of violence in that family to be highly likely? Somewhat likely? Unlikely? Why?

5. Are you personally more inclined to believe statistics, like these, than to believe a news story like "Shaken Baby Cases on the Increase" (p. 104)? Why or why not?

My Inheritance

Meera Nair

Is there a point in life at which all family woes involving money disappear for good? Even death is not exempt from becoming an occasion for family strife about money — especially regarding the terms of a will. This sad truth pertains around the world, as the piece below attests.

Although this piece is a memoir (a true memory), its author, Meera Nair, is primarily a writer of fiction. She won the Asian-American Literary Award for her collection of short stories titled *Video* (2003).

Several years ago, a man named Mr. Lal Bihari, in the Indian state of Uttar Pradesh, petitioned the government to proclaim him alive. His uncle had bribed bureaucrats to list him in various official records as legally dead so that he could appropriate Mr. Bihari's share of the family's ancestral farmlands. Expunged from legal reckoning, rendered deceased in the eyes of the government, Mr. Bihari found himself unable to accomplish simple tasks — like getting a bank loan.

Mr. Bihari was not the type of man to let his so-called demise go unchallenged. He started a lobbying group called the Association of Dead People, registered in his village of Azamgarh. This august body soon attracted hundreds of others who had suffered similar losses at the hands of venal° relatives. Accompanied by his fellow living dead, Mr. Bihari marched in raucous parades. He and his association held a mock funeral for themselves in Lucknow, the state's capital. He tried to get arrested, ran for office, and sued people in an attempt to get the powers that be to acknowledge what had been taken from him.

When I first read about Mr. Bihari, I clipped the article and put it in a file I keep of strange and wonderful news stories that come out of India. The circumstances themselves didn't surprise me. After all, there are one billion of my countrymen crammed into an area about four and a half times the size of Texas. It is easy to see where the longing for land, any land, comes from. Add corruption and bribery into the mix, and Mr. Bihari's plight, though unusual, is still only an extreme variation on a theme. Everything is for sale in India, if you know which official to bribe for it.

What pulls me back to the news story, though, is the photograph that accompanies it. In it, Mr. Bihari, dressed in a long-sleeved striped shirt, sits on a cot opposite one of the relatives who helped rob him of his official existence. Mr. Bihari is smiling at him. I have looked at his

---

venal: susceptible to bribery, corruptible.

expression again and again, trying to puzzle out the emotions behind it. It affects me in ways that I struggle to understand, that smile. Does it signal forgiveness? Or something more complicated?

• • •

My great-grandfather lay in a coma for five years. When I was a child, 5
going to see him was an unavoidable part of my summer vacation. To visit him, we had to travel for days by train and bus to get to my family's ancestral home, a farm in a tiny village in Kerala. The trip was long and miserable, but I knew protesting was futile — in our family we did our duty, we met expectations.

It is late afternoon by the time we arrive at his house and step gingerly over the raised threshold of the door into the dark well of the room. The trees outside the many windows are loud with birds, yet only one window stands open because his wife is afraid he'll catch cold.

She waves me in and I approach silently. My great-grandfather lies flat on his back on the canopied bed, a huge man with a bald head that looks too big even for his substantial body. I avoid looking at his mouth hanging open in his fleshy, shining face. Even now, I sometimes have nightmares in which he opens his eyes and stares at me.

There is a full-length portrait hanging in the corridor outside his room. In it, he stands soldier-straight in a Western-style suit; his chin raised pugnaciously,° ferocious eyes staring into the distance under his *sola topee*, the kind of pith helmet the British favored.

Before he fell ill, he was a district agricultural officer, a bureaucrat aware of his power and unashamed to use it. He owned acres and acres of land, mansions and stores in town, and farmlands and plantations of mangoes and coconuts on its outskirts. He was known for his terrible temper, a man who thought nothing of slapping his subordinates for the slightest misdemeanor. His sons grew up terrified of him and of the switch he used to keep behind his rocking chair at all times. Everything I've heard about him makes me glad not to have known him when he was well.

His wife, a short woman with white hair that fluffs about her face, 10
crushes me into her billowy chest, then releases me. She fusses with his sheets and wipes his face with a wet rag, pattering nonstop like a saleswoman pressing her wares.

"Look who's here. Our Bhanu's granddaughter — you remember her? She got the first rank in her class — ten out of ten in English composi-

pugnaciously: combatively, like a fighter.

tion." She turns to me. "Why don't you recite something to him — How about Wordsworth? You know 'Daffodils'?" She pats my shoulder in encouragement, but I can't bring myself to perform. Then she asks me to look for flies. Her manner as she relinquishes the whisk to me clearly indicates that this is a privilege, a reward for having made the pilgrimage. I walk around the bed inspecting my great-grandfather's feet and palms, which lie open, pink, plump, and unresisting as any baby's against the flies that dare to alight on him. My great-grandmother watches to make sure I do it right.

Every day since he'd fallen ill, she'd performed such duties without complaint. When medicine, both Western and ayurvedic,° failed to revive him, she brought in exorcists, astrologers, and magicians; masseurs who soaked her husband's body in herbal oils; and priests who lit huge blazing fires in the courtyard and chanted mantras° to the unresponsive gods through the night. She only left his side to bring him his meals — liquidized rice with tomatoes or tender coconut water that she dripped drop by drop down his throat. By the time breakfast was done, it was time for lunch.

When my great-grandfather died, his wife of fifty-four years discovered that he had changed his mind about his bequest° to his family. Her sons produced a new document, an annotated, meticulous will with her husband's signature ratifying every page. Every yard of land he owned, every store, every mansion, every plantation, was divided up among them. The only thing his wife and her only daughter, my grandmother, received was a share each in the house that he had died in, where two of her sons still lived.

Until the will was read, my great-grandmother must have presumed that everything he owned would be hers to distribute among her children. She had lived in the house all her life, given birth to her children and helped bring her grandchildren into the world under its roof. She didn't have anywhere else to go. Her share in the house would at least let her live there until she died, but her daughter would have to defer her inheritance until her brothers felt like selling the house.

What made our situation doubly scandalous was that my family is 15 part of the Nair community. We were, not so long ago, one of the few matrilineal° societies on the planet. And although the matrilineal system was abolished in 1976, its effects and traditions still linger. In our community, the right of inheritance passes from the mother to

ayurvedic: related to a very old tradition of medicine in India.
mantras: sacred prayers or formulas believed to have magical power.
bequest: something that is bequeathed, a legacy.
matrilineal: based on descent from one's mother, rather than from one's father.

her children and their children. Before new laws of Hindu succession decreed that property be equally divided among all children, the women got the lion's share of all family wealth. If the will hadn't been changed, my great-grandmother would have passed much of her inheritance on to her daughter, who would have passed it on to my mother and her sisters, and eventually some portion might have fallen to me.

The will my granduncles created is undeniably legal, authorized by a lawyer, a drinking buddy of theirs. Because of our family's prominence, most of the residents in that very small town knew that my great-grandfather had lain as one dead for many years and could not have produced that will. Yet the town's only notary stamped and signed it. There was nothing the women in my family, the suddenly dispossessed, could do.

> There was nothing the women in my family, the suddenly dispossessed, could do.

* * *

And yet my grandmother laughs fondly whenever she speaks of her youngest brother, the one the rest of us believe masterminded the new will. "He used to kick me in my stomach whenever I carried him. He was two years old, and I was nine months pregnant with your mother at the time," she tells me.

My grandmother is eighty-two now, and she's been looking out for her brothers all her life, even after she married and moved fifty miles away to her husband's farm. Even after we install a telephone at the farm, they arrive unannounced from her hometown, a convulsion of large, bald men heaving out of the car, and yell, "Edathir" in unison from the courtyard, as if they can't wait to see their big sister until they are decently inside the house. They come bearing gifts — sticky-sweet *jilebis*, expensive grapes, news of the world outside the farm. My serene grandmother, who normally professes a profound indifference to the workings of the kitchen, rushes to the cook and starts firing off instructions about lunch. A lifelong vegetarian, she dispatches farm-hands to chase down and slay chickens. She has a perfect memory for every brother's favorite dish from their childhood, and it falls to my mother or one of her sisters to persuade the by now thoroughly disgruntled cook to make at least some of them.

Her brothers spend the day eating and drinking, shaking out handkerchiefs big as tea towels to mop their sweating foreheads, competing with one another to entertain us. The youngest one was once the brother my mother always wanted. He taught her to whistle, to fight and use a slingshot, and to climb fences and steal mangoes from the baskets passing vendors carried on their heads. The middle one wiggles his hairy ears back and forth to make my young cousins scream with delight. They are collectively charming and worldly, born raconteurs° who mesmerize us with their stories. My frail, pretty grandmother grows pink with laughter as she listens. She is girlish in their presence, beside herself, squeezing any grandchild within reach too tight in her happiness. Her giddiness drives my mother and her sisters insane.

The moment the men leave, quiet, like the aftermath of a thunderstorm, returns to the bright, whitewashed rooms, and my mother flees upstairs to her bedroom with her two younger sisters at her heels. There, out of my grandmother's earshot, all hell breaks loose. 20

"They have smiles on their faces and poison in their hearts, but she'll never see that," my mother, ever dramatic, rails through clenched teeth. If I so much as giggle, she turns on me.

"And you, I saw you laughing like a fool at their jokes. Just like her. And they were not even so funny." I had noticed her laughing once or twice, too, but I know better than to say anything.

In private, my mother and aunts forget the lessons in humility and respect that they have always dinned into me and my cousins. They lampoon my grandmother — exaggerating the way she shakes her head at a brother in mock exasperation, as if at a naughty but beloved child, and parodying the silly diminutive° she calls them. Their mouths twist in rancor.

"How can she? How can she?" the sisters question one another, collapsed in the same bed, prostrate from anger. They search one another's impressions of the day, dissect every sentence, and weigh every expression, wanting answers, seeking even more ways to be outraged.

My cousins and I all have heard the facts — the stolen fortune, the 25 cheating, the litany of what could have been. It is a mountain we have climbed before. The story comes up without fail every time the family gets together. We arrive from cities scattered across the country, full of news of our different lives, yet end up listening to our mothers repeat our history, the narrative in all its twists and turns, as reliable and as unavoidable as rain in the monsoons.°

---

raconteurs: gifted storytellers.
diminutive: the kind of affectionate name one might use with a child.
monsoons: the big weather systems that produce wet seasons in India and southern Asia.

Our mothers take it upon themselves to keep the memory of our misfortunes alive and immediate, to keep the pain from passing. They don't allow us to question the facts, which are immutable, chiseled in stone long ago at some point in our family's journey from fabulous wealth to ordinariness. They need this legend, this loss; it welds my mother and her sisters together. One night, lying on the cool floor, I listen to them talk about the old house, the one they don't visit any-more. My mother and her sisters fall asleep one by one, then snort awake to continue the conversation without a break. In the dark, their voices are similar, their yearnings interchangeable; they are all my mother and loved as such. I am jealous of their closeness.

When my father has a stroke that leaves him partially paralyzed and unemployed, my parents come back to my grandmother's village. My father has retired early, and they hope to cobble together a new life on the farm, but his medical expenses soon wear our savings down to terrifying lows. My aunts are experiencing hardships as well. One of my cousins cannot get into a good college because he needs thousands of rupees to pay the "donations" they demand. It is in times like this of financial crisis that the wails of "if only" and "what if" grow louder. My mother weeps at the injustice that has been perpetuated on us, nineteen, twenty years after the fact. She blames our broken luck, our privations, on her uncles. Her sisters, I hear from my cous-ins, do the same. I am astonished and a little frightened at the tenac-ity of their memory and the resentment that keeps it alive.

And yet they rarely express their feelings in front of my grand-mother. When my mother, in her place as the eldest daughter, brings it up one night, she is circumspect, tiptoeing around the topic of how she and her sisters feel. "Perhaps it would be better if the uncles didn't come around as much," she says, "though no one wishes to dwell on the past."

"Yes, it was not right what they did," my grandmother says. "May God grant them good sense. I'll tell them to stop coming, if that is what you and your sisters want." She agrees and agrees; she can't stop agreeing. What she wants is for the conversation to be over.

My mother is halfway to the kitchen when my grandmother calls 30 her back. "Radha-Sudha-Indira!" she says. My mother is Indira. Her sisters are Radha and Sudha. My grandmother has never been able to say any one daughter's name alone — the three names spill out to-gether, no matter which one she is calling to her side. She tells her she wants her daughters to be like the three stones of the hearth after she dies. It is something I have heard her wish for before. Her language is often lyrical, full of metaphor, the only thing about her that tends toward extravagance. "You can't balance a pot if any one of the stones is missing," she explains. My mother strikes her forehead with her hand. "Ayyo! Do be quiet, Mother," she says.

My granduncle was one of my father's best friends when they were in college. Once, he convinced my father to come to a family wedding with him. My father fell in love at the celebration. The girl was beautiful, with curly, waist-length hair. The first time he saw her she was holding a tray full of flowers to welcome the bride. "I warned him — that's my niece and don't you dare so much as think about her," my granduncle always says when he comes to this part of the story. It is one I never tire of hearing. He was the reason my parents met and married each other. He had a hand in my existence, I tell my mother. But she wants to forget all these connections.

● ● ●

Whenever my granduncles visit, my mother and her sisters wait to see what happens. They hover. They eavesdrop. I know what my mother and her sisters want. I've heard it often enough. They want my grandmother to toss her brothers on their rear, order them to never darken our doors again. For them, only melodrama on a Bollywood° scale will suffice — shamefaced departures, triumphant laughter, recrimination and its satisfying aftermath, the four men fallen at their sister's feet cringing for forgiveness. Instead, my grandmother offers them tea and cake, unconditional absolution. When her brothers finally pile back into the car and leave, my grandmother stands at the doorstep, hands raised in blessing, just like her mother used to, until the taillights disappear.

Sometimes, as I watch them drive away, I wonder which one practiced my great-grandfather's signature until he got it right. How did they decide, as they sat upstairs drinking in their mother's house all those years ago, that their sister wasn't worth giving anything to? . . .

● ● ●

In 2002, a year after her husband died, my grandmother executed her will.° After her demise, her daughters would get the farm and the surrounding land. The house would go to my mother, the only one without one to call her own. The will is a model of fair distribution, beyond

Bollywood: India's film industry.
execute a will: put a will into effect.

complaint. At least that is what my mother and her sisters think in the beginning.

But one night, my aunts argue over the will, each accusing the other of scheming to take over more than the allotted acreage. At issue is a long, narrow French-loaf-shaped piece of property hemming Aunt Radha's property. Thirty-seven feet altogether, to be exact. It has five coconut palms growing any which way on it, making it impossible to decide whom they belonged to. Aunt Sudha thinks that the land and the trees should be hers. Land supervisors are brought in, measurements taken and disputed. Brutal, irredeemable things are said until the sisters stop talking altogether. The quarrel strains credibility, and at first I do not believe it is serious.

But when I visit India, the two of them come separately to see me. On our usual evening walks along the fields, each one sobs, heartbroken, women in their fifties with grown sons and daughters. They miss each other. Who would think this could happen to us? To this family, after all we have lost over the years? They say this as if they have no control over their desires, their egos, their dreams for their children. They are obsessed with this new outrage, this latest so-called land-grab. My grandmother says nothing to them, even though I beg her — she seems unable to summon the resources for another fight. I wonder if she is in shock, deeply disappointed that her daughters have not heeded the one lesson she tried to teach them all these years, the importance of forgiveness.

Instead, they are stuck in the flypaper of their natures, unable to rise above the hurt and the pain of the words that they have recklessly flung about, unable to see what really matters. They blame each other and dredge up petty arguments and childhood incidents as if they were portents predicting this exact break, this spendthrift pouring away of their love.

Listening to their stories, I am so angry that I cannot breathe. They are confused, taken aback when I lecture them, rip their arguments apart, condemn their behavior. I am ashamed of them for the first time in my life, I say, and I am laughing in relief as I say it, refusing to see it their way, reckless in my disrespect for my elders. I am not, I decide, going to allow thirty-seven feet of land to divide us. I am not my mother's daughter.

My grandmother will die soon. She waits for her time to come. My mother waits with her, the two women alone in the echoing rooms. My aunts visit them sometimes, but never together. I don't know if my harsh words got through to them, but I did hear that my aunts called each other recently. They had very little to say beyond Happy New

Year, but three sentences is a conversation, I tell myself. It's a beginning at least. I am waiting for the day when all of us, aunts, cousins, grandmothers, and grandchildren, will get together again, scarred, a little unsure of our reception, but smiling at each other like our lives depended on it.

Understanding the Text

1. In paragraph 4 of this memoir, Meera Nair stares at the mystifying smile of a man victimized by greedy relatives. Later, she puzzles over the mystifying smile of her grandmother, also a victim of family greed. What do you make of those smiles?

2. Do Nair's mother and aunts behave any better than Nair's granduncles did, in the preceding generation? Explain.

Reflection and Response

3. The vast majority of readers will agree that Nair's granduncles acted despicably in robbing Nair's grandmother of her inheritance — an event with repercussions felt by three generations. Agreement is harder to achieve, however, when it comes to the behavior of Nair's grandmother herself or the very different behavior of Nair's mother and aunts. Do any of them deal wisely with the granduncles' act of theft? If so, which ones? If not, what would a wise response look like? Why?

   In answering, take into account all that you find in the Nair memoir, including:

   - Nair's grandmother's metaphor of "the three stones of the hearth" (paragraph 30)
   - Nair's curious description of her grandmother as "loving and ineffectual"
   - the behavior of Nair's mother and aunts after they receive their inheritance from Nair's grandmother (paragraphs 35 and 36)
   - the closing words, ". . . like our lives depended on it."

Making Connections

4. Could new laws prevent the kind of selfish mischief that wrought havoc in Nair's family? Spell out your reasoning.

5. Find a roommate, classmate, or friend who would be willing to be interviewed — strictly anonymously — on money and relationships.

   Has that person seen up close, or been caught in, strife like

   - what David Amsden describes in "What's a Little Money between Friends?" (p. 92)?
   - what Mary Loftus describes in "Till Debt Do Us Part" (p. 99)?
   - what Carey Goldberg describes in "Shaken Baby Cases on the Increase" (p. 104)?
   - or what Meera Nair describes in "My Inheritance" above?

Have your interviewee give you as much of his/her story as possible, while you take notes. Write a paper based on the interview: What light, if any, does it shed on the pertinent reading? Does it tend to confirm the conclusions reached or implied in that reading? Does it call those conclusions into question or complicate them?

Be sure to do as you have promised and protect your interviewee's anonymity.

6. Even where the prospect of inheritance doesn't lead to action that tears a family apart, it can transform familial relations in subtle ways. Comment on the quote below by Miguel de Cervantes, the seventeenth-century Spaniard who wrote *Don Quixote*. Does it ring true to you? What experiences that you've had or know about contribute to your reaction?

> There is a strange charm in the thoughts of a good legacy, or the hopes of an estate, which wondrously removes or at least alleviates the sorrow that men would otherwise feel for the death of friends.

3

Is Money
to Blame for
Unethical
Conduct?

You have no doubt heard the expression "Money is the root of all evil." Thirty years ago, the magazine *Psychology Today* ran a survey on the things people would be willing to do for a million dollars. Most respondents said that, for a million dollars, they would take a job they didn't like. Many (roughly 20 percent of the men, 10 percent of the women) said they would participate in illegal acts, such as theft and bribery.

Survey results like these lead one to wonder if the net effect of money on society is positive or negative.

Most of the readings in this section speak to whether the attraction of money motivates people in business to treat customers and the general public well.

The author of the famous novel *Ragged Dick* seems to vote yes.

The authors of "Cheating in a Bottom-line Economy" and "Pinto Madness" dwell on the dark, amoral side of business.

The author of "The Social Responsibility of Business Is to Increase Its Profits" is a bit harder to classify, since he approaches the question indirectly and implicitly.

Business, however, isn't the only area of public life where the attraction of money can have negative effects. The authors of "You Can't Evict an Idea Whose Time Has Come," "CSI USA: Who Killed the American Dream?" and "Unfree Speech: The Folly of Campaign Finance Reform" set forth opposing views on the question "Does money corrupt politics?"

From Ragged Dick

Horatio Alger

With the possible exception of Benjamin Franklin, no one has done more than the author Horatio Alger to foster the belief that monetary success is the world's reward for virtue and hard work. Few books have achieved the popularity his *Ragged Dick* enjoyed for many years in post–Civil War America.

Before establishing himself as a writer, Alger was briefly a Unitarian pastor.

As the excerpt below begins, Alger's hero, Dick, has been sharing a rented room with Fosdick, a fellow bootblack (shoeshine boy). In return for Dick's paying their entire rent, Fosdick teaches Dick reading and arithmetic.

Chapter 26

An Exciting Adventure

Dick now began to look about for a position in a store or counting room. Until he should obtain one he determined to devote half the day to blacking boots, not being willing to break in upon his small capital. He found that he could earn enough in half a day to pay all his necessary expenses, including the entire rent of the room. Fosdick desired to pay his half; but Dick steadily refused, insisting upon paying so much as compensation for his friend's services as instructor.

It should be added that Dick's peculiar way of speaking and use of slang terms had been somewhat modified by his education and his intimacy with Henry Fosdick. Still he continued to indulge in them to some extent, especially when he felt like joking, and it was natural to Dick to joke, as my readers have probably found out by this time. Still his manners were considerably improved, so that he was more likely to obtain a situation than when first introduced to our notice.

Just now, however, business was very dull, and merchants, instead of hiring new assistants, were disposed to part with those already in their employ. After making several ineffectual applications, Dick began to think he should be obliged to stick to his profession until the next season. But about this time something occurred which considerably improved his chances of preferment.

This is the way it happened.

As Dick, with a balance of more than a hundred dollars in the savings bank, might fairly consider himself a young man of property, he thought himself justified in occasionally taking a half holiday from business, and going on an excursion. On Wednesday afternoon Henry Fosdick was sent by his employer on an errand to that part of Brooklyn near Greenwood Cemetery. Dick hastily dressed himself in his best, and determined to accompany him.

The two boys walked down to the South Ferry, and, paying their two cents each, entered the ferryboat. They remained at the stern, and stood by the railing, watching the great city, with its crowded wharves, receding from view. Beside them was a gentleman with two children, — a girl of eight and a little boy of six. The children were talking gaily to their father. While he was pointing out some object of interest to the little girl, the boy managed to creep, unobserved, beneath the chain that extends across the boat, for the protection of passengers, and, stepping incautiously to the edge of the boat, fell over into the foaming water.

At the child's scream, the father looked up, and, with a cry of horror sprang to the edge of the boat. He would have plunged in, but, being unable to swim, would only have endangered his own life, without being able to save his child.

"My child!" he exclaimed in anguish, — "who will save my child? A thousand — ten thousand dollars to any one who will save him!"

There chanced to be but few passengers on board at the time, and nearly all these were either in the cabins or standing forward. Among the few who saw the child fall was our hero.

Now Dick was an expert swimmer. It was an accomplishment which 10 he had possessed for years, and he no sooner saw the boy fall than he resolved to rescue him. His determination was formed before he heard the liberal offer made by the boy's father. Indeed, I must do Dick the justice to say that, in the excitement of the moment, he did not hear it at all, nor would it have stimulated the alacrity with which he sprang to the rescue of the little boy.

Little Johnny had already risen once, and gone under for the second time, when our hero plunged in. He was obliged to strike out for the boy, and this took time. He reached him none too soon. Just as he was sinking for the third and last time, he caught him by the jacket. Dick was stout and strong, but Johnny clung to him so tightly, that it was with great difficulty he was able to sustain himself.

"Put your arms round my neck," said Dick.

The little boy mechanically obeyed, and clung with a grasp strengthened by his terror. In this position Dick could bear his weight better. But the ferryboat was receding fast. It was quite impossible to reach it. The father, his face pale with terror and anguish, and his hands clasped in suspense, saw the brave boy's struggles, and prayed with agonizing fervor that he might be successful. But it is probable, for they were now midway of the river, that both Dick and the little boy whom he had bravely undertaken to rescue would have been drowned, had not a rowboat been fortunately near. The two men who were in it witnessed the accident, and hastened to the rescue of our hero.

"Keep up a little longer," they shouted, bending to their oars, "and we will save you."

Dick heard the shout, and it put fresh strength into him. He battled   15 manfully with the treacherous sea, his eyes fixed longingly upon the approaching boat.

"Hold on tight, little boy," he said. "There's a boat coming."

The little boy did not see the boat. His eyes were closed to shut out the fearful water, but he clung the closer to his young preserver. Six long, steady strokes, and the boat dashed along side. Strong hands seized Dick and his youthful burden, and drew them into the boat, both dripping with water.

> Dick's great ambition to "grow up 'spectable" seemed likely to be accomplished after all. . . .

"God be thanked!" exclaimed the father, as from the steamer he saw the child's rescue. "That brave boy shall be rewarded, if I sacrifice my whole fortune to compass it." . . .

The boat at once headed for the ferry wharf on the Brooklyn side. The captain of the ferryboat, seeing the rescue, did not think it necessary to stop his boat, but kept on his way. The whole occurrence took place in less time than I have occupied in telling it.

The father was waiting on the wharf to receive his little boy, with   20 what feeling of gratitude and joy can be easily understood. With a burst of happy tears he clasped him to his arms. Dick was about to withdraw modestly, but the gentleman perceived the movement, and, putting down the child, came forward, and, clasping his hand, said with emotion, "My brave boy, I owe you a debt I can never repay. But for your timely service I should now be plunged into an anguish which I cannot think of without a shudder."

Our hero was ready enough to speak on most occasions, but always felt awkward when he was praised.

"It wasn't any trouble," he said, modestly. "I can swim like a top."

"But not many boys would have risked their lives for a stranger," said the gentleman. "But," he added with a sudden thought, as his glance rested on Dick's dripping garments, "both you and my little boy will take cold in wet clothes. Fortunately I have a friend living close at hand, at whose house you will have an opportunity of taking off your clothes, and having them dried."

Dick protested that he never took cold; but Fosdick, who had now joined them, and who, it is needless to say, had been greatly alarmed at Dick's danger, joined in urging compliance with the gentleman's proposal, and in the end our hero had to yield. His new friend secured a hack, the driver of which agreed for extra recompense to receive the dripping boys into his carriage, and they were whirled rapidly to a pleasant house in a side street, where matters were quickly explained, and both boys were put to bed.

"I ain't used to goin' to bed quite so early," thought Dick. "This is the 25 queerest excursion I ever took."

Like most active boys Dick did not enjoy the prospect of spending half a day in bed; but his confinement did not last as long as he anticipated.

In about an hour the door of his chamber was opened, and a servant appeared, bringing a new and handsome suit of clothes throughout.

"You are to put on these," said the servant to Dick; "but you needn't get up till you feel like it."

"Whose clothes are they?" asked Dick.

"They are yours." 30

"Mine! Where did they come from?"

"Mr. Rockwell sent out and bought them for you. They are the same size as your wet ones."

"Is he here now?"

"No. He bought another suit for the little boy, and has gone back to New York. Here's a note he asked me to give you."

Dick opened the paper, and read as follows, — 35

Please accept this outfit of clothes as the first installment of a debt which I can never repay. I have asked to have your wet suit dried, when you can reclaim it. Will you oblige me by calling tomorrow at my counting room, No. — , Pearl Street.
   Your friend,
   James Rockwell

Chapter 27

Conclusion

When Dick was dressed in his new suit, he surveyed his figure with pardonable complacency. It was the best he had ever worn, and fitted him as well as if it had been made expressly for him.

"He's done the handsome thing," said Dick to himself; "but there wasn't no 'casion for his givin' me these clothes. My lucky stars are shinin' pretty bright now. Jumpin' into the water pays better than shinin' boots; but I don't think I'd like to try it more'n once a week."

About eleven o'clock the next morning Dick repaired to Mr. Rockwell's counting room on Pearl Street. He found himself in front of a large and handsome warehouse. The counting room was on the lower floor. Our hero entered, and found Mr. Rockwell sitting at a desk. No sooner did that gentleman see him than he arose, and, advancing, shook Dick by the hand in the most friendly manner.

"My young friend," he said, "you have done me so great a service that I wish to be of some service to you in return. Tell me about yourself, and what plans or wishes you have formed for the future."

Dick frankly related his past history, and told Mr. Rockwell of his 40
desire to get into a store or counting room, and of the failure of all his applications thus far. The merchant listened attentively to Dick's statement, and, when he had finished, placed a sheet of paper before him, and, handing him a pen, said, "Will you write your name on this piece of paper?"

Dick wrote, in a free, bold hand, the name Richard Hunter. He had very much improved his penmanship . . . and now had no cause to be ashamed of it.

Mr. Rockwell surveyed it approvingly.

"How would you like to enter my counting room as clerk, Richard?" he asked.

Dick was about to say "Bully," when he recollected himself, and answered, "Very much."

"I suppose you know something of arithmetic, do you not?" 45
"Yes, sir."

"Then you may consider yourself engaged at a salary of ten dollars a week. You may come next Monday morning."

"Ten dollars!" repeated Dick, thinking he must have misunderstood.

"Yes; will that be sufficient?"

"It's more than I can earn," said Dick, honestly. 50

"Perhaps it is at first," said Mr. Rockwell, smiling; "but I am willing to pay you that. I will besides advance you as fast as your progress will justify it."

Dick was so elated that he hardly restrained himself from some demonstration which would have astonished the merchant; but he exercised self-control, and only said, "I'll try to serve you so faithfully, sir, that you won't repent having taken me into your service."

"And I think you will succeed," said Mr. Rockwell, encouragingly. "I will not detain you any longer, for I have some important business to attend to. I shall expect to see you on Monday morning."

Dick left the counting room, hardly knowing whether he stood on his head or his heels, so overjoyed was he at the sudden change in his fortunes. Ten dollars a week was to him a fortune, and three times as much as he had expected to obtain at first. Indeed he would have been glad, only the day before, to get a place at three dollars a week. He reflected that with the stock of clothes which he had now on hand, he could save up at least half of it, and even then live better than he had been accustomed to do; so that his little fund in the savings bank, instead of being diminished, would be steadily increasing. Then he was to be advanced if he deserved it. It was indeed a bright prospect for a boy who, only a year before, could neither read nor write, and depended for a night's lodging upon the chance hospitality of an alleyway or old wagon. Dick's great ambition to "grow up 'spectable" seemed likely to be accomplished after all. . . .

Understanding the Text

1. What personal attributes seem to account for Dick's success? Do you include diligence, honesty, and generosity on your list? Why or why not?

2. Which came first, the chicken or the egg? Did the prospect of earning more money *make* Dick moral and upstanding, or did his inborn temperament happen to fit with what the world rewarded? How can you tell?

Reflection and Response

3. Aside from Dick's case, can you ordinarily tell when a businessperson is a genuinely good human being, rather than someone putting on a show to attract more business?

4. In real life, is it most often the individual who resembles Dick that prospers? How does Dick's story compare with what you know of friends, members of your family, and figures in the news?

Making Connections

5. The lifetimes of renowned lawyer Clarence Darrow and novelist Horatio Alger overlapped by more than 40 years, but their views on the reasons for personal success and failure in life were sharply at odds. In 1902, Darrow told an audience of prison inmates that, morally speaking, they were no worse than people of the highest standing in society, such as the oil tycoon John D. Rockefeller. With the help of your librarian or a Web search engine, find a copy of Darrow's address to the prisoners in Cook County Jail. Then, imagine what comments Darrow might have written to himself in the margins of the excerpt from *Ragged Dick* above. Write those comments out, together with the lines from *Ragged Dick* to which they refer.

In what respects does your own response to *Ragged Dick* coincide with what you have imagined Darrow's would be? In what respects does your response differ from that?

6. Even if Dick's finer qualities were put on for the sake of profit, the charade might have been praiseworthy. Find out what Aristotle thought of "acting like someone better than you are," as expressed in his *Nicomachean Ethics*, Book 2, Section 1. Do his opinions surprise you? Write a response explaining why or why not.

Cheating in a Bottom-line Economy

David Callahan

David Callahan's book *The Cheating Culture* deals with all the factors at play in our times that induce people to violate traditional values of fairness and honesty. This reading is excerpted from his chapter on the new pressures in business to increase profits.

Callahan co-founded Demos, a public policy think tank where he is a senior fellow. Besides *The Cheating Culture,* he has authored *The Moral Center* and *Fortunes of Change: The Rise of the Liberal Rich and the Remaking of America.*

Picture yourself as an auto mechanic who works for a national chain of repair shops. You never went to college, but you got some vocational training and you're making about $30,000 a year. In the old days, when your dad was your age, a mechanic's paycheck would have been big enough to afford the down payment on a modest house. It would have been big enough to allow your wife to stay home with the kids, and maybe even big enough to afford a boat.

Those days are long gone. Your paycheck just gets you by, and nothing more. On the other hand, working for a chain ensures a fair level of security. Customers flock to the chains because they trust them more, and heavy advertising and promotions keep drivers coming back. The work is steady and straightforward. Cars come in; you check them out and tell your manager what needs to be done. Then you fix them. When the day ends, the job doesn't come home with you.

Then abruptly something changes. A new set of marching orders is handed down to the repair centers from the chain's corporate headquarters. You're informed that all mechanics and managers will henceforth have their base pay sharply reduced and will have to make up the difference every month depending on how much work they perform. Once you and the other mechanics do the math, you realize that headquarters is expecting everyone to work harder for the same amount of money. Management also makes it clear that anyone who doesn't meet the quotas may be fired. The scant good news in all of this is that if you work really hard, a special incentive in the new system will allow you to make more money than you did before.

Your job becomes very different. You work harder during the day and worry more at night about whether you'll hit your monthly quota. You also face some dicey choices that didn't exist before. Whenever a customer brings a car in you can proceed in one of two ways: The right thing to do is to take a look and say, honestly, exactly what the car needs. This is your instinct and what you'd prefer to do. After all, you consider yourself an honest person. You've never been in trouble with the law and, except for speeding in your lovingly restored '75 Mustang, you pretty much play by the rules. The problem is that doing the right thing has suddenly gotten a lot harder. You'll suffer a pay cut and risk losing your job if you don't meet your quota — and there's a nice carrot dangling in front of you if you do rack up a lot of extra work.

So gradually you start handling things differently. When a car comes 5 in you take a look, say what the car needs, and then also call for a couple of other repairs that weren't necessary. Maybe the car only needs new brakes, but you say that the struts are also shot and should be replaced. Maybe the sputtering of the engine only requires a good tune-up; but you say that a new carburetor or fuel injection system is in order. Ninety-nine percent of customers don't know the first thing about how cars work, so the chances of getting caught seem next to nil. Also, the other mechanics are doing the same thing, and your manager actually encourages the practice. He's under even more pressure than you are.

Pretty soon, everyone at your shop is cheating customers nearly every day and nobody is giving it much thought. It's just the way things are done now that everyone is hustling so hard to keep their head above water. And your shop is nothing unusual. Some estimates of the cost nationwide of auto-repair fraud run as high as $40 billion a year. Maybe none of the customers at your shop ever catch on and this new way of doing business is never challenged. Or maybe state law enforcement agencies get tipped off to the fraud and they mount a sting operation — as happened with Sears.

During the 1990s, Sears was caught up in a huge scandal regarding its automotive repair chain. The circumstances paralleled the hypothetical situation just described. The scandal underscores how a new and intense focus on the bottom line in American business often spawns more cheating, eroding the integrity of people who would rather be playing by the rules.

Twenty years ago, Sears, Roebuck, & Company reigned as one of America's most well-known and beloved large retailers. For over a century it had prospered in good times and weathered hard times. Sears built more than brand loyalty; it shaped America's popular culture. But times became tougher for Sears in the 1980s as it faced challenges from Wal-Mart and Kmart. Then came the economic downturn at the end of that decade, and Sears confronted a serious falloff in earnings as the 1990s began.

In earlier business eras, like the '50s and '60s, the ups and downs of major companies did not have the consequences they do today. Corporations were firmly controlled by their top executives and often employees had a strong voice through labor unions. A company experiencing hard times could decide internally how to deal with the challenge.

All this changed in the 1970s and 1980s, as large outside investors   10 and Wall Street came to wield increasing power over publicly held companies. A company's stock price became the all-important indicator of success, and businesses were expected to do whatever it took to improve their bottom line — now defined not as healthy performance over a period of years but as strong earnings every quarter of every year.

This meant that a company's leadership no longer had much leeway in handling problems. When earnings fell off, intense pressure mounted to take drastic action. Which is exactly what Sears did as its earnings slid. It announced that it would cut 48,000 jobs and it also instituted a new compensation system for those employees who were spared the ax.

What happens when bottom-line practices put ordinary people under intense financial pressure — but provide them with a cheating option that can relieve that pressure?

The Sears auto repair chain was the largest in the country at the time, servicing 20 million cars annually. Within a year of the new policies taking effect, complaints from customers were rolling in to consumer groups and state watchdog agencies. People complained of getting billed for repairs they didn't want or need, and of pervasive dishonesty at the Sears repair centers. Sears became the target of official investigations in forty-four states and eighteen class action suits were filed against the company. "We had an all-American relationship with Sears," said Michael J. Stumpf, one angry customer. That relationship ended when Stumpf and his fiancée got stuck with a $650 bill for what should have been an $89 strut job. "Trust shaken is not easily gained back," Stumpf said.

The Sears mechanics and sales staff spoke out about how the new bottom-line focus had forced them to make unpleasant ethical choices at work. One mechanic talked of being "torn between moral integrity, losing my job, and trying to figure out how to work all this out" and others talked of the "pressure, pressure, pressure to get the dollars."

The evidence unearthed by investigators found nearly identical reports of cheating at one Sears auto repair shop after another. It was almost as if Sears's high command had constructed the perfect natural experiment around personal ethics. Want to know what happens when bottom-line practices put ordinary people under intense financial pressure — but provide them with a cheating option that can relieve that pressure? The answer is not very surprising: They will sacrifice their integrity before their economic security.

. . . The shadow that now hangs over Sears's reputation is rather 15
remarkable, given the company's history. Sears had cultivated a successful love affair with the American consumer for a century. It got through the Depression and many smaller economic downturns without betraying that trust or experiencing serious scandals. And then, during a period of less than fifteen years, Sears squandered public trust, incurred numerous criminal charges and multiple lawsuits, and paid fines and settlements that ultimately totaled over $2 billion. These problems didn't arise because of uniquely bad management or a suicidal impulse on the part of Sears's top executives.

The company and its employees were simply changing with the times.

• • •

The white-shoe corporate law firms of Manhattan wouldn't seem to bear even a passing resemblance to Sears auto repair centers. These firms operate in a rarefied strata of money and power — managing the legal affairs of some of America's largest companies. They are filled with well-compensated professionals bound by oath to abide by a rigorous code of ethics. And yet life at such firms often entails an ongoing clash between integrity and economic well-being not unlike what occurred in the Sears auto centers. Ordinary people are subjected to intense pressure and high financial stakes — all the while enjoying the option to cheat. And how do many lawyers behave under these circumstances? Not any better than the Sears auto mechanics did.

. . . To be a young law associate at a white-shoe New York firm is both a great privilege and a grueling experience. Associates enter a world of dramatic disparities in pay and power, and they are subjected to incredible stress. First-year associates start with a pay package that seems impressive: $125,000 a year and a signing bonus as high as $40,000. This pay becomes less impressive when one considers that associates can spend up to eighty hours a week in the office, the average one-bedroom apartment in New York City costs about $2,200 a month, and the typical law school grad is carrying over $80,000 in student loans. The entry-level pay is not why people join the corporate law world. They join with the hope that someday they will be able to make partner. The average partner at Cravath, Swaine & Moore took home nearly $2 million in bonus pay in 2002. Partners at Wachtell, Lipton, Rosen & Katz took home even bigger bonuses.[1]

But one of the first things associates at top firms learn is that their chances of ascending to partner are next to nil. Only a tiny fraction of associates have any prospect of making partner. The age is long gone when a brilliant young associate could pretty much bank on being elevated to partner. "People will get rejected who are extraordinary lawyers, who have worked long and hard and then get screwed," says a former associate who worked at one of New York's most prestigious firms in the late 1990s. "It's awful and there's awful pressure. For the people really gunning for partner there is a pressure, in addition to working inhuman hours, of trying to beat odds that are incredibly difficult to beat."

Associates at top firms put in insanely long hours in reality — and often longer hours on paper. "You're supposed to bill in tenths of an hour — six minute increments," explains the former associate. "But nobody sits there with a stopwatch. You always round up. If you worked seven minutes, you bill twelve; one minute, you bill six. . . . Everybody does it at some point."

The anonymity of corporate law makes the corner cutting less troubling. Unlike the old days, there's little loyalty between law firms and clients. "You're part of a sea of lawyers, you have no contact with anyone related to the client," says the former associate. "Why not err on the side of a higher [billing] number? There's no accountability at all for it in that situation. It never comes back to you in any personal way. All these firms charge by the hour. There's an incentive to over-bill for work not done or for things that are unnecessary. There's an incentive not to staff things efficiently.° It's true everywhere."

. . . Lisa Lerman is one of the nation's leading experts on corruption in law. She is director of the Law Public Policy program at Catholic University in Washington, D.C., and her research specialty is candor and deception in the legal profession. She has extensively examined over-billing and other abuses at major law firms, interviewing scores of lawyers. Lerman says that very few lawyers can actually meet the common billing requirements these days of 2,200 to 2,400 hours. "What I've heard over and over again is people say that they can't bill more than 1,700 or 1,800 hours a year honestly, and their bosses remonstrate them. Everyone knows who's billing the most, and it is not always

staff things efficiently: to assign only as many staff members to a task as are really needed to do it.
_____
[1] "The AM 100," *American Lawyer* (July 2003).

20

the one who's working the most. The ones who are willing to play with the numbers are more likely to achieve their goals." Lawyers who don't meet their billing requirements place year-end bonuses at risk and, in hard times, are more likely to be downsized.

So how do so many lawyers manage to bill the hours? They simply make up the numbers, according to Lerman, William Ross, Macklin Fleming, and many other veteran observers of the legal profession. They round their time upward and forget about the many things they did all day that weren't billable, like arguing with their wife on the phone about why they were going to miss dinner yet again. Says Fleming about the liberal allowances more and more lawyers make on their time sheets: "This development may be described as the new math."[2]

New associates at corporate law firms find themselves sprawling down a slippery slope as they learn the true rules that govern their universe. "Let me tell you how you will start acting unethically," wrote a law school dean, Patrick J. Schiltz, in an article addressed to law students. "One day, not too long after you start practicing law, you will sit down at the end of a long, tiring day, and you just won't have much to show for your efforts in terms of billable hours. It will be near the end of the month. You will know that all of the partners will be looking at your monthly time report in a few days, so what you'll do is pad your time sheet just a bit. Maybe you will bill a client for ninety minutes for a task that really took you only sixty minutes to perform. However, you will promise yourself that you will repay the client at the first opportunity by doing thirty minutes for the client for 'free.' In this way, you will be 'borrowing,' not stealing. And then what will happen is that it will become easier and easier to take these little loans against future work. And then, after a while, you will stop paying back these little loans. . . . You will continue to rationalize your dishonesty to yourself in various ways until one day you stop doing even that. And before long — it won't take you much more than three or four

---

[2] Macklin Fleming, *Lawyers, Money, and Success* (Westport, Conn.: Quorum Books, 1997), 36. For Lerman's findings, as well as more on the problem of overbilling, see Lerman, "The Slippery Slope from Ambition to Greed"; and Lerman, "Blue-Chip Bilking: Regulation of Billing and Expense Fraud by Lawyers," *Georgetown Journal of Legal Ethics* 12, no. 2 (winter 1999): 205–365; Lerman et al., "Unethical Billing Practices," *Rutgers Law Review* 50, no. 4 (summer 1998): 2153–226; and William G. Ross, "The Ethics of Hourly Billing by Attorneys," *Rutgers Law Review* 44 (fall 1991): 13; William G. Ross, *The Honest Hour: The Ethics of Time-Based Billing by Attorneys* (Durham, N.C.: Carolina Press, 1996); and Andre Gharakhanian and Yvonne Krywyj, "The Gunderson Effect and the Billable Mania: Trends in Overbilling and the Effect of New Wages," *Georgetown Journal of Legal Ethics* 14 (summer 2001): 1001–18.

years — you will be stealing from your clients almost every day, and you won't even notice it."[3]

   . . . It's easy for lawyers to get away with outrageous things, and   25 legal experts say that law firms may deliberately pad the bills of clients that are known to be less vigilant. The general laxity around bills is the only way to explain some of the charges that lawyers have tried to slip by their clients. Leona Helmsley once found that her lawyer had billed her for a forty-three-hour day. A lawyer named James Spiotto achieved brief notoriety in the 1990s when he revealed he had billed 6,000 hours a year for four years straight. He claimed his problem was not dishonesty but workaholism. A Los Angeles health-care company found that three different lawyers working on a project had submitted bills for more than fifty hours a day. An Annapolis lawyer named Edward Digges, Jr., a Princeton grad with a 300-acre Maryland estate to maintain, billed a client for $500,000 of nonexistent work and $66,000 for Lexis research that actually cost $394. In one of the biggest overbilling scandals of all, the Federal Deposit Insurance Corporation estimated in the early 1990s that it had been overbilled by as much as $100 million by the private law firms it used for outside contract work. Overbilling was found at nearly every firm the FDIC audited. One lawyer named William Duker overbilled the FDIC and the Resolution Trust Corporation by $1.4 million over a two-year period.

   And then there's Webster Hubbell, a confidante of the Clintons who was a partner at the Rose Law Firm and went on to be deputy attorney general. Hubbell bilked clients of hundreds of thousands of dollars during the 1980s and early 1990s. He later explained that the fraud occurred after he had "become overwhelmed" by personal debts and other problems.

   In 1998, investigators made public a taped telephone conversation between the imprisoned Hubbell and his wife, Suzanna.

   "You didn't actually do that, did you? Mark up time for the client, did you?" Suzanna asked.

   "Yes, I did," answered Hubbell. "So does every lawyer in the country."[4]

---

[3] Patrick J. Schiltz, "On Being a Happy, Healthy, and Ethical Member of an Unhappy, Unhealthy, and Unethical Profession," *Vanderbilt Law Review* 52, no. 871 (1999): 807.

[4] On Helmsley overbilling, see Darlene Ricker, "Greed, Ignorance, and Overbilling," *ABA Journal* (August 1994): 63. On Spiotto's billing, see Lerman, "The Slippery Slope from Ambition to Greed," 905. On L.A. healthcare company, see Amy Stevens, "As Some Clients Grow Bill Savvy, Others May Find They Get the Tab," *Wall Street Journal*, 11 February 1994, B5. On FDIC overbilling, see Linda Himelstein, "FDIC Counsel Routinely Overbill, Audit Finds," *New Jersey Law Journal*, 10 February 1992, 4. On Webster Hubbell's problems and rationales, see Ellen Joan Pollock, "Hubbell Receives

* * *

. . . "Your entire frame of reference will change," says Patrick Schiltz of 30 what happens to people who spend even a short amount of time within a cheating culture. "You will still be making dozens of quick, instinctive decisions every day, but those decisions, instead of re-flecting the notions of right and wrong by which you conduct your personal life, will instead reflect the set of values by which you will conduct your professional life — a set of values that embodies not what is right and wrong, but what is profitable, and what you can get away with. The system will have succeeded in replacing your values with the system's values, and the system will be profiting as a result."[5]

The bottom-line emphasis of laissez-faire ideology is not new in the United States. American culture — with its classless mythology and frontier ethos — has proved uniquely hospitable to seductive market ideas about the power of individuals to shape their own economic destiny. Horatio Alger, a Harvard grad and the son of a Unitarian pastor, made a fortune writing inspirational books about overcoming hardship. The United States lagged decades behind European nations in developing a social safety net that could buffer Americans from the harsh ups and downs of a capitalist economy.

The market's dominance in American life began to ebb with the rise of Progressivism and Liberalism in the first three decades of the twentieth century. Then came the national emergencies of the Great Depression, World War II, and the Cold War, which helped justify an activist federal government and locked into place a new liberal order.

But a resurgence of market ideology began during the economic turmoil of the 1970s. This decade witnessed the rising influence of conservative economic ideas, a fierce backlash to decades of govern-ment activism, and a growing view within business that companies needed to get leaner and meaner to cope with foreign competition.

. . . Before these changes, back in the 1950s and 1960s, corporate life was pretty laid back. As Paul Krugman writes: "America's great cor-porations behaved more like socialist republics than like cutthroat capitalist enterprises, and top executives behaved more like public-spirited bureaucrats than like captains of industry." An implicit social

---

21-Month Prison Sentence for Bilking His Law Firm and Clients," *Wall Street Journal* 29 June 1995, B4; and Adam Liptak, "Stop the Clock? Critics Call the Billable Hour a Legal Fiction," *New York Times,* 29 October 2002, G7.

[5] Schiltz, "On Being a Happy, Healthy, and Ethical Member of an Unhappy, Unhealthy, and Unethical Profession," 807.

contract at most companies bonded workers and management in a web of loyalty. Workers committed themselves to the firm and, in turn, management treated them well. An ethos of equity ruled in what has been called "managerial capitalism," and salaries at the top of the firm were not grossly inflated in comparison to salaries at the bottom. Powerful labor unions helped enforce the terms of this social contract. Many companies also had strong ties to the community, which they saw as another stakeholder, and played a leading role in civic affairs. "The job of management is to maintain an equitable and working balance among the claims of the various directly interested groups," said Frank Abrams in 1951. Abrams was neither a union agitator nor a liberal intellectual. He was chairman of Standard Oil Company.[6]

By the 1980s the social contract in business was largely defunct. 35 The top ranks of business management began catering mainly to just two constituencies: shareholders and themselves. Large institutional shareholders like pensions and mutual funds got new clout in the 1980s as a vast amount of money poured into the stock market. The managers of these large funds were under constant pressure to show results from their stock picks and they leaned on corporate leaders to boost profits — over a period not of many years, but of every quarter. To show these profits, corporate leaders became even more focused on being lean and mean. As "investor capitalism" replaced "managerial capitalism," mid-twentieth-century notions of loyalty within the firm were tossed aside.

Corporate leaders also grew more intent on feathering their own nests. The demise of labor unions in the '70s and '80s meant that workers had less leverage over how company profits were spread around. Social norms about pay equity within companies withered during this time. The top ranks of management could effectively behave however they wanted and pay themselves whatever they wanted — as long as the stock did well and investors stayed happy. "Downsizing" became common, even in good times, and the salaries of CEOs rose dramatically. In the late 1940s, no executive in America made over half a million dollars a year in official compensation. By 1968, after two decades of explosive growth and record corporate profits, CEO salaries had climbed only modestly. General Motors chairman James M. Roche was the highest-paid executive in America that year, making $795,000. But ten years later, during a period of sluggish growth, David

---

[6] Paul Krugman, "For Richer," *New York Times Magazine*, 20 October 2002, 62. Abrams quoted in Robert Reich, *The Future of Success* (New York: Vintage Books, 2002), 71.

Mahoney, chairman of Norton Simon, was the top earner among corporate chiefs, making $3 million a year. By 1988, Michael Eisner, the CEO of Walt Disney Company, made the most of any executive, taking home $40.1 million. Eisner was number one again ten years later, but this time he took home $575.6 million.[7] The new freedom of top executives to funnel more profits into their own pockets gave them an immense incentive to worship the leanest and meanest version of the bottom line, since every new "efficiency" translated directly into personal gain.

The point here is to show how an obsession with competition and profits steamrolled into American life starting in the 1970s. This obsession partly reflected changes in the economy, but it also reflected a shift in values and norms. "The ideal of a free, self-regulating market is newly triumphant," declared Robert Kuttner in his 1996 book *Everything for Sale.* "Unfettered markets are deemed both the essence of human liberty, and the most expedient route to prosperity."[8] . . . As a booming economy pumped rivers of cash into every kind of business organization — and as the carrots for the Winning Class got bigger — bad behavior became more tempting.

---

[7] "Executive Pay: Up, Up and Away," *Businessweek Online*, 19 April 1999.

[8] Robert Kuttner, *Everything for Sale* (New York: Knopf, 1996), 3. For an excellent overview of the triumph of market ideas in American society during the 1980s and 1990s, see Zachary Karabell, *A Visionary Nation: Four Centuries of American Dreams and What Lies Ahead* (New York: Harper-Collins, 2001), 119–57. See also Thomas Frank, *One Market under God: Extreme Capitalism, Market Populism, and the End of Economic Democracy* (New York: Doubleday, 2000); and David Bollier, *Silent Theft: The Private Plunder of Our Common Wealth* (New York: Routledge, 2002).

Understanding the Text

1. Why do you suppose Callahan pairs an example of cheating in the blue collar world (Sears auto repair shops) with examples in the white collar world (top law firms)?

2. The last seven paragraphs of the Callahan excerpt are devoted to the *history* behind today's cheating in business. Summarize that history in one paragraph.

Reflection and Response

3. Are the blue collar and white collar examples used by Callahan truly parallel instances of cheating? Make your case.

4. Here is a memory that a student retold in a paper:

    "How does this look on me? Be honest." She walks out of the dressing room, and I hope she has not seen the look of horror that just flashed across my face. Her outfit is less than flattering, but instead of telling her so, I muster up an encouraging smile and say, "You look great." It is not that I want this woman to go out in public in an unattractive outfit, and if it were any other day, I would discourage her from buying it. However, I only have a half hour left on my shift, and I have yet to meet my daily goal. . . . My hours and pay all depend on how much I sell, and if I consistently miss my daily goals, I will lose my job. I am not committing any type of fraud or breaking into the system and changing my numbers, I am simply telling someone that a shirt looks good on them when it really does not.

Does this story fit one of the patterns of cheating laid out by Callahan?

Have you or someone you know had such experiences, too? Were they less subtle instances of cheating? More subtle ones?

5. Fictionalize the dilemma of a young newcomer to a company who soon realizes that success there depends on behaving dishonestly, although no one explicitly says so. Write a short story either (a) in the voice of that newcomer or (b) in the voice of his/her superior, a manager who silently observes the newcomer's adjustment to the "facts of life" at the company.

Making Connections

6. How would Horatio Alger's character Dick (p. 121) have fared if he had gotten jobs in the different business settings Callahan describes?

7. Some "A" students now make money by selling their term papers to online companies that resell them at a profit to other students. How do you imagine the buyers and the sellers of these papers justify their actions to themselves?

Pinto Madness

Mark Dowie

In the 1970s, hundreds of people lost their lives due to a defect in a popular car model. Here is an account of that story that lays special emphasis on the role played by corporate greed. Author Mark Dowie's investigative reporting has garnered him four National Magazine awards and a Pulitzer Prize nomination. Books he has authored include *Losing Ground: American Environmentalism at the Close of the Twentieth Century*.

One evening in the mid-1960s, Arjay Miller was driving home from his office in Dearborn, Michigan, in the four-door Lincoln Continental that went with his job as president of the Ford Motor Company. On a crowded highway, another car struck his from the rear. The Continental spun around and burst into flames. Because he was wearing a shoulder-strap seat belt, Miller was unharmed by the crash, and because his doors didn't jam he escaped the gasoline-drenched, flaming wreck. But the accident made a vivid impression on him. Several months later, on July 15, 1965, he recounted it to a U.S. Senate subcommittee that was hearing testimony on auto safety legislation. "I still have burning in my mind the image of that gas tank on fire," Miller said. He went on to express an almost passionate interest in controlling fuel-fed fires in cars that crash or roll over. He spoke with excitement about the fabric gas tank Ford was testing at that very moment. "If it proves out," he promised the senators, "it will be a feature you will see in our standard cars."

Almost seven years after Miller's testimony, a woman, whom for legal reasons we will call Sandra Gillespie, pulled onto a Minneapolis highway in her new Ford Pinto. Riding with her was a young boy, whom we'll call Robbie Carlton. As she entered a merge lane, Sandra Gillespie's car stalled. Another car rear-ended hers at an impact speed of 28 miles per hour. The Pinto's gas tank ruptured. Vapors from it mixed quickly with the air in the passenger compartment. A spark ignited the mixture and the car exploded in a ball of fire. Sandra died in agony a few hours later in an emergency hospital. Her passenger, 13-year-old Robbie Carlton, is still alive; he has just come home from another futile operation aimed at grafting a new ear and nose from skin on the few unscarred portions of his badly burned body. (This accident is real; the details are from police reports.)

Why did Sandra Gillespie's Ford Pinto catch fire so easily, seven years after Ford's Arjay Miller made his apparently sincere pronouncements, the same seven years that brought more safety improvements to cars than any other period in automotive history? An extensive investigation by *Mother Jones* over the past six months has found these answers:

- Fighting strong competition from Volkswagen for the lucrative small-car market, the Ford Motor Company rushed the Pinto into production in much less than the usual time.

- Ford engineers discovered in pre-production crash tests that rear-end collisions would rupture the Pinto's fuel system extremely easily.

- Because assembly-line machinery was already tooled when engineers found this defect, top Ford officials decided to manufacture the car anyway — exploding gas tank and all — *even though Ford owned the patent on a much safer gas tank.*

- For more than eight years afterwards, Ford successfully lobbied, with extraordinary vigor and some blatant lies, against a key government safety standard that would have forced the company to change the Pinto's fire-prone gas tank.

By conservative estimates Pinto crashes have caused 500 burn deaths to people who would not have been seriously injured if the car had not burst into flames. The figure could be as high as 900. Burning Pintos have become such an embarrassment to Ford that its advertising agency, J. Walter Thompson, dropped a line from the end of a radio spot that read "Pinto leaves you with that warm feeling."

Ford knows the Pinto is a firetrap, yet it has paid out millions to   5
settle damage suits out of court, and it is prepared to spend millions more lobbying against safety standards. With a half million cars rolling off the assembly lines each year, Pinto is the biggest-selling subcompact in America, and the company's operating profit on the car is fantastic. Finally, in 1977, new Pinto models have incorporated a few minor alterations necessary to meet that federal standard Ford managed to hold off for eight years. Why did the company delay so long in making these minimal, inexpensive improvements?

Ford waited eight years because its internal "cost-benefit analysis," *which places a dollar value on human life,* said it wasn't profitable to make the changes sooner.

Before we get to the question of how much Ford thinks your life is worth, let's trace the history of the death trap itself. Although this particular story is about the Pinto, the way in which Ford made its decision is typical of the U.S. auto industry generally. There are plenty of similar stories about other cars made by other companies. But this case is the worst of them all.

The next time you drive behind a Pinto (with over two million of them on the road, you shouldn't have much trouble finding one), take a look at the rear end. That long silvery object hanging down under the bumper is the gas tank. The tank begins about six inches forward of the bumper. In late models the bumper is designed to withstand a collision of only about five miles per hour. Earlier bumpers may as well not have been on the car for all the protection they offered the gas tank.

Mother Jones has studied hundreds of reports and documents on rear-end collisions involving Pintos. These reports conclusively reveal that if you ran into that Pinto you were following at over 30 miles per hour, the rear end of the car would buckle like an accordion, right up to the back seat. The tube leading to the gas-tank cap would be ripped away from the tank itself, and gas would immediately begin sloshing onto the road around the car. The buckled gas tank would be jammed up against the differential housing (that big bulge in the middle of your rear axle), which contains four sharp, protruding bolts likely to gash holes in the tank and spill still more gas. Now all you need is a spark from a cigarette, ignition, or scraping metal, and both cars would be engulfed in flames. If you gave that Pinto a really good whack — say, at 40 mph — chances are excellent that its doors would jam and you would have to stand by and watch its trapped passengers burn to death.

This scenario is no news to Ford. Internal company documents in 10 our possession show that Ford has crash-tested the Pinto at a top-secret site more than 40 times and that *every* test made at over 25 mph without special structural alteration of the car has resulted in a ruptured fuel tank. Despite this, Ford officials denied under oath having crash-tested the Pinto.

Eleven of these tests, averaging a 31-mph impact speed, came before Pintos started rolling out of the factories. Only three cars passed the test with unbroken fuel tanks. In one of them an inexpensive lightweight plastic baffle was placed between the front of the gas tank and the differential housing, so those four bolts would not perforate the tank. (Don't forget about that little piece of plastic, which costs one dollar and weighs one pound. It plays an important role in our story later on.) In another successful test, a piece of steel was placed between the tank and the bumper. In the third test car the gas tank was lined with a rubber bladder. But none of these protective alterations was used in the mass-produced Pinto.

In pre-production planning, engineers seriously considered using in the Pinto the same kind of gas tank Ford uses in the Capri. The Capri tank rides over the rear axle and differential housing. It has been so successful in over 50 crash tests that Ford used it in its Experimental Safety Vehicle, which withstood rear-end impacts of 60 mph. So why wasn't the Capri tank used in the Pinto? Or, why wasn't that plastic baffle placed between the tank and the axle — something that would have saved the life of Sandra Gillespie and hundreds like her? Why was a car known to be a serious fire hazard deliberately released to production in August of 1970?

• • •

Whether Ford should manufacture subcompacts at all was the subject of a bitter two-year debate at the company's Dearborn headquarters. The principals in this corporate struggle were the then-president Semon "Bunky" Knudsen, whom Henry Ford II had hired away from General Motors, and Lee Iacocca, a spunky Young Turk who had risen fast within the company on the enormous success of the Mustang. Iacocca argued forcefully that Volkswagen and the Japanese were going to capture the entire American subcompact market unless Ford put out its own alternative to the VW Beetle. Bunky Knudsen said, in effect: let them have the small-car market; Ford makes good money on medium and large models. But he lost the battle and later resigned. Iacocca became president and almost immediately began a rush program to produce the Pinto.

Like the Mustang, the Pinto became known in the company as "Lee's car." Lee Iococca wanted that little car in the showrooms of America with the 1971 models. So he ordered his engineering vice president, Bob Alexander, to oversee what was probably the shortest production planning period in modern automotive history. The normal time span from conception to production of a new car model is about 43 months. The Pinto schedule was set at just under 25.

A quick glance at the bar chart below will show you what that speed-up meant. Design, styling, product planning, advance engineering and quality assurance all have flexible time frames, and engineers can pretty much carry these on simultaneously. Tooling, on the other hand, has a fixed time frame of about 18 months. Normally, an auto company doesn't begin tooling until the other processes are almost over: you don't want to make the machines that stamp and press and grind metal into the shape of car parts until you know all those parts will work well together. *But Iacocca's speed-up meant Pinto tooling went on at the same time as product development.* So when crash tests revealed a serious defect in the gas tank, it was too late. The tooling was well under way.

When it was discovered the gas tank was unsafe, did anyone go to Iacocca and tell him? "Hell no," replied an engineer who worked on the Pinto, a high company official for many years, who, unlike several others at Ford, maintains a necessarily clandestine concern for safety. "That person would have been fired. Safety wasn't a popular subject around Ford in those days. With Lee it was taboo. Whenever a problem was raised that meant a delay on the Pinto, Lee would chomp on his cigar, look out the window and say 'Read the product objectives and get back to work.'"

The product objectives are clearly stated in the Pinto "green book." This is a thick, top-secret manual in green covers containing a step-by-step production plan for the model, detailing the metallurgy, weight, strength and quality of every part in the car. The product objectives for the Pinto are repeated in an article by Ford executive F. G. Olsen published by the Society of Automotive Engineers. He lists these product objectives as follows:

1. TRUE SUBCOMPACT
   - Size
   - Weight

2. LOW COST OF OWNERSHIP
   - Initial price
   - Fuel consumption
   - Reliability
   - Serviceability

3. CLEAR PRODUCT SUPERIORITY
   - Appearance
   - Comfort
   - Features
   - Ride and handling
   - Performance

Safety, you will notice, is not there. It is not mentioned in the entire article. As Lee Iacocca was fond of saying, "Safety doesn't sell."

Heightening the anti-safety pressure on Pinto engineers was an important goal set by Iacocca known as "the limits of 2,000." The Pinto was not to weigh an ounce over 2,000 pounds and not to cost a cent over $2,000. "Iacocca enforced these limits with an iron hand," recalls the engineer quoted earlier. So, even when a crash test showed that that one-pound, one-dollar piece of plastic stopped the puncture of the gas tank, it was thrown out as extra cost and extra weight.

People shopping for subcompacts are watching every dollar. "You 20 have to keep in mind," the engineer explained, "that the price elasticity on these subcompacts is extremely tight. You can price yourself right out of the market by adding $25 to the production cost of the model. And nobody understands that better than Iacocca."

Dr. Leslie Ball, the retired safety chief for the NASA manned space program and a founder of the International Society of Reliability Engineers, recently made a careful study of the Pinto. "The release to production of the Pinto was the most reprehensible decision in the history of American engineering," he said. Ball can name more than 40 European and Japanese models in the Pinto price and weight range with safer gas-tank positioning. Ironically, many of them, like the Ford Capri, contain a "saddle-type" gas tank riding over the back axle. *The patent on the saddle-type tank is owned by the Ford Motor Co.*

Los Angeles auto safety expert Byron Bloch has made an in-depth study of the Pinto fuel system. "It's a catastrophic blunder," he says. "Ford made an extremely irresponsible decision when they placed such a weak tank in such a ridiculous location in such a soft rear end. It's almost designed to blow up — premeditated."

A Ford engineer, who doesn't want his name used, comments: "This company is run by salesmen, not engineers; so the priority is styling, not safety." He goes on to tell a story about gas-tank safety at Ford:

Lou Tubben is one of the most popular engineers at Ford. He's a friendly, outgoing guy with a genuine concern for safety. By 1971 he had grown so concerned about gas-tank integrity that he asked his boss if he could prepare a presentation on safer tank design. Tubben and his boss had both worked on the Pinto and shared a concern for its safety. His boss gave him the go-ahead, scheduled a date for the presentation and invited all company engineers and key production planning personnel. When time came for the meeting, a grand total of two people showed up — Lou Tubben and his boss.

"So you see," continued the anonymous Ford engineer ironically, 25 "there *are* a few of us here at Ford who are concerned about fire safety." He adds: "They are mostly engineers who have to study a lot of accident reports and look at pictures of burned people. But we don't talk about it much. It isn't a popular subject. I've never seen safety on the agenda of a product meeting and, except for a brief period in 1956, I can't remember seeing the word safety in an advertisement. I really don't think the company wants American consumers to start thinking too much about safety — for fear they might demand it, I suppose."

Asked about the Pinto gas tank, another Ford engineer admitted: "That's all true. But you miss the point entirely. You see, safety isn't the issue, trunk space is. You have no idea how stiff the competition is over trunk space. Do you realize that if we put a Capri-type tank in the Pinto you could only get one set of golf clubs in the trunk?"

● ● ●

Blame for Sandra Gillespie's death, Robbie Carlton's unrecognizable face and all the other injuries and deaths in Pintos since 1970 does not rest on the shoulders of Lee Iacocca alone. For, while he and his associates fought their battle against a safer Pinto in Dearborn, a larger war against safer cars raged in Washington. One skirmish in that war involved Ford's successful eight-year lobbying effort against Federal Motor Vehicle Safety Standard 301, the rear-end provisions of which would have forced Ford to redesign the Pinto.

But first some background:

During the early '60s, auto safety legislation became the *bête-noire* of American big business. The auto industry was the last great un-regulated business, and if *it* couldn't reverse the tide of government regulation, the reasoning went, no one could.

People who know him cannot remember Henry Ford II taking a 30 stronger stand than the one he took against the regulation of safety design. He spent weeks in Washington calling on members of Con-gress, holding press conferences and recruiting business cronies like W. B. Murphy of Campbell's Soup to join the anti-regulation battle. Displaying the sophistication for which today's American corporate leaders will be remembered, Murphy publicly called auto safety "a hula hoop, a fad that will pass." He was speaking to a special lun-cheon of the Business Council, an organization of 100 chief execu-tives who gather periodically in Washington to provide "advice" and "counsel" to government. The target of their wrath in this instance was the Motor Vehicle Safety Bills introduced in both houses of Con-gress, largely in response to Ralph Nader's *Unsafe at Any Speed.*

By 1965, most pundits and lobbyists saw the handwriting on the wall and prepared to accept government "meddling" in the last bas-tion of free enterprise. Not Henry. With bulldog tenacity, he held out for defeat of the legislation to the very end, loyal to his grandfather's invention and to the company that makes it. But the Safety Act passed the House and Senate unanimously, and was signed into law by Lyndon Johnson in 1966.

While lobbying for and against legislation is pretty much a process of high-level back-slapping, press-conferencing and speech-making, fighting a regulatory agency is a much subtler matter. Henry headed home to lick his wounds in Grosse Pointe, Michigan, and a planeload of the Ford Motor Company's best brains flew to Washington to start the "education" of the new federal auto safety bureaucrats.

Their job was to implant the official industry ideology in the minds of the new officials regulating auto safety. Briefly summarized, that ideology states that auto accidents are caused not by cars, but by 1) people and 2) highway conditions.

This philosophy is rather like blaming a robbery on the victim. Well, what did you expect? You were carrying money, weren't you? It is an extraordinary experience to hear automotive "safety engineers" talk for hours without ever mentioning cars. They will advocate spending billions educating youngsters, punishing drunks and redesigning street signs. Listening to them, you can momentarily begin to think that it is easier to control 100 million drivers than a handful of manufacturers. They show movies about guardrail design and advocate the clear-cutting of trees 100 feet back from every highway in the nation. If a car is unsafe, they argue, it is because its owner doesn't properly drive it. Or, perhaps, maintain it.

In light of an annual death rate approaching 50,000, they are forced 35 to admit that driving is hazardous. But the car is, in the words of Arjay Miller, "the safest link in the safety chain."

Before the Ford experts left Washington to return to drafting tables in Dearborn they did one other thing. They managed to informally reach an agreement with the major public servants who would be making auto safety decisions. This agreement was that "cost-benefit" would be an acceptable mode of analysis by Detroit and its new regulators. And, as we shall see, cost-benefit analysis quickly became the basis of Ford's argument against safer car design.

Cost-benefit analysis was used only occasionally in government until President Kennedy appointed Ford Motor Company president Robert McNamara to be Secretary of Defense. McNamara, originally an accountant, preached cost-benefit with all the force of a Biblical zealot. Stated in its simplest terms, cost-benefit analysis says that if the cost is greater than the benefit, the project is not worth it — no matter what the benefit. Examine the cost of every action, decision, contract part or change, the doctrine says, then carefully evaluate the benefits (in dollars) to be certain that they exceed the cost before you begin a program or — and this is the crucial part for our story — pass a regulation.

As a management tool in a business in which profits matter over everything else, cost-benefit analysis makes a certain amount of sense. Serious problems come, however, when public officials who ought to have more than corporate profits at heart apply cost-benefit analysis to every conceivable decision. The inevitable result is that they must place a dollar value on human life.

> Ever wonder what your life is worth in dollars?

Ever wonder what your life is worth in dollars? Perhaps $10 million? Ford has a better idea: $200,000.

Remember, Ford had gotten the federal regulators to agree to talk auto safety in terms of cost-benefit analysis. But in order to be able to argue that various safety costs were greater than their benefits, Ford needed to have a dollar value figure for the "benefit." Rather than be so uncouth as to come up with such a price tag itself, the auto industry pressured the National Highway Traffic Safety Administration to do so. And in a 1972 report the agency decided a human life was worth $200,725. Inflationary forces have recently pushed the figure up to $278,000.

Furnished with this useful tool, Ford immediately went to work using it to prove why various safety improvements were too expensive to make.

Nowhere did the company argue harder that it should make no changes than in the area of rupture-prone fuel tanks. Not long after the government arrived at the $200,725-per-life figure, it surfaced, rounded off to a cleaner $200,000, in an internal Ford memorandum. This cost-benefit analysis argued that Ford should not make an $11-per-car improvement that would prevent 180 fiery deaths a year. (This minor change would have prevented gas tanks from breaking so easily both in rear-end collisions, like Sandra Gillespie's, and in rollover accidents, where the same thing tends to happen.)

Ford's cost-benefit table is buried in a seven-page company memorandum entitled "Fatalities Associated with Crash-Induced Fuel Leakage and Fires." The memo argues that there is no financial benefit in complying with proposed safety standards that would admittedly result in fewer auto fires, fewer burn deaths and fewer burn injuries. Naturally, memoranda that speak so casually of "burn deaths" and "burn injuries" are not released to the public. They are very effective, however, with Department of Transportation officials indoctrinated in McNamarian cost-benefit analysis.

All Ford had to do was convince men like John Volpe, Claude Brinegar and William Coleman (successive Secretaries of Transportation during the Nixon-Ford years) that certain safety standards would add so much to the price of cars that fewer people would buy them. This could damage the auto industry, which was still believed to be the bulwark of the American economy. "Compliance to these standards," Henry Ford II prophesied at more than one press conference, "will shut down the industry."

The Nixon Transportation Secretaries were the kind of regulatory 45 officials big business dreams of. They understood and loved capitalism and thought like businessmen. Yet, best of all, they came into office uninformed on technical automotive matters. And you could talk "burn injuries" and "burn deaths" with these guys, and they didn't seem to envision children crying at funerals and people hiding in their homes with melted faces. Their minds appeared to have leapt right to the bottom line — more safety meant higher prices, higher prices meant lower sales and lower sales meant lower profits.

So when J. C. Echold, Director of Automotive Safety (which means chief anti-safety lobbyist) for Ford, wrote to the Department of Transportation — which he still does frequently, at great length — he felt secure attaching a memorandum that in effect says it is acceptable to kill 180 people and burn another 180 every year, *even though we have the technology that could save their lives for $11 a car.*

Furthermore, Echold attached this memo, confident, evidently, that the Secretary would question neither his low death/injury statistics nor his high cost estimates. But it turns out, on closer examination, that both these findings were misleading.

First, note that Ford's table shows an equal number of burn deaths and burn injuries. This is false. All independent experts estimate that for each person who dies by an auto fire, many more are left with charred hands, faces and limbs. Andrew McGuire of the Northern California Burn Center estimates the ratio of burn injuries to deaths at ten to one instead of the one to one Ford shows here. Even though Ford values a burn at only a piddling $67,000 instead of the $200,000 price of a life, the true ratio obviously throws the company's calculations way off.

The other side of the equation, the alleged $11 cost of a fire-prevention device, is also a misleading estimation. One document that was *not* sent to Washington by Ford was a "Confidential" cost analysis *Mother Jones* has managed to obtain, showing that crash fires could be largely prevented for considerably *less* than $11 a car. The cheapest method involves placing a heavy rubber bladder inside the gas tank to keep the fuel from spilling if the tank ruptures. Goodyear had developed the bladder and had demonstrated it to the automotive industry. We have in our possession crash-test reports showing that the Goodyear bladder worked well. On December 2, 1970 (*two years before* Echold sent his cost-benefit memo to Washington), Ford Motor Company ran a rear-end crash test on a car with the rubber bladder in the gas tank. The tank ruptured, but no fuel leaked. On January 15, 1971, Ford again tested the bladder and again it worked. The total purchase and installation cost of the bladder would have been $5.08 per car. That $5.08 could have saved the lives of Sandra Gillespie and several hundred others.

• • •

When a federal regulatory agency like the National Highway Traffic 50 Safety Administration (NHTSA) decides to issue a new standard, the law usually requires it to invite all interested parties to respond before the standard is enforced — a reasonable enough custom on the surface. However, the auto industry has taken advantage of this process and has used it to delay lifesaving emission and safety standards for years. In the case of the standard that would have corrected that fragile Pinto fuel tank, the delay was for an incredible eight years.

The particular regulation involved here was Federal Motor Vehicle Safety Standard 301. Ford picked portions of Standard 301 for strong opposition way back in 1968 when the Pinto was still in the blueprint stage. The intent of 301, and the 300 series that followed it, was to protect drivers and passengers *after* a crash occurs. Without question the worst post-crash hazard is fire. So Standard 301 originally proposed that all cars should be able to withstand a fixed barrier impact of 20 mph (that is, running into a wall at that speed) without losing fuel.

When the standard was proposed, Ford engineers pulled their crash-test results out of their files. The front ends of most cars were no problem — with minor alterations they could stand the impact without losing fuel. "We were already working on the front end," Ford engineer Dick Kimble admitted. "We knew we could meet the test on the front end." But with the Pinto particularly, a 20-mph rear-end standard meant redesigning the entire rear end of the car. With the Pinto scheduled for production in August of 1970, and with $200 million worth of tools in place, adoption of this standard would have created a minor financial disaster. So Standard 301 was targeted for delay, and, with some assistance from its industry associates, Ford succeeded beyond its wildest expectations: the standard was not adopted until the 1977 model year. Here is how it happened:

There are several main techniques in the art of combating a government safety standard: a) make your arguments in succession, so the feds can be working on disproving only one at a time; b) claim that the real problem is not X but Y (we already saw one instance of this in "the problem is not cars but people"); c) no matter how ridiculous each argument is, accompany it with thousands of pages of highly technical assertions it will take the government months or, preferably, years to test. Ford's large and active Washington office brought these techniques to new heights and became the envy of the lobbyists' trade.

The Ford people started arguing against Standard 301 way back in 1968 with a strong attack of technique b). Fire, they said, was not the real problem. Sure, cars catch fire and people burn occasionally. But statistically auto fires are such a minor problem that NHTSA should really concern itself with other matters.

Strange as it may seem, the Department of Transportation 55 (NHTSA's parent agency) didn't know whether or not this was true. So it contracted with several independent research groups to study auto fires. The studies took months, which was just what Ford wanted.

The completed studies, however, showed auto fires to be more of a problem than Transportation officials ever dreamed of. Robert Nathan and Associates, a Washington research firm, found that 400,000 cars were burning up every year, burning more than 3,000 people to death. Furthermore, auto fires were increasing five times as fast as building fires. Another study showed that 35 per cent of all fire deaths in the U.S. occurred in automobiles. Forty per cent of all fire department calls in the 1960s were to vehicle fires — a public cost of $350 million a year, a figure that, incidentally, never shows up in cost-benefit analyses.

Another study was done by the Highway Traffic Research Institute in Ann Arbor, Michigan, a safety think-tank funded primarily by the auto industry (the giveaway there is the words "highway traffic" rather than "automobile" in the group's name). It concluded that 40 per cent of the lives lost in fuel-fed fires could be saved if the manufacturers complied with proposed Standard 301. Finally, a third report was prepared for NHTSA by consultant Eugene Trisko entitled "A National Survey of Motor Vehicle Fires." His report indicates that the Ford Motor Company makes 24 per cent of the cars on the American road, yet these cars account for 42 per cent of the collision-ruptured fuel tanks.

Ford lobbyists then used technique a) — bringing up a new argument. Their line then became: yes, perhaps burn accidents do happen, but rear-end collisions are relatively rare (note the echo of technique b) here as well). Thus Standard 301 was not needed. This set the NHTSA off on a new round of analyzing accident reports. The government's findings finally were that rear-end collisions were seven and a half times more likely to result in fuel spills than were front-end collisions. So much for that argument. By now it was 1972; NHTSA had been researching and analyzing for four years to answer Ford's objections. During that time, nearly 9,000 people burned to death in flaming wrecks. Tens of thousands more were badly burned and scarred for life. And the four-year delay meant that well over 10 million new unsafe vehicles went on the road, vehicles that will be crashing, leaking fuel and incinerating people well into the 1980s.

Ford now had to enter its third round of battling the new regulations. On the "the problem is not X but Y" principle, the company had to look around for something new to get itself off the hook. One might have thought that, faced with all the latest statistics on the horrifying number of deaths in flaming accidents, Ford would find the task difficult. But the company's rhetoric was brilliant. The problem was not burns, but . . . impact! Most of the people killed in these fiery accidents, claimed Ford, would have died whether the car burned or not. They were killed by the kinetic force of the impact, not the fire.

And so once again, as in some giant underwater tennis game, 60 the ball bounced into the government's court and the absurdly pro-industry NHTSA began another slow-motion response. Once again it began a time-consuming round of test crashes and embarked on a study of accidents. The latter, however, revealed that a large and growing number of corpses taken from burned cars involved in rear-end crashes contained no cuts, bruises or broken bones. They clearly would have survived the accident unharmed if the cars had not caught fire. This pattern was confirmed in careful rear-end crash tests performed by the Insurance Institute for Highway Safety. A University of Miami study found an inordinate number of Pintos burning on rear-end impact and concluded that this demonstrated "a clear and present hazard to all Pinto owners."

Pressure on NHTSA from Ralph Nader and consumer groups began mounting. The industry–agency collusion was so obvious that Senator Joseph Montoya (D-N.M.) introduced legislation about Standard 301. NHTSA waffled some more and again announced its intentions to promulgate a rear-end collision standard.

Waiting, as it normally does, until the last day allowed for response, Ford filed with NHTSA a gargantuan batch of letters, studies and charts now arguing that the federal testing criteria were unfair. Ford also argued that design changes required to meet the standard would take 43 months, which seemed like a rather long time in light of the fact that the entire Pinto was designed in about two years. Specifically, new complaints about the standard involved the weight of the test vehicle, whether or not the brakes should be engaged at the moment of impact and the claim that the standard should only apply to cars, not trucks or buses. Perhaps the most amusing argument was that the engine should not be idling during crash tests, the rationale being that an idling engine meant that the gas tank had to contain gasoline and that the hot lights needed to film the crash might ignite the gasoline and cause a fire.

Some of these complaints were accepted, others rejected. But they all required examination and testing by a weak-kneed NHTSA, meaning more of those 18-month studies the industry loves so much. So the complaints served their real purpose — delay; all told, an eight-year delay, while Ford manufactured more than three million profitable, dangerously incendiary Pintos. To justify this delay, Henry Ford II called more press conferences to predict the demise of American civilization. "If we can't meet the standards when they are published," he warned, "we will have to close down. And if we have to close down some production because we don't meet standards we're in for real trouble in this country."

While government bureaucrats dragged their feet on lifesaving Standard 301, a different kind of expert was taking a close look at the Pinto — the "recon man." "Recon" stands for reconstruction; recon men reconstruct accidents for police departments, insurance companies and lawyers who want to know exactly who or what caused an accident. It didn't take many rear-end Pinto accidents to demonstrate the weakness of the car. Recon men began encouraging lawyers to look beyond one driver or another to the manufacturer in their search for fault, particularly in the growing number of accidents where passengers were uninjured by collision but were badly burned by fire.

Pinto lawsuits began mounting fast against Ford. Says John Versace, 65 executive safety engineer at Ford's Safety Research Center, "Ulcers are running pretty high among the engineers who worked on the Pinto. Every lawyer in the country seems to want to take their depositions." (The Safety Research Center is an impressive glass and concrete building standing by itself about a mile from Ford World Headquarters in Dearborn. Looking at it, one imagines its large staff protects consumers from burned and broken limbs. Not so. The Center is the technical support arm of Jack Echold's 14-person anti-regulatory lobbying team in World Headquarters.)

When the Pinto liability suits began, Ford strategy was to go to a jury. Confident it could hide the Pinto crash tests, Ford thought that juries of solid American registered voters would buy the industry doctrine that drivers, not cars, cause accidents. It didn't work. It seems that juries are much quicker to see the truth than bureaucracies, a fact that gives one confidence in democracy. Juries began ruling against the company, granting million-dollar awards to plaintiffs.

"We'll never go to a jury again," says Al Stechter in Ford's Washington office. "Not in a fire case. Juries are just too sentimental. They see those charred remains and forget the evidence. No sir, we'll settle."

Settlement involves less cash, smaller legal fees and less publicity, but it is an indication of the weakness of their case. Nevertheless, Ford has been settling when it is clear that the company can't pin the blame on the driver of the other car. But, since the company carries $2 million deductible product-liability insurance, these settlements have a direct impact on the bottom line. They must therefore be considered a factor in determining the net operating profit on the Pinto. It's impossible to get a straight answer from Ford on the profitability of the Pinto and the impact of lawsuit settlements on it — even when you have a curious and mildly irate shareholder call to inquire, as we did. However, financial officer Charles Matthews did admit that the company establishes a reserve for large dollar settlements. He would not divulge the amount of the reserve and had no explanation for its absence from the annual report.

Until recently, it was clear that, whatever the cost of these settlements, it was not enough to seriously cut into the Pinto's enormous profits. The cost of retooling Pinto assembly lines and of equipping each car with a safety gadget like that $5.08 Goodyear bladder was, company accountants calculated, greater than that of paying out millions to survivors like Robbie Carlton or to widows and widowers of victims like Sandra Gillespie. The bottom line ruled, and inflammable Pintos kept rolling out of the factories.

In 1977, however, an incredibly sluggish government has at last 70 instituted Standard 301. Now Pintos will have to have rupture-proof gas tanks. Or will they?

• • •

To everyone's surprise, the 1977 Pinto recently passed a rear-end crash test in Phoenix, Arizona, for NHTSA. The agency was so convinced the Pinto would fail that it was the first car tested. Amazingly, it did not burst into flame.

"We have had so many Ford failures in the past," explained agency engineer Tom Grubbs, "I felt sure the Pinto would fail."

How did it pass?

Remember that one-dollar, one-pound plastic baffle that was on one of the three modified Pintos that passed the pre-production crash tests nearly ten years ago? Well, it is a standard feature on the 1977 Pinto. In the Phoenix test it protected the gas tank from being perforated by those four bolts on the differential housing.

We asked Grubbs if he noticed any other substantial alterations in 75 the rear-end structure of the car. "No," he replied, "the [plastic baffle] seems to be the only noticeable change over the 1976 model."

But was it? What Tom Grubbs and the Department of Transportation didn't know when they tested the car was that it was manufactured in St. Thomas, Ontario. Ontario? The significance of that becomes clear when you learn that Canada has for years had extremely strict rear-end collision standards. Tom Irwin is the business manager of Charlie Rossi Ford, the Scottsdale, Arizona, dealership that sold the Pinto to Tom Grubbs. He refused to explain why he was selling Fords made in Canada when there is a huge Pinto assembly plant much closer by in California. "I know why you're asking that question, and I'm not going to answer it," he blurted out. "You'll have to ask the company."

But Ford's regional office in Phoenix has "no explanation" for the presence of Canadian cars in their local dealerships. Farther up the line in Dearborn, Ford people claim there is absolutely no difference between American and Canadian Pintos. They say cars are shipped back and forth across the border as a matter of course. But they were hard pressed to explain why some Canadian Pintos were shipped all the way to Scottsdale, Arizona. Significantly, one engineer at the St. Thomas plant did admit that the existence of strict rear-end collision standards in Canada "might encourage us to pay a little more attention to quality control on that part of the car."

The Department of Transportation is considering buying an American Pinto and running the test again. For now, it will only say that the situation is under investigation.

• • •

Whether the new American Pinto fails or passes the test, Standard 301 will never force the company to test or recall the more than two million pre-1977 Pintos still on the highway. Seventy or more people will burn to death in those cars every year for many years to come. If the past is any indication, Ford will continue to accept the deaths.

According to safety expert Byron Bloch, the older cars could quite 80 easily be retrofitted with gas tanks containing fuel cells. "These improved tanks would add at least 10 mph improved safety performance to the rear end," he estimated, "but it would cost Ford $20 to $30 a car, so they won't do it unless they are forced to." Dr. Kenneth Saczalski, safety engineer with the Office of Naval Research in Washington, agrees. "The Defense Department has developed virtually fail-safe fuel systems and retrofitted them into existing vehicles. We have shown them to the auto industry and they have ignored them."

Unfortunately, the Pinto is not an isolated case of corporate malpractice in the auto industry. Neither is Ford a lone sinner. There probably isn't a car on the road without a safety hazard known to its manufacturer. And though Ford may have the best auto lobbyists in Washington, it is not alone. The anti-emission control lobby and the anti-safety lobby usually work in chorus form, presenting a well-harmonized message from the country's richest industry, spoken through the voices of individual companies — the Motor Vehicle Manufacturers Association, the Business Council and the U.S. Chamber of Commerce.

Furthermore, cost-valuing human life is not used by Ford alone. Ford was just the only company careless enough to let such an embarrassing calculation slip into public records. The process of willfully trading lives for profits is built into corporate capitalism. Commodore Vanderbilt publicly scorned George Westinghouse and his "foolish" airbrakes while people died by the hundreds in accidents on Vanderbilt's railroads.

The original draft of the Motor Vehicle Safety Act provided for criminal sanction against a manufacturer who willfully placed an unsafe car on the market. Early in the proceedings the auto industry lobbied the provision out of the bill. Since then, there have been those damage settlements, of course, but the only government punishment meted out to auto companies for noncompliance to standards has been a minuscule fine, usually $5,000 to $10,000. One wonders how long the Ford Motor Company would continue to market lethal cars were Henry Ford II and Lee Iacocca serving 20-year terms in Leavenworth for consumer homicide.

Understanding the Text

1. In paragraph 37, we learn that the Ford Motor Company assigned a dollar value to a human life. How was that dollar amount determined? Did it represent the value of a life to the person living it? To that person's family? If not, what, then, did it represent?

2. How did money factor into Ford's decision to rush its car into production?

Reflection and Response

3. One student who read this article wrote the following comment to himself in the margin:

    It's hard to imagine how these things happen!

    Do you share his astonishment? Why or why not?

4. Dowie's article was originally published in *Mother Jones,* an unabashedly left-leaning magazine. Does knowing that affect your willingness to credit it with being accurate? Why or why not?

Making Connections

5. How could you verify the information contained in the article, to be more certain about it?

6. Both Mark Dowie, in "Pinto Madness," and David Callahan, in "Cheating in a Bottom-line Economy" (p. 126), set forth the consequences of bad corporate behavior. However, the consequences in the Pinto case are far graver than those in Callahan's cases. Is that because the behavior in the Pinto case goes beyond what Callahan calls "cheating"?

The Social Responsibility of Business Is to Increase Its Profits

Milton Friedman

This is the best known essay of the most influential economist of the 1980s and the Reagan Revolution.

Milton Friedman was awarded the 1976 Nobel Prize in Economics for "achievements in the field of consumption analysis, monetary history and theory, and for his demonstration of the complexity of stabilization policy." He was a champion of free markets, unfettered by government intrusion.

When I hear businessmen speak eloquently about the "social responsibilities of business in a free-enterprise system," I am reminded of the wonderful line about the Frenchman who discovered at the age of seventy that he had been speaking prose all his life. The businessmen believe that they are defending free enterprise when they declaim that business is not concerned "merely" with profit but also with promoting desirable "social" ends; that business has a "social conscience" and takes seriously its responsibilities for providing employment, eliminating discrimination, avoiding pollution, and whatever else may be the catchwords of the contemporary crop of reformers. In fact they are — or would be if they or anyone else took them seriously — preaching pure and unadulterated° socialism. Businessmen who talk this way are unwitting puppets of the intellectual forces that have been undermining the basis of a free society these past decades. The discussion of the "social responsibilities of business" are notable for their analytical looseness and lack of rigor. What does it mean to say that "business" has responsibilities? Only people can have responsibilities. A corporation is an artificial person and in this sense may have artificial responsibilities, but "business" as a whole cannot be said to have responsibilities, even in this vague sense. The first step toward clarity to examining the doctrine of the social responsibility of business is to ask precisely what it implies for whom.

> What does it mean to say that "business" has responsibilities? Only people can have responsibilities.

Presumably, the individuals who are to be responsible are businessmen, which means individual proprietors or corporate executives. Most

unadulterated: pure.

of the discussion of social responsibility is directed at corporations, so in what follows I shall mostly neglect the individual proprietors and speak of corporate executives.

In a free-enterprise, private-property system, a corporate executive is an employee of the owners of the business. He has direct responsibility to his employers. That responsibility is to conduct the business in accordance with their desires, which generally will be to make as much money as possible while conforming to the basic rules of the society, both those embodied in law and those embodied in ethical custom. Of course, in some cases his employers may have a different objective. A group of persons might establish a corporation for an eleemosynary° purpose — for example, a hospital or a school. The manager of such a corporation will not have money profit as his objectives but the rendering of certain services.

In either case, the key point is that, in his capacity as a corporate executive, the manager is the agent of the individuals who own the corporation or establish the eleemosynary institution, and his primary responsibility is to them.

Needless to say, this does not mean that it is easy to judge how well   5
he is performing his task. But at least the criterion of performance is straightforward, and the persons among whom a voluntary contractual arrangement exists are clearly defined.

Of course, the corporate executive is also a person in his own right. As a person, he may have many other responsibilities that he recognizes or assumes voluntarily — to his family, his conscience, his feelings of charity, his church, his clubs, his city, his country. He may feel impelled by these responsibilities to devote part of his income to causes he regards as worthy, to refuse to work for particular corporations, even to leave his job, for example, to join his country's armed forces. If we wish, we may refer to some of these responsibilities as "social responsibilities." But in these respects he is acting as a principal, not an agent; he is spending his own money or time or energy, not the money of his employers or the time or energy he has contracted to devote to their purposes. If these are "social responsibilities," they are the social responsibilities of individuals, not of business.

What does it mean to say that the corporate executive has a "social responsibility" in his capacity as businessman? If this statement is not pure rhetoric, it must mean that he is to act in some way that is not in the interest of his employers. For example, that he is to refrain from increasing the price of the product in order to contribute to the social

eleemosynary: for charity.

objective of preventing inflation° even though a price increase would be in the best interests of the corporation. Or that he is to make expenditures on reducing pollution beyond the amount that is in the best interests of the corporation or that is required by law in order to contribute to the social objective of improving the environment. Or that, at the expense of corporate profits, he is to hire "hardcore" unemployed instead of better qualified available workmen to contribute to the social objective of reducing poverty.

In each of these cases, the corporate executive would be spending someone else's money for a general social interest. Insofar as his actions in accord with his "social responsibility" reduce returns to stockholders, he is spending their money. Insofar as his actions raise the price to customers, he is spending customers' money. Insofar as his actions lower the wages of some employees, he is spending their money.

The stockholders or the customers or the employees could separately spend their own money on the particular action if they wished to do so. The executive is exercising a distinct "social responsibility," rather than serving as an agent of the stockholders or the customers or the employees, only if he spends the money in a different way than they would have spent it.

But if he does this, he is in effect imposing taxes, on the one hand, 10 and deciding how the tax proceeds shall be spent, on the other.

This process raises political questions on two levels: principle and consequences. On the level of political principle, the imposition of taxes and the expenditure of tax proceeds are governmental functions. We have established elaborate constitutional, parliamentary, and judicial provisions to control these functions, to assure that taxes are imposed so far as possible in accordance with the preferences and desires of the public — after all, "taxation without representation" was one of the battle cries of the American Revolution. We have a system of checks and balances to separate the legislative function of imposing taxes and enacting expenditures from the executive function of collecting taxes and administering expenditure programs and from the judicial function of mediating disputes and interpreting the law.

Here the businessman — self-selected or appointed directly or indirectly by stockholders — is to be simultaneously legislator, executive, and jurist. He is to decide whom to tax by how much and for what purpose, and he is to spend the proceeds — all this guided only by

---

inflation: a general rise of prices in the economy.

general exhortations from on high to restrain inflation, improve the environment, fight poverty, and so on and on.

The whole justification for permitting the corporate executive to be selected by the stockholders is that the executive is an agent serving the interests of his principal. This justification disappears when the corporate executive imposes taxes and spends the proceeds for "social" purposes. He becomes in effect a public employee, a civil servant, even though he remains in name an employee of a private enterprise. On grounds of political principle, it is intolerable that such civil servants — insofar as their action in the name of social responsibility are real and not just window dressing — should be selected as they are now. If they are to be civil servants, then they must be elected through a political process. If they are to impose taxes and make expenditures to foster "social" objectives, then political machinery must be set up to make the assessment of taxes and to determine through a political process the objectives to be served.

This is the basic reason why the doctrine of "social responsibility" involves the acceptance of the socialist view that political mechanisms, not market mechanisms, are the appropriate way to determine the allocation of scarce resources to alternative uses.

On the grounds of consequences, can the corporate executive in   15
fact discharge his alleged "social responsibilities"? On the one hand, suppose he could get away with spending the stockholders' or customers' or employees' money. How is he to know how to spend it? He is told that he must contribute to fighting inflation. How is he to know what action of his will contributes to that end? He is presumably an expert in running his company — in producing a product or selling it or financing it. But nothing about his selection makes him an expert on inflation. Will his holding down the price of his product reduce inflationary pressure? Or, by leaving more spending power in the hands of his customers, simply divert it elsewhere? Or, by forcing him to produce less because of the lower price, will it simply contribute to shortages? Even if he could answer these questions, how much cost is he justified in imposing on his stockholders, customers, and employees for this social purpose? What is his appropriate share and what is the appropriate share of others?

And, whether he wants to or not, can he get away with spending his stockholders', customers', or employees' money? Will not the stockholders fire him? (Either the present ones or those who take over when his actions in the name of social responsibility have reduced the corporation's profits and the price of its stock.) His customers and his employees can desert him for other producers and employers less scrupulous in exercising their social responsibilities.

This facet of "social responsibility" doctrine is brought into sharp relief when the doctrine is used to justify wage restraint by trade unions. The conflict of interest is naked and clear when union officials are asked to subordinate the interest of their members to some more general purpose. If union officials try to enforce wage restraint, the consequence is likely to be wildcat strike,° rank-and-file revolts, and the emergence of strong competitors for their jobs. We thus have the ironic phenomenon that union leaders — at least in the United States — have objected to government interference with the market far more consistently and courageously than have business leaders. The difficulty of exercising "social responsibility" illustrates, of course, the great virtue of private competitive enterprise — it forces people to be responsible for their own actions and makes it difficult for them to "exploit" other people for either selfish or unselfish purpose. They can do good — but only at their own expense.

Many a reader who has followed the argument this far may be tempted to remonstrate that it is all well and good to speak of government's having the responsibility to impose taxes and determine expenditures for such "social" purposes as controlling pollution or training the hard-core unemployed, but that the problems are too urgent to wait on the slow course of political processes, that the exercise of social responsibility by businessmen is a quicker and surer way to solve pressing current problems.

Aside from the question of fact — I share Adam Smith's skepticism about the benefits that can be expected from "those who affect to trade for the public good" — this argument must be rejected on the grounds of principle. What it amounts to is an assertion that those who favor the taxes and expenditures in question have failed to persuade a majority of their fellow citizens to be of like mind and that they are seeking to attain by undemocratic procedures what they cannot attain by democratic procedures. In a free society it is hard for "evil" people to do "evil," especially since one man's good is another's evil.

I have, for simplicity, concentrated on the special case of the cor-   20 porate executive, except only for the brief digression on trade unions. But precisely the same argument applies to the newer phenomenon of calling upon stockholders to require corporations to exercise social

wildcat strike: a walkout of workers that has not been sanctioned by the union leadership.

responsibility (the recent GM crusade for example). In most of these cases, what is in effect involved is some stockholders trying to get other stockholders (or customers or employees) to contribute against their will to "social" causes favored by the activists. Insofar as they succeed, they are again imposing taxes and spending the proceeds.

The situation of the individual proprietor is somewhat different. If he acts to reduce the returns of his enterprise in order to exercise his "social responsibility," he is spending his own money, not someone else's. If he wishes to spend his money on such purposes, that is his right, and I cannot see that there is any objection to his doing so. In the process, he, too, may impose costs on employees and customers. However, because he is far less likely than a large corporation or union to have monopolistic power, any such side effects will tend to be minor.

Of course, in practice the doctrine of social responsibility is frequently a cloak for actions that are justified on other grounds rather than a reason for those actions.

To illustrate, it may well be in the long-run interest of a corporation that is a major employer in a small community to devote resources to providing amenities to that community or to improving its government. That may make it easier to attract desirable employees, it may reduce the wage bill or lessen losses from pilferage° and sabotage or have other worthwhile effects. Or it may be that, given the laws about the deductibility of corporate charitable contributions, the stockholders can contribute more to charities they favor by having the corporation make the gift than by doing it themselves, since they can in that way contribute an amount that would otherwise have been paid as corporate taxes.

In each of these — and many similar — cases, there is a strong temptation to rationalize these actions as an exercise of "social responsibility." In the present climate of opinion, with its widespread aversion to "capitalism," "profits," and the "soulless corporation" and so on, this is one way for a corporation to generate goodwill as a by-product of expenditures that are entirely justified in its own self-interest.

It would be inconsistent of me to call on corporate executives to   25
refrain from this hypocritical window-dressing because it harms the foundations of a free society. That would be to call on them to exercise a "social responsibility"! If our institutions, and the attitudes of the public make it in their self-interest to cloak their actions in this way, I cannot summon much indignation to renounce them. At the same time, I can express admiration for those individual proprietors

pilferage: petty theft.

or owners of closely held corporations or stockholders of more broadly held corporations who disdain such tactics as approaching fraud.

Whether blameworthy or not, the use of the cloak of social responsibility, and the nonsense spoken in its name by influential and prestigious businessmen, does clearly harm the foundations of a free society. I have been impressed time and again by the schizophrenic character of many businessmen. They are capable of being extremely farsighted and clearheaded in matters that are internal to their businesses. They are incredibly shortsighted and muddle-headed in matters that are outside their businesses but affect the possible survival of business in general. This shortsightedness is strikingly exemplified in the calls from many businessmen for wage and price guidelines or controls or income policies. There is nothing that could do more in a brief period to destroy a market system and replace it by a centrally controlled system than effective governmental control of prices and wages.

The shortsightedness is also exemplified in speeches by businessmen on social responsibility. This may gain them kudos in the short run. But it helps to strengthen the already too prevalent view that the pursuit of profits is wicked and immoral and must be curbed and controlled by external forces. Once this view is adopted, the external forces that curb the market will not be the social consciences, however highly developed, of the pontificating executives; it will be the iron fist of government bureaucrats. Here, as with price and wage controls, businessmen seem to me to reveal a suicidal impulse.

The political principle that underlies the market mechanism is unanimity. In an ideal free market resting on private property, no individual can coerce any other, all cooperation is voluntary, all parties to such cooperation benefit or they need not participate. There are no values, no "social" responsibilities in any sense other than the shared values and responsibilities of individuals. Society is a collection of individuals and of the various groups they voluntarily form.

The political principle that underlies the political mechanism is conformity. The individual must serve a more general social interest — whether that be determined by a church or a dictator or a majority. The individual may have a vote and say in what is to be done, but if he is overruled, he must conform. It is appropriate for some to require others to contribute to a general social purpose whether they wish to or not.

Unfortunately, unanimity is not always feasible. There are some 30 respects in which conformity appears unavoidable, so I do not see how one can avoid the use of the political mechanism altogether.

But the doctrine of "social responsibility" taken seriously would extend the scope of the political mechanism to every human activity. It does not differ in philosophy from the most explicitly collectivist doctrine. It differs only by professing to believe that collectivist° ends can be attained without collectivist means. That is why, in my book *Capitalism and Freedom*, I have called it a "fundamentally subversive doctrine" in a free society, and I have said that in such a society, "there is one and only one social responsibility of business — to use its re-sources and engage in activities designed to increase its profits so long as it stays within the rules of the game, which is to say, engages in open and free competition without deception or fraud."

collectivist: pertaining to the belief that all economic activity should be controlled by the people as a whole.

Understanding the Text

1. Is the title of this essay an adequate summary of it? Is Friedman's point more complex than that? Elaborate.

2. Why does Friedman contend that business executives who preach social responsibility are suicidal?

3. In Friedman's view, whose job is it to promote the general welfare? Is it the job of individuals? Businesses? The government? (He doesn't explicitly address this moral question. Which specific statements in the essay have you based your answer on?)

Reflection and Response

4. Do you agree with Friedman? Somewhat agree? Disagree?

   Do you find yourself confused by Friedman — wanting him to clarify certain points or to provide more information? Where?

5. How do you react to Friedman's use of phrases like "pure and unadulterated socialism" (paragraph 1)? Explain.

Making Connections

6. Would Friedman have approved of the conduct of executives at the Ford Motor Company, as described by Mark Dowie in "Pinto Madness" (p. 139)?

7. Here are the title and opening paragraph of one student's response to the Friedman essay. (The entire paper, by Sanford Boxerman, was published in the book *Student Writers at Work — The Bedford Prizes*.)

   Not So Fast, Milton Friedman!

   Businessmen should love Milton Friedman. With one stroke of his Nobel Prize–winning pen, Friedman grants executives and managers free reign to indulge in profit-maximizing activities to their hearts' content. Get all you can while the getting's good — just don't break the law, he exhorts. The suggestion that business has an obligation that goes beyond making money, that it has a basic responsibility to the society in which it operates, evokes indignation and cries of "Socialist!" from Friedman.

How would you rate the title of this paper? Did it work as a hook to lure you? If so, why?

Would you agree that the paper's opening is energetic? If so, what seem to be the secrets of its vitality?

What tone of voice comes through in the opening?

Does the tone of voice give you confidence that the student writer will treat Friedman objectively and fairly? If not, is there still a place for this type of writing?

You Can't Evict an Idea Whose Time Has Come

Occupy Wall Street

Theoretically, the United States is a democracy where no person's interests or views count more heavily than anyone else's. In recent years, however, many Americans have wondered if, in fact, their country has become a plutocracy, where the views and interests of the wealthy hold sway over those of the majority. In 2011, thousands of people "occupied Wall Street" — created open-air encampments near the New York Stock Exchange, as well as at locations around the United States, to protest what they perceived to be the greedy role of the super-rich — the top 1 percent — in creating the great "meltdown" of 2008 and in blocking reforms meaningful enough to prevent a recurrence of the crisis. The protesters referred to themselves as members of "the 99 percent."

At 1:36 in the morning of November 15, 2011, Occupy Wall Street activists posted the notice below online.

A massive police force is presently evicting Liberty Square, home of Occupy Wall Street for the past two months and birthplace of the 99% movement that has spread across the country.

The raid started just after 1:00 AM. Supporters and allies are mobilizing throughout the city, presently converging at Foley Square. Supporters are also planning public actions for the coming days, including occupation actions.

You can't evict an idea whose time has come.

Our political structures should serve us, the people — all of us, not just those who have amassed great wealth and power.

Two months ago a few hundred New Yorkers set up an encampment at the doorstep of Wall Street. Since then, Occupy Wall Street has become a national and even international symbol — with similarly styled occupations popping up in cities and towns across America and around the world. The Occupy movement was inspired by simliar occupations and uprisings such as those during Arab Spring, and in Spain, Greece, Italy, France, and the UK.

A growing popular movement has significantly altered the national narrative about our economy, our democracy, and our future. Americans are talking about the consolidation of wealth and power in our society, and the stranglehold that the top 1% have over our political system. More and more Americans are seeing the crises of our economy and our democracy as systemic problems that require collective action to remedy. More and more Americans are identifying as part of the 99%, and saying "enough!"

This burgeoning movement is more than a protest, more than an occupation, and more than any tactic. The "us" in the movement is far broader than those who are able to participate in physical occupation. The movement is everyone who sends supplies, everyone who talks to their friends and families about the underlying issues, everyone who takes some form of action to get involved in this civic process.

This movement is nothing short of America rediscovering the strength we hold when we come together as citizens to take action to address crises that impact us all.

Such a movement cannot be evicted. Some politicians may physically remove us from public spaces — our spaces — and, physically, they may succeed. **But we are engaged in a battle over ideas. Our idea is that our political structures should serve us, the people — all of us,** not just those who have amassed great wealth and power. We believe that is a highly popular idea, and that is why so many people have come so quickly to identify with Occupy Wall Street and the 99% movement.

You cannot evict an idea whose time has come.

Understanding the Text

1. This post is not a call-to-arms against the police who, at that very moment, were evicting protesters. What is its purpose, then? On what parts of the text do you base your answer?

2. Why does the line that reads, "This burgeoning movement is more than a protest, more than an occupation, and more than any tactic" appear in boldface type?

Reflection and Response

3. If all you knew of the Occupy Wall Street movement was the information in this post, what questions would you be left with?

4. Do you approve of civil disobedience as a means of protest? If not ever, why? If only under certain conditions, what are those conditions — and again, why?

Making Connections

5. When you contemplate the CBPP chart "Income Gains at the Top" (p. 210), would you say that the division of American society into "the 1 percent" and "the 99 percent" is apt? Explain.

6. Some observers call the Occupy Wall Street movement a form of class warfare,
    pitting one economic stratum of the population against another. They say it
    could fray the very fabric of American society. Others disagree. Still others say,
    in effect, "If it *is* class warfare, it was started by the other side, which had to be
    opposed." Look into the matter — maybe going online with search terms like
    "class warfare" and "Occupy Wall Street" — and weigh in.

CSI USA: Who Killed the American Dream?

Arianna Huffington

In an ideal America, elected officials would serve the best interests of all citizens, not just those of supporters with deep pockets. Arianna Huffington claims our government falls far short of that vision at this time. She contends that it is money that talks in Washington, D.C.; poor and middle-class Americans' needs are neglected.

Huffington is most well-known as the creator of the provocative blog *The Huffington Post.* Since the 1990s, she has gone from taking conservative positions to espousing liberal views. She was born in Greece.

So how did we get here?

How did we get to a place where our infrastructure° is well past its sell-by date, our schools are failing, our middle class is on life support, and the American Dream is turning into a mirage?

Who took control of our national GPS and set as our ultimate destination the coordinates° of a Third World° future? Casting about for answers, the knee-jerk response is to point a finger and hurl an enraged "j'accuse!"° at Washington. And, in this case, the knee-jerk response is right. But for all the wrong reasons.

Listen to the punditocracy° and they'll tell you — loudly and often — that our politics is "broken" and "paralyzed." That government no longer works because of bipartisan bickering and polarization. That the parties have moved so far to their respective extremes on the left and the right that collaboration and consensus are no longer possible.

And while the GOP's decision to respond to the election of Presi- 5 dent Obama by transforming itself into the Party of No certainly gives that slice of conventional wisdom the surface patina° of insight, dig a little deeper and you'll discover the much uglier truth: Over the past thirty years, the two parties have actually become much more alike — both deeply in the pocket of the big-business masters who fill their campaign coffers.

infrastructure: the public works — such as roads and bridges — that enable commerce and other activities to take place.
coordinates: numbers used to pinpoint a location.
Third World: a phrase used for the technologically undeveloped nations of the world.
j'accuse! a public accusation (French for "I accuse").
punditocracy: Huffington's word for the many people who publish or broadcast their analyses of issues and events.
patina: surface appearance.

American politics is indeed "broken" — but not because our leaders are at one another's throats. It's broken because the founding democratic principle of "one man, one vote"° has been replaced by the arithmetic of special interest politics: Thousands of lobbyists plus billions of dollars equal access and influence out of the reach of ordinary Americans.

The consequences of this corporate takeover of our democracy couldn't be more profound and far-reaching, affecting every aspect of our lives — from the cleanliness of the air we breathe and the water we drink to the safety of the food we eat, the medications we take, and the products we buy, to the stability of the economy that allows us to keep our jobs, afford our houses, and pursue our dreams.

> Some people look at laws and ask, "Why?" or "Why not?"
> I look at laws and ask, "Who paid for them?"

All of these and more are being dictated by a system of government that determines its priorities in a bazaar of influence peddling.

There's an old joke about a cop who comes upon a drunk crawling around under a streetlight. "What are you doing?" he asks.

"Looking for my keys," the drunk answers.   10

"Where did you lose them?"

"Over there."

"Well, why are you looking for them here?"

"Because the lighting is better."

Do you ever find yourself wondering why laws that make no   15
sense get passed while laws that would seem like no-brainers never make it out of committee? Why some issues get pushed to the front of the line, while others die from lack of attention? The answer is simple. Like the drunk following the light, politicians follow the money and the clamor of noisy special interest groups — leaving the interests of middle-class Americans, like so many car keys, forgotten and left behind.

Some people look at laws and ask, "Why?" or "Why not?" I look at laws and ask, "Who paid for them?"

There Are No Lobbyists for the American Dream

Since 1964, the American National Election Studies at the University of Michigan has regularly asked voters whether they think the U.S.

"one man, one vote": the idea that no citizen should influence the outcome of an election more than other citizens do.

government is run "for the benefit of all" or "by a few big interests."[1] In the mid-1960s, only 29 percent thought "big interests" ran the nation.[2] By the mid-1990s, that number had climbed to 76 percent. And in 2008, 80 percent of Americans surveyed told the Program on International Policy Attitudes that they believed government was controlled by "a few big interests looking out for themselves."[3]

That shouldn't be a surprise: Over the years there has been an explosion in the number of lobbyists in Washington and the money they spend. In 2009,[4] more than 13,700 registered lobbyists spent a record $3.5 billion swaying government policy the special interests' way, double the amount lobbyists spent as recently as 2002.[5]

With 535 members of the Senate and the House, that means lobbyists in the halls of power outnumber our elected representatives almost 26 to 1. If we divide $3.5 billion evenly among the 535, it means each member of the legislative branch was at the receiving end of $6.5 million worth of special interest arm-twisting over the course of the year.

And that's just the money corporate America is spending on lobbying. Millions more are given directly to politicians and the political parties. From 1974 to 2008[6] the average amount it took to run for reelection to the House went from $56,000 to more than $1.3 million.[7]

For an example of how special interests took advantage of this inflated price tag, let's look at the financial sector, which was front and center in the fund-raising explosion.[8] Over the past two decades, it was the top contributor to political campaigns. According to Simon Johnson and James Kwak in their book, *13 Bankers*, from 1998 to 2008

20

---

[1] *Since 1964 the American National Election Studies:* American National Election Studies, "The ANES Guide to Public Opinion and Electoral Behavior," 27 Nov. 2005, www.electionstudies.org.

[2] *In the mid-1960s, only 29 percent:* Ibid.

[3] *And in 2008, 80 percent of Americans surveyed:* "World Publics Say Governments Should Be More Responsive to the Will of the People," 12 May 2008, www.worldpublicopinion .org.

[4] *In 2009, more than 13,700 registered lobbyists:* Dave Levinthal, "Federal Lobbying Climbs in 2009 as Lawmakers Execute Aggressive Congressional Agenda," 12 Feb. 2010, www .opensecrets.org.

[5] *double the amount lobbyists spent:* Center for Responsive Politics, "Lobbying Database," 25 Apr., 2010, www.opensecrets.com.

[6] *From 1974 to 2008 the average amount:* Alan R. Grant, *The American Political Process,* 7th ed. (New York: Routledge, 2004), 252.

[7] *to more than 1.3 million:* Center for Responsive Politics, "Big Picture: Price of Admission," www.opensecrets.org.

[8] *For an example of how special interests took advantage:* Simon Johnson and James Kwak, "Too Big for Us to Fail," 26 Apr. 2010, www.prospect.org.

"the financial sector spent $1.7 billion on campaign contributions and $3.4 billion on lobbying expenses."[9] And the money was, of course, targeted to where it would have the most effect: the campaign coffers of such Senate Banking Committee powerhouses as Phil Gramm, Alfonse D'Amato, Chris Dodd, and Chuck Schumer.[10] Notice that the bankers' money rained down on both sides of the aisle° To paraphrase Matthew, the rain falleth on the left and on the right.

The investment paid off in spades with the rollback of the financial regulations that had kept the worst excesses of corporate greed in check since the Great Depression, leaving in their place a shaky edifice of self-policing and cowed regulators powerless to rein in the galloping bulls of Wall Street. The results for corporate America: record profits, record pay packages, and record bonuses. The results for the rest of us: the savings and loan crisis, the corporate scandals of the Enron era, and the economic collapse we are still struggling to dig our way out of.

That collapse, by the way, has only caused the banking lobbyists to redouble their efforts in an all-hands-on-deck effort to thwart financial reform. Over the course of the debate about reforming Wall Street, the finance industry — which has been bailed out with trillions of taxpayer dollars and cheap loans from the Fed — has spent an estimated $1.4 million a day to convince our lawmakers to kill real reform.[11]

For instance, when the Senate was crafting its financial reform bill, it included absolutely no reform of Fannie Mae and Freddie Mac°[12] This despite the fact that in just the first quarter of 2010 Freddie — one-half of what the *New York Times's* Gretchen Morgenson calls "the elephant in the bailout" — reported a loss of $6.7 billion.[13]

As of May 2010, according to Morgenson, "serious delinquencies in 25 Freddie's single-family conventional loan portfolio — those more than 90 days late — came in at 4.13 percent, up from 2.41 percent for the

---

the aisle: the line dividing Democrats from Republicans.
Fannie Mae and Freddie Mac: two big holders of home mortgages in the United States.

[9] *According to Simon Johnson and James Kwak in their book:* Simon Johnson and James Kwak, *13 Bankers: The Wall Street Takeover and the Next Financial Meltdown* (New York: Pantheon, 2010), 91.
[10] *And the money was, of course, targeted:* Ibid.
[11] *Over the course of the debate:* Brian Wingfield, "Wall Street Overhaul Not So Bad for Wall Street," 17 May 2010, www.forbes.com.
[12] *For instance, when the Senate was crafting its financial reform bill:* "Fannie, Freddie Need to Be Part of Reform: Corker," 18 May 2010, www.cnbc.com.
[13] *This despite the fact that in just the first quarter of 2010:* Gretchen Morgenson, "Ignoring the Elephant in the Bailout," 7 May 2010, www.nytimes.com.

period a year earlier."[14] And the number of foreclosed units Freddie controlled stood at nearly 54,000, up from 29,145 at the end of March 2009.

"I don't understand why people are not talking about it," says Dean Baker of the Center for Economic and Policy Research.[15] "It seems to me the most fundamental question is, have they on an ongoing basis been paying too much for loans even since they went into conservatorship?"°

And why would they do that?[16] It's part of what Baker calls a "back-door bailout" of the banks. In other words, an under-the-radar way to continue shoveling money from struggling tax-payers over to the richest Americans.

This unseemly link between money and political influence is the dark side of capitalism. And like a swarm of termites reducing a house to sawdust, moneyed interests and their lobbyists are making a meal out of the foundations of our democracy.

In 2008, the American people voted for change. But there's been a change in the plans for change. The detour was created by D.C. lobbyists who, since President Obama took office, have watered down, gutted, or out-and-out killed ambitious plans for reforming Wall Street, energy, and health care.

The media like to pretend that something's at stake when a big bill 30 is being debated on the House or Senate floor, but the truth is that by then the game is typically already over. The real fight happens long before. And the lobbyists usually win.

This disconnect between perception and reality reminds me of the time a friend took a family trip on a cruise ship. Her ten-year-old son kept pestering the crew, begging for a chance to drive the massive ocean liner. The captain finally invited the family up to the bridge, whereupon the boy grabbed hold of the wheel and began vigorously turning it. My friend panicked — until the captain leaned over and told her not to worry, that the ship was on autopilot, and that her son's maneuvers would have no effect.

And that's the way it is with our leaders. They stand on the bridge making theatrical gestures they claim will steer us in a new direction while, down in the control room, the autopilot, programmed by politicians in the pocket of special interests, continues to guide the ship of

---

conservatorship: an arrangement whereby a failing institution is temporarily put into the hands of outsiders to manage.

---

[14] *As of May 2010, according to Morgenson:* Ibid.
[15] *"I don't understand why people are not talking about it":* Ibid.
[16] *And why would they do that:* Ibid.

state along its predetermined course. America won't be able to change
the disastrous direction it's heading in until the people elected to represent us go down into the boiler room and disengage the autopilot — which
means taking on the hordes of lobbyists who continue to dictate policy
in D.C.

Unfortunately, the middle class doesn't have a gaggle° of lobbyists
patrolling the corridors of power, offering cash incentives to Congress
and the White House to protect the American people from the corporate crooks fattening their bottom lines (and filling their personal
coffer°) while our jobs, our houses, and our pensions disappear.

There are no lobbyists for the American Dream.

Democracy Goes on the Auction Block

The epic struggle between financial powerhouses and the American   35
democratic experiment — between the wealthy few and the struggling
many — is as old as the country itself.

From the trust busting° of Theodore Roosevelt to the major banking reforms put in place by FDR in the wake of the Great Depression,
from the monopoly that was Standard Oil to today's Goldman Sachs,
there have always been powerful special interests pitted against the
interests of the public.

Indeed, as far back as 1910, Roosevelt warned about the danger of
corporations exerting influence on the body politic: "There can be no
effective control of corporations while their political activity remains.
To put an end to it will be neither a short nor an easy task. . . ."[17] Of
course, far from being put to an end, corporate political activity has
only gotten more pervasive, more aggressive, more ruthless, and
more effective. Not only have we failed to control corporations, corporations have flipped the equation and taken control of us.

Teddy Roosevelt must have been spinning in his grave in January
2010 when the Supreme Court, in *Citizens United v. Federal Election
Commission*, voted 5–4 to extend the right of free speech to corporations and unions, lifting any limits on so-called independent expenditures on political campaigns.[18] President Obama called the decision "a

gaggle: a flock, as of geese.
coffer: a strongbox or other place for keeping money.
trust busting: eliminating business monopolies.

[17] *Indeed, as far back as 1910, Roosevelt warned:* Theodore Roosevelt, *The New National-
ism* (New York: The Outlook Company, 1910), 13.
[18] *Teddy Roosevelt must have been spinning in his grave:* Adam Liptak, "Justices, 5–4,
Reject Corporate Spending Limit," 21 Jan. 2010, www.nytimes.com.

major victory for Big Oil, Wall Street banks, health insurance companies, and the other powerful interests that marshal their power every
day in Washington to drown out the voices of everyday Americans."[19]

This decision will allow the giant pharmaceutical companies that
knowingly permit unsafe drugs to remain on the shelves, the people
running chemical plants releasing deadly toxins into the water and
air, and the factory farm conglomerates filling our food with steroids
to spend unlimited amounts of money to get their water carriers° into
office and defeat the all-too-rare candidates who actually stand up for
the public good.

It has now become even easier to auction off our democracy to the   40
highest bidder.

Foxes Guarding the Henhouse

Not content with controlling politicians and kneecapping effective
government oversight and regulations, corporate America has taken
things one step further.[20] As Janine Wedel, author of *Shadow Elite,* and
Linda Keenan put it, "businesses aren't just *sidestepping* or fighting
regulators. Their M.O. is to try to make *themselves* the de facto regulators of their own self-interested conduct. . . ."

That's something else that the mining, oil, and financial industries
share: the revolving door between regulators and those they're supposed to be regulating. The names of the Wall Streeters who have
moved into positions of power in Washington are familiar: Hank Paul-
son, Robert Rubin, Josh Bolten, Neel Kashkari, Mark Patterson — and
that's just from Goldman Sachs.[21]

But the revolving door between Wall Street and Washington goes
far beyond these marquee names. The finance industry has 70 former
members of Congress and over 900 former federal employees on its
lobbying payroll.[22] This includes 33 chiefs of staff, 54 staffers of the
House Financial Services Committee and Senate Banking Committee (or a current member of those committees), and 28 legislative

---

water carriers: people who advocate for others.

[19] *President Obama called the decision "a major victory . . .":* Ibid.

[20] *Not content with controlling politicians and kneecapping:* Linda Keenan and Janine R.
Wedel, "Shadow Elite: Think BP's the Bad Guy? Think Bigger, Way Bigger," 13 May
2010, www.huffingtonpost.com.

[21] *The names of the Wall Streeters:* Matthew Vadum, "Goldman Sachs Government," 16
Oct. 2008, www.spectator.org.

[22] *The finance industry has 70 former members of Congress:* Public Citizen, "Stop Congress'
Revolving Door of Corruption," www.citizen.org.

directors.[23] Five of Senate Banking Committee chair Chris Dodd's former staffers are now working as banking lobbyists, as are eight former staffers for Senate Banking Committee heavyweights Richard Shelby and Chuck Schumer.[24] Of course, the revolving door spins both ways: 18 percent of current House Financial Services committee staffers used to work on K Street.[25]

On the mining front, former Massey chief operating officer Stanley Suboleski was appointed to be a commissioner of the Federal Mine Safety and Health Review Commission in 2003, and four years later was nominated to run the U.S. Department of Energy's Office of Fossil Energy.[26] At the time of the Upper Big Branch accident he was back on Massey's board.[27] And President Bush named Massey executive Richard Stickler to head the Mine Safety and Health Administration in 2006.[28] Stickler had such a lousy safety record at the companies he'd run, his nomination was twice rejected by senators from both parties, forcing Bush to sneak him in the back door with a recess appointment.[29] In other words, the guy Bush tapped to protect miners was precisely the kind of executive the head of the MSHA is supposed to protect miners from.

Picking foxes to guard the henhouse was standard operating procedure during the Bush years, when appointments to federal regulatory agencies were often used as a payback mechanism for rewarding major political donors, with industry hacks getting key government positions not because they were the best people to protect the public interest but because they were willing to protect the very industries they were meant to supervise.

That's what happened when Bush put Edwin Foulke, a lawyer with a long history of open hostility to health and safety regulations, in

45

[23] *This includes 33 chiefs of staff, 54 staffers of the House:* Arthur Delaney, "Big Bank Takeover: Report Blames Revolving Door for 'Too Big to Fail,'" 11 May 2010, www.huffingtonpost.com.
[24] *Five of Senate Banking Committee chair Chris Dodd's:* Kevin Connor, "Big Bank Takeover: How Too-Big-to-Fail's Army of Lobbyists Has Captured Washington," Institute for America's Future, 11 May 2010, www.ourfuture.org.
[25] *Of course, the revolving door spins both ways:* Arthur Delaney, "Big Bank Takeover: Report Blames Revolving Door for 'Too Big to Fail,'" 11 May 2010, www.huffingtonpost.com.
[26] *On the mining front, former Massey chief operating officer:* Brad Johnson, "Don Blankenship's Record of Profits over Safety: 'Coal Pays the Bills,'" 8 Apr. 2010, www.thinkprogress.org.
[27] *At the time of the Upper Big Branch accident he was:* Ibid.
[28] *And President Bush named Massey executive Richard Stickler:* Ibid.
[29] *Stickler had such a lousy safety record:* Ibid.

charge of the Occupational Safety and Health Administration (OSHA), the agency meant to oversee workplace safety.[30] Earlier in his career, while serving as chairman of the federal agency that hears appeals from companies cited by OSHA, Foulke led a successful effort to weaken OSHA's enforcement power.[31] With Foulke in charge of his former target, OSHA, not surprisingly, issued fewer significant standards than at any time in its history.

Then there was Bush's choice of Mary Sheila Gall to head the Consumer Product Safety Commission, despite her tendency to blame consumers rather than manufacturers when defective products injured or killed.[32] In her ten years on the commission, Gall voted against regulating baby walkers, infant bath seats, flammable pajamas, and children's bunk beds.[33] She even adopted a "Let them eat marbles" stance on the need for toy labeling, voting against choke-hazard warnings on marbles, small balls, and balloons.[34] Consumers, she argued, are aware of "the well-known hazard of very young children putting marbles in their mouths."

In other words, if a kid chokes on a small toy, it's because the parent is defective, not the product. And while I'm all for slapping warnings on defective parents, Gall's attitude dishonors the lives of the twenty thousand people, many of them children, who are killed every year by defective products — to say nothing of the close to thirty million people a year who are injured by them.[35] Thankfully, the Senate refused to confirm Gall.[36] Undeterred, Bush filled the slot with Harold Stratton, a vocal opponent of states pursuing consumer protection cases.[37]

---

[30] *That's what happened when Bush put Edwin Foulke:* Stephen Labaton, "OSHA Leaves Worker Safety in Hands of Industry," 25 Apr. 2007, www.nytimes.com.

[31] *Earlier in his career, while serving as chairman:* Ibid.

[32] *Then there was Bush's choice of Mary Sheila Gall:* "Mary Sheila Gall Named to Chair CPSC," 20 Apr. 2001, www.cansumeraffairs.com.

[33] *In her ten years on the commission:* Lizette Alvarez, "Consumer Product Safety Chief Sets Deadline to Resign," 9 Aug. 2001, www.nytimes.com.

[34] *She even adopted a "Let them eat marbles" stance:* Hearing on the nomination of Mary Sheila Gall to chair the Consumer Product Safety Commission before the Committee on Commerce, Science, and Transportation, U.S. Senate, 25 Jul. 2001, www.gpo.gov.

[35] *And while I'm all for slapping warnings:* Matthew Robinson and Daniel Murphy, *Greed Is Good: Maximization and Elite Deviance in America* (Lanham, MD: Rowman & Littlefield, 2009), 94–95.

[36] *Thankfully, the Senate refused to confirm Gall:* Caroline E. Mayer, "Senate Panel Rejects Bush's Choice for Consumer Job," 3 Aug. 2001, www.sfgate.com.

[37] *Undeterred, Bush filled the slot with Harold Stratton:* Daphne Eviatar, "Toy Story," 3 Jan. 2008, www.thenation.com.

The Food and Drug Administration is another agency that has long had an overly cozy relationship with the very companies it is supposed to oversee — in this case, the pharmaceutical industry. This dysfunctional dynamic has proved especially deadly over the years, with numerous drugs pulled off the market after causing deaths and serious injuries to patients.

Following the money once again, we see that Big Pharma contrib- 50
uted more than $124 million to federal candidates between 2000 and 2008.[38] In return, the Bush administration served up FDA commissioners such as Lester Crawford, who was forced to resign after failing to disclose that he owned stock in companies regulated by his agency.[39]

And, if you want to see "overly cozy" run amok, look no further than the Minerals Management Service, which, according to government watchdog reports, featured "a culture of substance abuse and promiscuity" wherein government employees did drugs and had sexual relationships with oil and gas industry officials.[40] So not only is the fox guarding the henhouse, it's doing blow and sleeping with the hens. But it's middle-class Americans who are getting screwed.

We have a regulatory system in which corporate greed, political timidity, and a culture of cronyism have rendered the public good a quaint afterthought. . . .

---

[38] *Following the money once again:* Center for Responsive Politics, "Pharmaceuticals/ Health Products: Long-Term Contribution Trends," 1990–2010, www.opensecrets.org.
[39] *In return, the Bush administration served up:* Marc Kaufman, "Former FDA Chief Illegally Held Stocks," 17 Oct. 2006, www.washingtonpost.com.
[40] *And, if you want to see "overly cozy" run amok:* Charlie Savage, "Sex, Drug Use and Graft Cited in Interior Department," 10 Sep. 2008, www.nytimes.com.

Understanding the Text

1. In paragraph 7, Huffington refers to the "corporate takeover of our democracy." What does she mean by that? Elaborate on your answer with some of her own pieces of evidence.

2. What appears to be the point of Huffington's joke about the lost car keys (paragraphs 9–15)? Does it relate well to her argument?

3. What seems to be the point of her true story of the child who wanted to steer a cruise ship (paragraphs 31–32)? Once again, does it relate well to her argument?

Reflection and Response

4. Which of Huffington's claims seem to you to be amply supported? Which would require more evidence for you to accept them? Please explain.

5. Can you locate in this excerpt any "appeals to authority" — points at which Huffington argues by reporting that others agree with her, rather than by presenting hard facts?

   Do such appeals carry as much weight with you as specific concrete facts do? Why?

Making Connections

6. Would you agree or disagree with the following comparison between Huffington's piece and the Occupy Wall Street piece "You Can't Evict an Idea Whose Time Has Come" (p. 166)? Why?

   "You Can't Evict an Idea Whose Time Has Come" isn't an argument, it's a political flyer. Huffington's piece is an argument.

7. Here is the transcript of an actual voice-mail message left in 2010 by Congresswoman Eleanor Holmes Norton for a lobbyist whose client was a contractor likely to be affected by decisions made in a Congressional committee on which Norton sat:

   Hello, this is Eleanor Holmes Norton.

   Uhh, I noticed that you have given [campaign contributions] to other colleagues on the Transportation and Infrastructure Committee. I am a senior member, a twenty-year veteran [of the committee]. . . . I was . . . frankly surprised to see that we don't have a record, so far as I can tell, of your having given to me, despite my long and deep work . . . essentially in your sector. I'm simply candidly calling to ask for a contribution.

   She goes on to tell the lobbyist how to make his check out and what address to send it to.

   When the story of this message broke, Congresswoman Norton's staff put out the following press release targeting Andrew Breitbart, the blogger who made the voice mail public:

   He is circulating a voicemail of a standard request made by candidates to potential donors who do not know the candidates or their work. . . . Norton is a longtime supporter of public financing of campaigns, but barring that, candidates from all parties regularly raise funds in calls by first identifying who they are and what they have done. The call was made from campaign headquarters. Her request fully complied with legal and ethical requirements.

   What might Huffington say about this incident and the response? (Don't overlook the word "regularly" in the press release. How might that one word, among other things, register with Huffington?)

Unfree Speech: The Folly of Campaign Finance Reform

Bradley Smith

Are you someone convinced of the corrupting influence of money in politics? If so, gird yourself for an onslaught of reasons to rethink the issue.

A professor of law, Bradley Smith has been able to influence campaign finance regulation both as a writer (the book from which this excerpt is taken was actually cited in the Supreme Court's landmark 2010 decision on the issue, popularly known as "Citizens United") and as a political appointee. Between 2000 and 2005, he sat on the Federal Election Commission.

A fundamental tenet of the effort to further regulate campaign finance is that money has corrupted the legislative process. Encouraged by extreme language of the press and reform advocates, large numbers of Americans, according to polling data, have come to view campaign contributions as the dominant influence on policymaking. And experience and human nature tell us that legislators, like most people, are influenced by money, even, we might presume, when it goes into their campaign funds rather than into their pockets for personal use.

Many lawmakers and former lawmakers themselves have complained of the influence of money in the legislature. Former Arkansas senator Dale Bumpers is quoted as saying, "Every Senator knows I speak the truth when I say bill after bill after bill has been defeated in this body because of campaign money." Another senator, West Virginia's Robert Byrd, has been quoted as stating, "Money talks, and the perception is that money will talk here in this Senate. Money will open the door. Money will hold the balance of power."[1]

As we begin to analyze the truth or falsity of this assumption, we must first recognize that in the context of the debate over campaign finance reform, the term "corruption" takes on a special meaning. What is meant by "corruption" in this context is not the common definition of the term, that is to say, personal enrichment of a legislator in exchange for a vote, although some of the more demagogic reformers seem to hope that their audience interprets it in that way. That type of traditional corruption, after all, is prohibited by bribery

---

[1] Quoted in Wertheimer and Manes, "Campaign Finance Reform," 1,128–29. For more quotes, see Rosenkranz, "Faulty Assumptions," 876–80.

laws. What reformers mean by "corruption" is that legislators react to the wishes of constituents; or what, in other circumstances, might be called "responsiveness." What makes this particular incidence of responsiveness "corrupt" is that the constituents involved have taken an active role in supporting the candidate's campaign for election. Normally we would expect, and hardly consider it inappropriate, for candidates to take positions that reflect the views of their supporters or, to turn it around, for groups and individuals to support candidates who reflect their views. Thus we would not normally think anything amiss unless, as a starting point, it appeared that candidates adopt positions which they would not otherwise adopt for the primary purpose of obtaining campaign contributions. The starting point for finding corruption, it would seem, is to establish a causal link showing that contributions cause legislators to vote differently from the way they would otherwise.

Nevertheless, many reform advocates seem to consider it "corruption" if a lawmaker merely votes in a manner consistent with the desires of those groups or individuals that have contributed to his or her campaign — unless, of course, the reform-minded advocate thinks that the position is correct, in which case it becomes a vote on principle. Browse the web pages of pro-"reform" groups such as Common Cause, Public Campaign, and the Center for Responsive Politics, and one finds numerous "studies" of campaign giving that simply assume that a correlation between voting and contributions indicates corruption. For example, the September 1999 issue of *Capitol Eye*, the newsletter of the Center for Responsive Politics (CRP), notes that Senator Slade Gorton received a $1,000 contribution from the National Rifle Association in May of 1999, and then, "emerge[d] as a prominent supporter of the NRA in the [debate over a gun control bill]," as if this indicated the corrupting influence of money. However, even CRP acknowledged elsewhere that Gorton was "a longtime critic of proposed gun curbs." A Common Cause bulletin from November 1999, reports that the "sugar and peanut industries together" gave $14.2 million in political contributions between 1991 and 1997, and that, "in return, these industries have benefited from anti-competitive government policies."[2] No effort is made to show that any congressman or senator, let alone a majority, voted against his conscience or the wishes of his constituency in exchange for votes on the issue. This may be for good

---

[2] Holly Bailey, "Top Gun"; Dan Balz, "Why Consumers Should Care about Campaign Finance Reform."

reason — the total $14.2 million, given over two presidential elections and three congressional elections, to all candidates (including those who did not win election) and parties, totals substantially less than one-half of 1 percent of spending on federal campaigns in that time period.

A discrepancy occurs here in the way in which political results are 5 described. No group ever argues that it won a public policy debate because it outspent its opponents. It is only when we lose that we claim the other guy had some unfair advantage. For example, Democrats rarely complain that we periodically raise the minimum wage because Capital Hill is swarming with union lobbyists or because unions spend millions of dollars on political activities; and Republicans would never argue that a minimum wage increase was defeated thanks to the influence of business contributions, rather than sound economic considerations. Perhaps we should consider the possibility that the representatives believe what they say.

> Few could deny that campaign contributions may play a role in a legislator's complex calculations of how to vote and what to say and do. The question is how great a role.

More serious academic observers require more than mere correlation, of course, before putting forth cries of corruption. They agree that there must be a causal link between contributions and legislative behavior before the issue of corruption gains legitimacy. But how far does this take us? Few could deny that campaign contributions may play a role in a legislator's complex calculations of how to vote and what to say and do. The question is how great a role.

I find it implausible that this is really a major problem in American government. For one thing, the assertion that lawmakers vote to please financial contributors is simply not supported by the bulk of systematic evidence. Serious studies of legislative behavior have overwhelmingly concluded that campaign contributions play little role in floor voting,[3] and these conclusions are no longer seriously disputed by the would-be regulators.[4] Instead, it is now argued that

---

[3] See Thomas F. Burke, "The Concept of Corruption in Campaign Finance Law," 139 n. 45 and cites therein (indicating that "contributions do influence representatives, but less than many suppose"); see also Stephan G. Bronars and John R. Lott, Jr., "Do Campaign Donations Alter How a Politician Votes? Or, Do Donors Support Candidates Who Value the Same Things That They Do?" 346 (concluding that empirical data fail to support the notion that campaign contributions buy politicians' votes).

[4] See, for example, Rosenkranz, "Faulty Assumptions," 877.

the corruption exists where it is harder to see — in committee activities, in "the speech not given," and in prioritizing. Of course, if corruption cannot be measured or seen, this assertion cannot be disproven, which is something of a handicap for those skeptical of this justification. On the other hand, the assertion of widespread corruption is backed by bits of anecdotal evidence, usually quotes from present and former legislators explaining their support for campaign finance regulation or explaining why they were unable to accomplish certain legislative objectives. Typical, for example, is a quote by former representative Hamilton Fish: "Certainly amendments are influenced by campaign financing."[5] But even this "first-hand" evidence is not terribly persuasive, for there is a human tendency to blame defeat on "unfair" factors, such as corruption, rather than to admit that our ideas were not strong enough, our allies not numerous enough, or our side not organized enough, to gain legislative victory. Moreover, the fact is that the vast majority of current and former legislators do not make such comments, and indeed, there are similar types of anecdotal quotes running in the opposite direction, even from the supposedly unbiased former representatives with nothing left to hide. For example, the former senator and congressman Dan Coates, a twenty-two year Capitol Hill veteran, states, "Never, not once . . . have I witnessed or been informed of the exchange of dollars for political favors. Not by me or my supporters, not for any amount of money, and not by anyone I have known or served with."[6] In addition, there is the inability of regulatory advocates actually to name corrupt legislators or episodes of such corruption. The fact is, it is still shocking when episodes such as Abscam and the Keating Five come to light, precisely because such episodes are rare. Conventional wisdom aside, most people don't do it.

Part of the stubbornness behind the idea of hidden corruption is that experience and human nature warn us that legislators, like other people, are influenced by money, even when it does not go directly into their pockets but into their campaigns. Yet the idea that political donations play a relatively minor role in legislative behavior is also a matter of common sense, really. After all, all that a contribution can do is help a candidate try to persuade people to vote for him or her. Thus, adopting an unpopular position in exchange for a donation

---

[5] Quoted ibid., 876–77; see ibid., 875–77 for other, similar quotes.
[6] U.S. Congress, Senate, Committee on Rules and Administration, *Hearings on Campaign Contribution Limits*, 106th Cong. (March 24, 1999), 6.

will not generally be a wise course of action. It is votes, not dollars, that win elections. A candidate must get more votes. Contrary to the heated rhetoric of some reformers, the "wealthy" do not vote with their dollars. All they can do with their dollars is attempt to persuade others how to vote. That is free speech, and the essence of the First Amendment.

A further bit of reflection tells us why it is unlikely that money "corrupts" the legislature to any great extent. Campaign money is of little value if it cannot be turned into an electoral victory,[7] and it makes little sense to betray one's personal convictions, lose the support of one's party, and offend public opinion in order to obtain a contribution. It should not be surprising, therefore, that empirical studies show that the influence of contributions is dwarfed by that of party agenda, personal ideology, and constituent desires, as the latter is revealed in polls, letters, calls, and conversations with voters.[8] Common sense and experience tell us that money matters, but they also tell us that people who are attracted to public office generally do have strong personal views on issues. This rather obvious observation often seems lost on political observers, even those with an otherwise skeptical eye. For example, one skeptic of "reform" still found it "scandalous" that sixty-four Democrats in the House of Representatives voted for a capital gains tax cut in 1989, writing, "I cannot believe [they] would have voted for this bill . . . were they not so dependent on campaign contributions from the sector of the population most likely to benefit from the bill." This suggestion — that only contributions can explain this vote — seems little short of bizarre. It is hard to think of a contested legislative issue in which the arguments were so one-sided that *only* "corruption" could explain the votes of nearly 15 percent of the entire legislative body. In this case, though the issue was hotly debated, considerable literature suggested that a reduction in capital gains tax rates would actually increase government revenue. Perhaps these Democrats found such studies persuasive and merely wanted to cut the then sizeable federal budget deficit, or raise added revenue to fund social programs?[9]

---

[7] Bruce Cain, "Moralism and Realism in Campaign Finance Reform," 116.

[8] See for example, Sabato, "Real and Imagined Corruption," 160; Moussalli, *Campaign Finance Reform*, 6; Frank Sorauf, *Money in American Elections*, 316.

[9] Sanford Levinson, "Electoral Regulation; Some Comments," 412; See, for example, George Zodrow, "Economic Analysis of Capital Gains Taxation: Realizations, Revenues, Efficiency and Equity," 429–30.

On a personal level, for many years I have been associated with a 10
variety of public policy think tanks, and until recently sat on the Board
of Trustees of one such institution. Never have I known any of these
groups to take a position, or to avoid taking a position, in order to
please or to avoid offending donors. To the contrary, I have frequently
seen them take stands that incur the wrath of donors and cause major
declines in donations. In my role as a trustee, the only time I have
seen the questions of donors even come up is when discussing either
how to inform a donor of the position the organization intends to take,
or when discussing how to convince a donor that he or she should continue to contribute to the organization, despite its adoption of a position known to be at odds with the contributor's view. I believe that this
is how most of the professors who write on "reform," and most of the
staffers and board members of advocacy groups that champion more
regulation, conduct their affairs, as well. It strikes me as odd, if not of-
fensive, that these people assume that most members of Congress are
feckless suits, easily swayed by a few dollars to their campaign organizations, while they themselves are men and women of principle.

Second, there are institutional and political incentives to support
party positions. These include logistical and financial support, appeals
to party unity, rewards and punishment through such perks as committee assignments, and promises of support from party leaders on
other issues. All of these can be more valuable for pleasing constituents, gaining favorable press coverage, and accomplishing legislative
objectives than most campaign contributions could ever be.

Third, large campaign contributors are usually offset in legislative
debate by equally well-financed interests who contribute to a different group of candidates. Few candidates, especially incumbents, are
particularly reliant on one industry or source for campaign funds, so
that a vote that offends any particular interest is rarely, if ever, a potential death knell for future sources of funding. In fact, major contributors frequently suffer enormous losses in the legislative process.
For example, tobacco companies, often cited by regulatory advocates
as an example of an industry that "buys" votes in the legislature, have
been pummeled in recent congressional legislation.

Finally, money is not the only political commodity of value. For
example, in April 1999, as Congress was considering gun-control measures opposed by the National Rifle Association (NRA), Common Cause
issued a press release noting that from 1989 to 1998, the NRA had
contributed nearly $8.4 million to congressional campaigns. During
that same ten-year period, however, total spending by congressional
candidates and parties easily topped $4 billion, so the NRA's share of

the total congressional spending was less than two-tenths of 1 percent of the total. In this light, contributions hardly seem to be a realistic explanation for the NRA's alleged power. A more logical explanation is that, in addition to its PAC, the NRA also has over three million members who focus intently, or even solely, on Second Amendment and gun-ownership issues in their voting. In many congressional districts, the NRA is capable of shifting vote totals by as much as 5 percent. The NRA's power would seem to come more from votes than from dollars. However, to the extent that it comes from dollars, that, too, may be a function of votes. The group's large membership is part of what allows it to raise PAC money. Groups that advocate gun control often complain that the NRA outspends them, but rarely mention that the NRA also outvotes them.[10]

The NRA, with its large, ideological membership, of course, may not be the typical group. How do smaller, less ideological groups such as used-car dealers, sugar-beet growers, and the tobacco industry, to use three examples suggested by one critic, succeed? The answer is in much the same way as the NRA. For example, over 80,000 used-car dealers dot the American landscape, employing tens of thousands of workers. Sugar-beet growers can be found in every state from Ohio to California, and are often supported by a vast network of employees and suppliers. Coupled with the domestic corn syrup industry, sugar-beet growers provide over 420,000 jobs. These employees in turn have family members and friends, and in many small towns in the Midwest, the economy is contingent on the local processing facility. Similarly, the oft-maligned tobacco industry can call on large numbers of voters throughout the upper South, and even in parts of southern Ohio, Indiana, and Maryland, which are home to tobacco growers, processors, pickers, packagers, marketers, and more. Behind them stand millions of Americans who enjoy smoking, and may therefore oppose higher taxes, for example, on the product.[11] And it is certainly worth noting that many very influential groups, such as the American Association of Retired Persons or the American Bar Association, have no political action committee and make no political contributions at all.

Thus it is not surprising that personal ideology, party loyalty, and constituent views are far more important than the influence of cam- 15

---

[10] See, for example, Sorauf, *Inside Campaign Finance*, 166; Sorauf, *Money in American,* 307–17; Common Cause, "National Rifle Association Gives Large Amounts of Soft PAC Money."

[11] Daniel H. Lowenstein, *Election Law: Cases and Materials, Teachers Manual*, 116; Max Gates, "FTC Targets Buyer's Guide Violations"; David Hendee, "Defending the Sugar Program."

paign contributions on the legislature. Moreover, ideology, party, and constituency do not even begin to cover the myriad nonmonetary considerations that determine legislative activity.

Other factors that undoubtedly affect a legislator's actions might include anticipated newspaper endorsements or the slant of reporting, including deciding what qualifies as "news"; the opinions of staffers and personal friends and family, who are themselves likely to have strongly held views; perceptions of whether or not a stand on an issue could be distorted by an opponent into an effective campaign attack; potential endorsements by interest groups; and (I suspect) a host of other factors.

Consider just what it would mean for a legislator to act in a "corrupt" manner. For centuries, philosophers, political scientists, and others have debated how a legislator ought to make decisions; there is no consensus on the issue. However, democratic theorists have suggested a few ways of decision making which, I think, have enough legitimacy that even those who disagree with them would not suggest that they are "corrupt."

First, U.S. congresspersons or senators might choose to act according to the desires of a majority of their constituents, whether or not doing so comports with their own best judgment. Second, they might choose to act according to their own best judgment and ideological principles, whether or not doing so comports with the wishes of their constituents.[12] This would be a legitimate method of acting, whether the legislators are measuring the benefits according simply to what is best for their constituents or whether they are considering what is best for the nation as a whole. These do not exhaust the possibilities for legitimate legislative action. Legislators might also act legitimately (that is, non-"corruptly") in a manner opposed to both their own best judgment *and* the desires of a majority of their constituencies. For example, if a legislator thinks it would be a good idea to allow private discrimination against homosexuals in the rental housing market, and recognizes that a majority of his or her constituents hold a mild preference for allowing such private discrimination against homosexuals, he or she might still act in support of a law barring such

---

[12] See John Stuart Mill, "Considerations on Representative Government," 323, noting that some representatives "feel bound in conscience to let their conduct, on questions on which their constituents have a decided opinion, be the expression of that opinion rather than of their own"; Edmund Burke, "The English Constitutional System," 175, stating that although the opinion of constituents is "weighty and respectable," the notion that a representative is "bound blindly" to obey is "unknown to the law."

discrimination because of the much more intense preference of a minority of constituents who favor such legislation. This, too, is generally regarded as a legitimate mode of legislative action.

Which theory is best is, of course, a question for another day. At this point it is enough to note that a vote cast along any of these three lines cannot really be called "illegitimate" or "corrupt." In practice, I suspect that most legislators are frequently torn between these theories, and will usually vote their best judgment unless it means probable electoral defeat or, conversely, will usually vote with the constituency unless the legislators hold very strong opinions to the contrary.

In any case, to find "corruption," we must assume that the representative is acting against his or her own best judgment and principles, against the wishes of a majority of his or her constituents, and against the intense preferences of a minority, and that this is being done in order to gain a campaign contribution (as opposed to a media or other endorsement, favorable press coverage, or some other electoral advantage). How likely is any legislator to do such a thing for a mere contribution? Yet people express surprise that empirical studies fail to show that monetary contributions exert much influence. 20

So what, if anything, is the role of money? Why do donors give? The simple answer is that donors give primarily to elect candidates with whom they agree on issues important to the donor or, sometimes, simply because they are asked. And, we might add, it is hardly inappropriate for a legislator to vote in ways that please his or her constituents and that may, therefore, help the legislator to accumulate future campaign donations. Voters who do not like the legislator's record can record their votes at the next election.

Another reason that many donors themselves give for making political contributions is to assure access to legislators. Once again, regulatory advocates are quick to suggest that contributions play a dominant role in determing "access." Says former Representative Romano Mazzoli, "People who contribute get the ear of the member and the ear of the staff. They have the access." But like the "corruption" story, the "access" turns out not to be entirely true. The fact is, the vast majority of campaign contributors never seek access, and legislators meet regularly with people who have never made contributions. Nor does every contributor who seeks access get it.[13]

---

[13] See *Hearings on Campaign Contribution Limits*, testimony of former senator Dan Coates: "A contribution is by no means necessary to obtain a meeting, and a meeting by no means guarantees results."

To the extent that the access theory is true, however, it is hardly shocking. For one thing, such contributors are often well informed on public issues and provide valuable information to representatives. Whether or not such minor influence is good or bad will depend on one's views of the legislation. But certainly the exclusion of knowledgeable interests from the legislative process can just as easily lead to poor legislation with bad, unintended consequences, as can the inclusion of such interests. Those donors who expect their contributions to gain them particular legislative results not otherwise compatible with the lawmaker's ideology and constituency views are almost always disappointed. For example, after the 1996 presidential campaign, much was made of an arms dealer named Roger Tamraz, who made contributions to the Clinton campaign and confessed quite openly that he hoped to gain federal subsidies for a Caspian Sea oil pipeline. Less noted is that Tamraz's project was rejected by the president. As former Senator Coates says, "a contribution is by no means necessary to obtain a meeting, and a meeting by no means guarantees results."

The access question seems to rely on a romantic and highly implausible view of political life. There seems to be a notion that but for monetary contributions, the typical congressional representative would . . . well, would what? Randomly call citizens in his or her district to get their opinions? Or spend more time golfing? And if the added time was used to call constituents, would it be time well spent? Imagine the probable results of such phone calls: a large number of hang-ups, many more "I don't knows," and a great deal of off-the-cuff advice by persons with little knowledge of the issues the representative may be dealing with. But of course, legislators do meet regularly with concerned constituents. What evidence is there that legislators refuse access to constituents in order to meet only with donors? If meetings with contributors were eliminated, the most likely result, I think, is that the typical representative would spend more time with the people who already surround him or her most of the day, and who make up the single largest occupational group of witnesses in congressional committee hearings: other government employees and officials. If private contributions were banned we can be sure that the overwhelming majority of citizens would still never, ever, get to spend even two minutes discussing public affairs with their congressional representatives; and we could make a reasonable guess that the number of private citizens with whom that representative does discuss public affairs would almost certainly decline.

In recent years, the popular arguments of reform advocates have grown more and more specious. For example, one popular tactic has 25 been to lump together dozens, or even hundreds, of contributions, made over several years and several campaigns, by numerous donors who share one or more characteristic, which may or may not be their dominant characteristic.

A recent Common Cause report on the influence of the broadcast industry, for example, tells us in breathless prose that all broadcast interests, over a ten-year period ending in November 1996, gave about $9 million in total PAC contributions to candidates and soft-money contributions to parties. The report then suggests that this influence resulted in passage of legislation which, in Common Cause's eyes at least, was detrimental to the national interest. Of course, these contributions were made over five campaigns, with changing issues and candidates, and there are any number of reasons why contributions may have been made. The total includes contributions by interests frequently hostile to one another, such as Time-Warner and Turner Broadcasting, and by interests allied on some issues but opposed on others, such as networks and their affiliates, or in other instances, franchisers and franchisees. Further, Common Cause fails to point out that during this same decade, the recipient candidates and parties spent about $9 billion on political activity. So even assuming a unity of interest on the part of all "broadcast interests," broadcast contributions total about one-tenth of 1 percent of total national spending over this time. From this — one-tenth of 1 percent of total spending, over five campaigns, including contributions to persons no longer in Congress, contributions for state campaigns, including donations made for any reason whatsoever, we are to believe that a majority of Congress — more than 218 United States representatives and 51 senators — voted for a bill that they would otherwise have opposed and that they believed was against the interest of a majority of the voters they have to face in the next election. Meanwhile, more obvious reasons for any industry influence — that broadcasters own most of the broadcast outlets and so control reporting on campaigns — was ignored. Oddly enough, efforts to limit how much can be spent on political activity would only serve to strengthen the disproportionate influence of the broadcast and print media, as the overwhelming source of influence for these groups — broadcast time — would be untouched by reform. The Common Cause argument is not intended to be taken seriously. But Common Cause is hardly alone. In one report, typical of many on its web site, the Center for Responsive Politics casually lumps together all contributions by the insurance, securities, and banking industries, even while admitting, further on in the story, the substantially different interests among these industries. A variation of this tactic was done by Charles Lewis in his book, *The Buying of the President 2000*. Lewis lumped together all contributions from donors over a politician's career, to create a list of "career patrons" for each candidate, and suggested that the candidates are totally controlled by these donors.[14]

Indeed, unable to demonstrate "corruption" in any serious manner, reform groups have resorted to what might be called "guilt by innuendo." That is, they never say who is actually corrupt but simply hint that everyone is, or that the "system" is corrupt. But this is demonstrably not true. During the 1996 campaign, for example, the president's fund-raising tactics drew considerable public criticism — in particular a practice of allowing large campaign contributors to sleep in the Lincoln Bedroom at the White House. But it should be obvious that not every president does what the Clinton campaign did to raise funds in 1996. Furthermore, in November 1996, that same public ratified Clinton's substantive policies with a lopsided electoral victory, and his approval numbers continued to climb in 1997, even as the fund-raising "scandals" grew. Similarly, in the late 1980s, Senator John McCain was one of five senators caught up in what became known as the Keating Five scandal. The senators were accused of improperly interfering in regulatory decisions in order to assist campaign contributor Charles Keating. But what brought the Keating Five scandal to the public's attention and made it a scandal is that it was not typical. It was out of the ordinary. After the Keating Five scandal broke, the voters of Arizona twice returned Senator McCain to office by substantial margins — thanks, I am sure, to his many other virtues and his generally sound representation of the people of Arizona. And Senator McCain, far from being castigated by campaign reform advocates as "corrupt," was, by the mid-1990s, their single most prominent legislative hero, running a competitive campaign for the Republican presidential nomination in 2000. When challenged to name individuals corrupted by campaign contributions, reform advocates fall silent. Instead, they assert only that it is the "system" which is corrupt. But if we cannot name individuals corrupted by the system, on what basis should we conclude that the system is corrupt?

Ultimately, the claims of corruption seem to rest on the idea that legislators should respond to some notion of the "public good" that exists apart from the views of any particular group of voters. But leg-

---

[14] Common Cause, "Channeling Influence: The Broadcast Lobby and the $70-Billion Free Ride"; Center for Responsive Politics, "Banking Deregulation"; Charles Lewis, *The Buying of the President 2000*; Lewis, *The Buying of the President.*

islators respond disproportionately to the interests of select constituents all the time, depending, among other things, upon the intensity, the degree of organization, and the willingness of those constituents to vote on those interests, and those interests alone. To the extent that it is argued that a legislator might use Burkean judgment to resist the blandishments of powerful groups, or even the majority, in favor of what the legislator, with his or her added knowledge, believes to be good public policy, I support that notion. I am a Burkean. But to the extent that Common Cause or some other group not accountable at the polls claims to know what that good public policy is, and therefore to know when legislators are violating their trust — and to the extent that they then seek to justify limits on the political advocacy of others — such actions are very dangerous to First Amendment rights.

Understanding the Text

1. Describe the rhetorical situation here.
   - Whom does Smith believe he is addressing?
   - What has *occasioned* Smith's remarks? That is, what events — or remarks by others — have *moved* him to express himself?
2. What makes Smith leery of the word "corruption"?

Reflection and Response

3. How does it affect Smith's credibility that he starts by presenting a position that is not his own? (Could you tell that that's what he is doing in his opening? Could you tell exactly where he shifts to his own views? If not, look again.)
4. Which of Smith's points do you find most compelling? Which, least? Why?

Making Connections

5. Read Arianna Huffington's "CSI USA: Who Killed the American Dream" (p. 169). Overall, who makes the more persuasive case, Smith or Huffington? Why?
6. What questions raised by Huffington and Smith would you like answered? (For example, do the two sources contradict each other on certain facts, leaving you to wonder which author is more accurate?) How might the answers to these questions lead you to change your position?

   Tap your online resources — and/or the assistance of a reference librarian — to try to settle one of these questions. Describe your progress.
7. "Citizens United," the important Supreme Court decision to which Smith's thinking contributed, has been roundly criticized by many liberals in America — and even by the president, Barack Obama, in the middle of a State of the Union Address, with all Supreme Court members present. Find out what the critics and the supporters of the decision have to say, and stake out a position of your own concerning it.

4

Can Huge Differences in Wealth Be Justified?

Since the fall of the Soviet Union in 1991, few voices have been raised in support of Communism, a totalitarian system for equalizing wealth that is now generally regarded as incompatible with human nature. Still, the question of wealth's distribution in the world remains, as evidenced by the decibel level of debates about tax rates on the highest income brackets. As one student writes, "There are many people today who work very hard and do not receive in return [even] the substance required to live, while there are people who do nothing and live comfortable lives. . . ."

Does it matter that the gap between the poor and the rich in America continues to grow? The opening pieces of this section — the short work of fiction "The Lesson," the analytical article "Wealth, Race, and the Great Recession," the personal essay "Should Working-Class People Get B.A.'s and Ph.D.'s?" and the graph "Income Gains at the Top" — all appear to suggest that the gap cries out for action. However, the author of the analysis that comes next, "Inequality and (Un)happiness in America," does not concur.

After a look at items that shed different lights on wealth redistribution — three paintings and the opinion piece "Stop Coddling the Super-Rich" — the balance of this section is devoted to readings on humanity's least controversial form of spreading wealth, philanthropy, which turns out to raise questions enough. Those last readings are an excerpt from the *Mishneh Torah* and the daring essay "Rich and Poor."

The Lesson

Toni Cade Bambara

In this widely praised short story, a college-educated woman named Miss Moore takes a group of kids from a poor, inner-city neighborhood to perhaps the most expensive toy store in the world, F.A.O. Schwarz. The speaker of the story is Sylvia, one of those kids on Miss Moore's field trip.

Author Toni Cade Bambara played many roles in life besides that of writer. She was a civil rights advocate, a social worker, a recreation director, a film producer, and a college English teacher.

Back in the days when everyone was old and stupid or young and foolish and me and Sugar were the only ones just right, this lady moved on our block with nappy hair and proper speech and no makeup. And quite naturally we laughed at her, laughed the way we did at the junk man who went about his business like he was some big-time president and his sorry-ass horse his secretary. And we kinda hated her too, hated the way we did the winos who cluttered up our parks and pissed on our handball walls and stank up our hallways and stairs so you couldn't halfway play hide-and-seek without a goddamn gas mask. Miss Moore was her name. The only woman on the block with no first name. And she was black as hell, cept for her feet, which were fish-white and spooky. And she was always planning these boring-ass things for us to do, us being my cousin, mostly, who lived on the block cause we all moved North the same time and to the same apartment then spread out gradual to breathe. And our parents would yank our heads into some kinda shape and crisp up our clothes so we'd be presentable for travel with Miss Moore, who always looked like she was going to church, though she never did. Which is just one of the things the grown-ups talked about when they talked behind her back like a dog. But when she came calling with some sachet she'd sewed up or some gingerbread she'd made or some book, why then they'd all be too embarrassed to turn her down and we'd get handed out all spruced up. She'd been to college and said it only right that she should take responsibility for the young ones' education, and she not even related by marriage or blood. So they'd go for it. Specially Aunt Gretchen. She was the main gofer in the family. You got some ole dumb shit foolishness you want somebody to go for, you send for Aunt Gretchen. She been screwed into the go-along for so long, it's a blood-deep natural thing with her. Which is how she got saddled with me and Sugar and Junior in the first place while our mothers were in a la-de-da apartment up the block having a good ole time.

So this one day Miss Moore rounds us all up at the mailbox and it's puredee hot and she's knockin herself out about arithmetic. And school suppose to let up in summer I heard, but she don't never let up. And the starch in my pinafore scratching the shit outta me and I'm really hating this nappy-head bitch and her goddamn college degree. I'd much rather go to the pool or to the show where it's cool. So me and Sugar leaning on the mailbox being surly, which is a Miss Moore word. And Flyboy checking out what everybody brought for lunch. And Fat Butt already wasting his peanut-butter-and-jelly sandwich like the pig he is. And Junebug punchin on Q.T.'s arm for potato chips. And Rosie Giraffe shifting from one hip to the other waiting for somebody to step on her foot or ask her if she from Georgia so she can kick ass, preferably Mercedes'. And Miss Moore asking us do we know what money is, like we a bunch of retards. I mean real money, she say, like it's only poker chips or monopoly papers we lay on the grocer. So right away I'm tired of this and say so. And would much rather snatch Sugar and go to the Sunset and terrorize the West Indian kids and take their hair ribbons and their money too. And Miss Moore files that remark away for next week's lesson on brotherhood, I can tell. And finally I say we oughta get to the subway cause it's cooler and besides we might meet some cute boys. Sugar done swiped her mama's lipstick so we ready.

So we heading down the street and she's boring us silly about what things cost and what our parents make and how much goes for rent and how money ain't divided up right in this country. And then she gets to the part about we all poor and live in the slums, which I don't feature. And I'm ready to speak on that, but she steps out in the street and hails two cabs just like that. Then she hustles half the crew in with her and hands me a five-dollar bill and tells me to calculate 10 percent tip for the driver. And we're off. Me and Sugar and Junebug and Flyboy hangin out the window and hollering to everybody, putting lipstick on each other cause Flyboy a faggot anyway, and making farts with our sweaty armpits. But I'm mostly trying to figure how to spend this money. But they all fascinated with the meter ticking and Junebug starts laying bets as to how much it'll read when Flyboy can't hold his breath no more. Then

Sugar lays bets as to how much it'll be when we get there. So I'm stuck. Don't nobody want to go for my plan, which is to jump out at the next light and run off to the first bar-b-que we can find. Then the driver tells us to get the hell out cause we are there already. And the meter reads eighty-five cents. And I'm stalling to figure out the tip and Sugar say give him a dime. And I decide he don't need it bad as I do, so later for him. But then he tries to take off with Junebug foot still in the door so we talk about his mama something ferocious. Then we check out that we on Fifth Avenue and everybody dressed up in stockings. One lady in a fur coat, hot as it is. White folks crazy.

"This is the place," Miss Moore say, presenting it to us in the voice she uses at the museum. "Let's look in the windows before we go in."

"Can we steal?" Sugar asks very serious like she's getting the ground rules square sway before she plays. "I beg your pardon," say Miss Moore, and we fall out. So she leads us around the windows of the toy store and me and Sugar screamin, "This is mine, that's mine, I gotta have that, that was made for me, I was born for that," till Big Butt drowns us out.

"Hey, I'm goin to buy that there."

"That there? You don't even know what it is, stupid."

"I do so," he say punchin on Rosie Giraffe. "It's a microscope."

"Whatcha gonna do with a microscope, fool?"

"Look at things."

"Like what, Ronald?" ask Miss Moore. And Big Butt ain't got the first notion. So here go Miss Moore gabbing about the thousands of bacteria in a drop of water and the somethinorother in a speck of blood and the million and one living things in the air around us is invisible to the naked eye. And what she say that for? Junebug go to town on that "naked" and we rolling. Then Miss Moore ask what it cost. So we all jam into the window smudgin it up and the price tag say $300. So then she ask how long'd take for Big Butt and Junebug to save up their allowances. "Too long," I say. "Yeh," adds Sugar, "outgrown it by that time." And Miss Moore say no, you never outgrow learning instruments. "Why, even medical students and interns and," blah, blah, blah. And we ready to choke Big Butt for bringing it up in the first damn place.

"This here costs four hundred eighty dollars," say Rosie Giraffe. So we pile up all over her to see what she pointin out. My eyes tell me it's a chunk of glass cracked with something heavy, and different-color inks dripped into the splits, then the whole thing put into a oven or something. But for $480 it don't make sense.

"That's a paperweight made of semi-precious stones fused together under tremendous pressure," she explains slowly, with her hands doing the mining and all the factory work.

"So what's a paperweight?" asks Rosie Giraffe.

"To weigh paper with, dumbbell," say Flyboy, the wise man from the   15
East.

"Not exactly," say Miss Moore, which is what she say when you warm
or way off too. "It's to weigh paper down so it won't scatter and make
your desk untidy." So right away me and Sugar curtsy to each other
and then to Mercedes who is more the tidy type.

"We don't keep paper on top of the desk in my class," say Junebug,
figuring Miss Moore crazy or lyin one.

"At home, then," she say. "Don't you have a calendar and a pencil
case and a blotter and a letter-opener on your desk at home where
you do your homework?" And she know damn well what our homes
look like cause she nosys around in them every chance she gets.

"I don't even have a desk," say Junebug. "Do we?"

"No. And I don't get no homework neither," say Big Butt.   20

"And I don't even have a home," say Flyboy like he do at school to
keep the white folks off his back and sorry for him. Send this poor kid
to camp posters, is his speciality.

"I do," say Mercedes. "I have a box of stationery on my desk and a
picture of my cat. My godmother bought the stationery and the desk.
There's a big rose on each sheet and the envelopes smell like roses."

"Who want to know about your smelly-ass stationery," say Rosie
Giraffe fore I can get my two cents in.

"It's important to have a work area all your own so that . . ."

"Will you look at this sailboat, please," say Flyboy, cuttin her off and   25
pointin to the thing like it was his. So once again we tumble all over
each other to gaze at this magnificent thing in the toy store which is
just big enough to maybe sail two kittens across the pond if you strap
them to the posts tight. We all start reciting the price tag like we in
assembly. "Handcrafted sailboat of fiberglass at one thousand one hundred ninety-five dollars."

"Unbelievable," I hear myself say and am really stunned. I read it
again for myself just in case the group recitation put me in a trance.
Same thing. For some reason this pisses me off. We look at Miss Moore
and she lookin at us, waiting for I dunno what.

"Who'd pay all that when you can buy a sailboat set for a quarter at
Pop's, a tube of glue for a dime, and a ball of string for eight cents? It
must have a motor and a whole lot else besides," I say. "My sailboat cost
me about fifty cents."

"But will it take water?" say Mercedes with her smart ass.

"Took mine to Alley Pond Park once," say Flyboy. "String broke.
Lost it. Pity."

"Sailed mine in Central Park and it keeled over and sank. Had to ask my father for another dollar."   30

"And you got the strap," laugh Big Butt. "The jerk didn't even have a string on it. My old man wailed on his behind."

Little Q.T. was staring hard at the sailboat and you could see he wanted it bad. But he too little and somebody'd just take it from him. So what the hell. "This boat for kids, Miss Moore?"

"Parents silly to buy something like that just to get all broke up," say Rosie Giraffe.

"That much money it should last forever," I figure.

"My father'd buy it for me if I wanted it."   35

"Your father, my ass," say Rosie Giraffe getting a chance to finally push Mercedes.

"Must be rich people shop here," say Q.T.

"You are a very bright boy," say Flyboy. "What was your first clue?" And he rap him on the head with the back of his knuckles, since Q.T. the only one he could get away with. Though Q.T. liable to come up behind you years later and get his licks in when you half expect it.

"What I want to know is," I says to Miss Moore though I never talk to her, I wouldn't give the bitch that satisfaction, "is how much a real boat costs? I figure a thousand'd get you a yacht any day."

"Why don't you check that out," she says, "and report back to the group?" Which really pains my ass. If you gonna mess up a perfectly good swim day least you could do is have some answers. "Let's go in," she say like she got something up her sleeve. Only she don't lead the way. So me and Sugar turn the corner to where the entrance is, but when we get there I kinda hang back. Not that I'm scared, what's there to be afraid of, just a toy store. But I feel funny, shame. But what I got to be shamed about? Got as much right to go in as anybody. But somehow I can't seem to get hold on the door, so I step away for Sugar to lead. But she hangs back too. And I look at her and she looks at me and this is ridiculous. I mean, damn, I have never ever been shy about doing nothing or going nowhere. But then Mercedes steps up and then Rosie Giraffe and Big Butt crowd in behind and shove, and next thing we all stuffed into the doorway with only Mercedes squeezing past us, smoothing out her jumper and walking right down the aisle. Then the rest of us tumble in like a glued-together jigsaw done all wrong. And people lookin at us. And it's like the time me and Sugar crashed into the Catholic church on a dare. But once we got in there and everything so hushed and holy and the candles and the bowin and the handkerchiefs on all the drooping heads, I just couldn't go through with the plan. Which was for me to run up to the altar and do a tap dance   40 while Sugar played the nose flute and messed around in the holy water. And Sugar kept givin me the elbow. Then later teased me so bad I tied her up in the shower and turned it on and locked her in. And she'd be there till this day if Aunt Gretchen hadn't finally figured I was lying about the boarder takin a shower.

Same thing in the store. We all walkin on tiptoe and hardly touchin the games and puzzles and things. And I watched Miss Moore who is steady watchin us like she waitin for a sign. Like Mama Drewery watches the sky and sniffs the air and takes note of just how much slant is in the bird formation. Then me and Sugar bump smack into each other, so busy gazing at the toys, 'specially the sail-boat. But we don't laugh and go into our fat-lady bump-stomach routine. We just stare at that price tag. Then Sugar run a finger over the whole boat. And I'm jealous and want to hit her. Maybe not her, but I sure want to punch somebody in the mouth.

"Watcha bring us here for, Miss Moore?"

"You sound angry, Sylvia. Are you mad about something?" Give me one of them grins like she tellin a grown-up joke that never turns out to be funny. And she's lookin very closely at me like maybe she plannin to do my portrait from memory. I'm mad, but I won't give her that satisfaction. So I slouch around the store bein very bored and say, "Let's go."

Me and Sugar at the back of the train watchin' the tracks whizzin by large then small then gettin gobbled up in the dark. I'm thinkin about this tricky toy I saw in the store. A clown that somersaults on a bar then does chin-ups just cause you yank lightly at his leg. Cost $35. I could see me askin my mother for a $35 birthday clown. "You wanna who that costs what?" she'd say, cockin her head to the side to get a better view of the hole in my head. Thirty-five dollars could buy new bunk beds for Junior and Gretchen's boy. Thirty-five dollars and the whole household could go visit Granddaddy Nelson in the country. Thirty-five dollars would pay for the rent and the piano bill too. Who are these people that spend that much for performing clowns and $1,000 for toy sailboats? What kinda work they do and how they live and how come we ain't in on it? Where we are is who we are, Miss Moore always pointin out. But it don't necessarily have to be that way, she always adds then waits for somebody to say that poor people have to wake up and demand their share of the pie and don't none of us know what kind of pie she talkin about in the first damn place. But she ain't so smart cause I still got her four dollars from the taxi and she sure ain't gettin it. Messin up my day with this shit. Sugar nudges me in my pocket and winks.

Miss Moore lines us up in front of the mailbox where we started   45
from, seem like years ago, and I got a headache for thinkin so hard.
And we lean all over each other so we can hold up under the draggy-
ass lecture she always finishes us off with at the end before we thank
her for borin us to tears. But she just looks at us like she readin tea
leaves. Finally she say, "Well, what did you think of F.A.O. Schwarz?"

Rosie Giraffe mumbles, "White folks crazy."

"I'd like to go in there again when I get my birthday money," says
Mercedes, and we shove her out the pack so she has to lean on the
mailbox by herself.

"I'd like a shower. Tiring day," say Flyboy.

Then Sugar surprises me by saying, "You know, Miss Moore, I
don't think all of us here put together eat in a year what that sailboat
costs." And Miss Moore lights up like somebody goosed her. "And?"
she say, urging Sugar on. Only I'm standin on her foot so she don't
continue.

"Imagine for a minute what kind of society it is in which some   50
people can spend on a toy what would cost to feed a family of six or
seven. What do you think?"

"I think," say Sugar pushing me off her feet like she never done
before, cause I whip her ass in a minute, "that this is not much of a
democracy if you ask me. Equal chance to pursue happiness means
an equal crack at the dough, don't it?" Miss Moore is besides herself
and I am disgusted with Sugar's treachery. So I stand on her foot one
more time to see if she'll shove me. She shuts up, and Miss Moore looks
at me, sorrowfully I'm thinkin. And somethin weird is going on, I can
feel it in my chest.

"Anybody else learn anything today?" lookin dead at me. I walk away
and Sugar has to run to catch up and don't even seem to notice when
I shrug her arm off my shoulder.

"Well, we got four dollars anyway," she says.

"Uh hunh."

"We could go to Hascombs and get half a chocolate layer and then   55
go to the Sunset and still have plenty money for potato chips and ice-
cream sodas."

"Uh hunh."

"Race you to Hascombs," she say.

We start down the block and she gets ahead which is O.K. by me
cause I'm goin to the West End and then over to the Drive to think this
day through. She can run if she want to and even run faster. But ain't
nobody gonna beat me at nuthin.

Understanding the Text

1. Sylvia, the student in whose voice this story is told, does many things Miss Moore might disapprove of — like keeping four of the five dollars Miss Moore has given her for cab fare. Whom does Miss Moore blame for such behavior? What specific lines in the text lead you to say so?

2. If Miss Moore has taken the kids to F.A.O. Schwarz to impart a lesson to them, what exactly *is* that lesson? Where, if anywhere, does she or someone else spell it out?

3. What might explain the author's choice of a line to *end* the story on? Would you agree that the concluding line has more than one meaning?

Reflection and Response

4. Are you optimistic about Sylvia's future? Why or why not?

5. The language in which this story was written is one of the rich dialects of America. Should the author have "cleaned the language up" — either to make its meaning clearer at times or to keep some readers from being offended? Why or why not?

Making Connections

6. Here's a scene taken from the "money journal" of a student who worked the cash register at a drugstore in her hometown.

   A man came in with a small girl who looked to be five or six. As they walked the aisles, I heard the girl shriek, "Daddy, I want this!" and "Daddy, buy me this!" Each time, the dad would [at first] say no but in the end say yes, because of the girl's persistence. She never said "please" or "may I," just "give me" and "I want." Yet somehow she got everything she wanted without even one "thank you." When I finally rang them up, the dad had a pack of batteries for himself, and the rest was over fifty dollars' worth of toys, magazines, and candy that the girl had requested. As I finished bagging their products, I heard the dad say, "We're not doing this again the next time we go shopping." The girl simply squeaked, "Yes, we are, Daddy. You buy whatever I want." With that, they were out the door, and I was left to replay the scenario in my mind.

   You, too, have no doubt witnessed scenes like this. As one part of the introduction to a paper on "The Lesson," describe a real incident that either parallels Bambara's narrative or, like the incident above, provides a contrast to it.

7. Read Melanie Scheller's "On the Meaning of Plumbing and Poverty" (p. 85). Is Bambara's character Sylvia as conscious of how affluent people live as the young, real-life Melanie Scheller was? What details of the Bambara story and the Scheller memoir inform your answer? If one of these two girls was more aware of disparities in lifestyle between social classes, what might account for that greater awareness?

Wealth, Race, and the Great Recession

Michael Powell

In the 1860s, the Civil War ended slavery. In 1954, the Supreme Court declared racial segregation in schools unconstitutional. In the 1960s, Congress passed the landmark Civil Rights Acts. In 2008, the U.S. electorate put a black man in the White House. . . . Haven't Americans of color had good reason to expect that such milestones would lead to a closing of the gap in standard of living between the races? Michael Powell's column below deals with the sobering realities since 1983.

A former tenant organizer, Powell has reported on poverty, crime, politics, and diverse other subjects for *New York Newsday,* the *Washington Post,* and, currently, *The New York Times.* In 2009, he belonged to a team of reporters at *The Times* who jointly won the Pulitzer Prize.

The primal economic divide in America remains the chasm between the wealth of black and white families, and it has widened steadily over the last generation.

And that largely reckons — as demographic data trails a year or two behind economic reality — without the toll taken by the Great Recession, which several economists forecast will most likely deepen this divide. These conclusions arise from a study released today by Professor Thomas M. Shapiro and his colleagues at the Institute on Assets and Social Policy at Brandeis University. They studied the same 2,000 black and white families between 1983 and 2007, and found that the racial wealth gap "has more than quadrupled over the course of a generation."

Mr. Shapiro and his colleagues say their data points to a "stampede toward an escalating racial wealth gap." Other analysts might pick their own adjectives, but the bones of the study present a disturbing take.

White families saw "dramatic growth" in their financial assets, from a median value of $22,000 in 1983 to $100,000 in 2007; black families experienced only the slightest growth in wealth during this same period, measured in 2007 dollars. This held true even at higher income levels. Middle-income whites, for instance, accumulated $74,000 in assets by 2007, as opposed to high-income black families, whose median assets totaled just $18,000 in 2007. (For both races, middle income was defined as $40,000 to $70,000 in 2007 dollars.)

At the bottom of the economic pyramid, at least 25 percent of black 5 families in 2007 could draw on no assets whatsoever to see themselves through the economic storm.

Wealth begets wealth, and the lack of wealth perpetuates the same.

So why does this matter?

In short, wealth begets wealth, and the lack of wealth perpetuates the same. Black families — who save at the same rate as white families — have less money to pay for college tuition, less money to invest in business and less money to tide them through rough times. "The gap is opportunity denied and assures racial economic inequality for the next generation," Mr. Shapiro notes.

The reasons for this gap are rooted deep in this nation's racial history. Government policy shut many blacks out of homeownership during the depths of the Depression. And during the post–World War II boom years, federal, state and city policies, and discriminatory bank lending and real estate practices steered even higher-income blacks to segregated neighborhoods and towns, where real estate appreciation lagged far behind that of predominantly white areas.

Also, even high-income blacks most often hail from families of humble economic origins. These families had far fewer dollars to pass on to their children. (As any young person who has cadged a down payment from parents can attest, intergenerational wealth transfers are a particularly efficient way of gaining a foothold in homeownership and so building wealth.)

Government tax policy in the past three decades has broadened   10
this racial gap, even if inadvertently. When Congress cuts inheritance and capital gains taxes, its actions keep more money in the pockets of those families who already have it, which is to say disproportionately upper-income white families.

There is finally the looming question of the toll taken by the recession. Certainly, many millions of white families have suffered grievously, losing houses and jobs. At the low point in 2009, white families had lost more than $1 trillion in wealth.

But the recession fell even more heavily on blacks, as the average black family has far more of its wealth wrapped up in a home. (Whites, again for reasons of racial and economic history, tend to have diversified portfolios, with more stocks, pensions and the like.)

"Given differential employment rates, loss of wages, loss of health insurance, to the extent that all of these are worse for African-Americans, it has to make the wealth divide worse," said William A. Darity, a professor of African-American studies and economics at the Sanford School of Public Policy at Duke University. "All the arrows are pointing down."

Understanding the Text

1. Why does Michael Powell use the words "primal" and "chasm" in his first sentence?

2. Powell writes, ". . . the lack of wealth perpetuates the same." Why, according to him, is this so?

   How, according to Powell, have racist government policies and bank practices made the situation worse for poor African-Americans than for poor whites?

Reflection and Response

3. Were you shocked by the phrase "more than quadrupled" at the end of Powell's second paragraph? Why or why not?

4. Come up with a possible way to close the economic gap between races. Explain your plan of action, and indicate the questions you would need to get answered in order to be confident about it.

Making Connections

5. How well do the findings Powell reports square with those Elizabeth Warren reports in "The Vanishing Middle Class" (p. 64)?

6. What, exactly, *were* the racist government policies (during the Depression and post-war boom) and racist bank practices (in the post-war period) that Powell's article alludes to? Investigate, and report back.

Should Working-Class People Get B.A.'s and Ph.D.'s?

Briallen Hopper and Johanna Hopper

When it comes to distributing wealth, shouldn't those who "work hard and play by the rules" be rewarded accordingly? Since the economic downturn of 2008–2009, countless hard-working college graduates have found themselves asking just that question when they leave school and enter an unpromising job market.

Published in March 2012, here is a firsthand account of two sisters who made different decisions about pursuing a college degree.

W e are sisters from a working-class family: Our dad works in construction, and our mom is a licensed practical nurse with a GED. We are equally bookish and academically inclined, but we represent opposite ends of the educational spectrum.

Briallen has a Ph.D. from Princeton University and is a lecturer in the English department at Yale University. Johanna is a high-school graduate working full time at a bakery for slightly above minimum wage.

Recently, after reading Thomas B. Edsall's piece on "The Reproduction of Privilege" in *The New York Times*, we got into a lively and sometimes painful conversation about why academically qualified, working-class Americans might choose not to go to college, and about how the system sometimes fails them even when they do manage to go.

Edsall argues that college is no longer the force for class mobility that it used to be, and he laments that working-class students are less and less likely to pursue a B.A. We agree with a lot of what he says, but we believe he fails to fully explain why people like us might consciously choose not to get B.A.'s, and why we sometimes pay a high price when we do.

For both of us, decisions about education have been limited and 5 complicated by our class status.

Briallen worked in child care and food service for a while after high school, went to community college, and was accepted to a selective four-year college but was not offered enough financial aid to go. She finally graduated from a local college with the help of Pell Grants and a lot of debt. She can't imagine her life without higher education, but as a non-tenure-track academic in a tough job market, she has limited job security, and she owes more than $800 a month in student-loan payments. Her student debt makes it impossible for her to save money or start a family anytime soon, and she is entering her mid-30s.

Johanna is 20. She was an honor student at her Jesuit prep school and was considered to be obvious "college material" by her teachers, but she graduated after the 2008 crash and couldn't count on getting a job after college that would enable her to make student-loan payments. She got into many good institutions, including a nationally ranked private research university (which gave her a $25,000-a-year merit scholarship), a nationally ranked liberal-arts college (which nearly matched that offer), and the flagship public university in her state. But she would still have needed to take out between $50,000 to $100,000 in loans to go to any of them.

Johanna was wary of graduating with substantial debt and no family safety net, so she took a year off to work and save money and try applying to college again. Her financial-aid offers the next year were no better. She ended up taking classes at the local satellite campus of a state university while living at home and working long hours at a salon to pay her own way.

But after a couple of quarters she discovered that, because of the poor academic advising she had received, none of the introductory courses she had taken were actually required for her degree. Her AP credits from high school should have qualified her to start as a sophomore, but she was mistakenly placed in freshman-level courses.

After learning that she'd spent almost all of her hard-earned savings on classes she was not even required to take, Johanna lost her faith in the wisdom of investing in higher education. She left school and is now working full time for $13,000 a year. She's proudly debt-free and self-supporting, and in her limited free time she is pursuing reading, writing, and the free or cheap cultural and educational opportunities available to her.

Johanna hasn't ruled out college someday, but even community college would require money, time, and faith in the system that she doesn't yet have. Too many of her college-educated friends are living off of family and food stamps. She's determined to seek success and self-worth outside of the enormously expensive educational institutions that too often disregard the significant personal sacrifices students make to attend them.

We both agree that there are almost insurmountable obstacles to higher education for people like us, but we disagree about whether

There are almost insurmountable obstacles to higher education for people like us, but we disagree about whether college is a good or defensible option in those circumstances.

college is a good or defensible option in those circumstances. Briallen's life as a teacher and scholar would have been impossible without her expensive education, and she can't help believing in its worth. For five years she participated in outreach programs at Princeton and Yale, trying to help get underrepresented students into college and graduate school.

And even as she sells her books and clothes to make her student-loan payments, she still periodically tries to talk Johanna into going back to college. She believes higher education is valuable beyond the price, and she hopes it will even prove a good investment someday, if the economy improves.

Meanwhile Johanna believes that since the cost of college has become potentially ruinous for many qualified students, the choice not to go ought to be respected, and even encouraged, not lamented.

And she resists the pressure to define her life by college or its absence. As she says: "We all know that a B.A. can qualify you for an enormous number of valuable jobs that may otherwise be unavailable to you. However, it is not only a B.A. that can qualify you for a meaningful life. Thanks to the stigma, it actually took me more than a year to realize that I was not a college dropout. I was a 19-year-old, I was a salon receptionist, I was frugal, I was changing careers, I was a piano player, I was a little sister, and a daughter, and reader — I was so many things, yet the only label that stuck to me was 'college dropout.' You hear it said so often, you forget to question it. So a person didn't go to college. Well. What did they do instead?"

Although we both continue to struggle with the stressful economic implications of our different education levels, we are proud of each other and of our very different choices. We just wish we'd been given the opportunity to make them more freely.

Understanding the Text

1. In what different ways does money influence the thinking of the two Hopper sisters?
2. Like any true account of important decisions, the Hopper sisters' story involves multiple factors — their personal finances and the state of the economy are just two of them. What other factors contribute to their choices?

Reflection and Response

3. Are you more sympathetic with one sister than with the other? Explain.

4. How do the factors at play in these sisters' story compare with the considerations that affected your own decision to go to college, as well as your own choice of a college to attend?

Making Connections

5. Suppose for a moment that Sylvia, the girl who is the speaker of the story "The Lesson" (p. 195), eventually decided to "make something of herself" by going to college. What do you predict would happen? Why? (In your response, work in references to one or both of the Hopper sisters, if only to set up a clarifying contrast with the situation Sylvia is in.)

   If your prediction came true, would that fact bolster or call into doubt America's description of itself as a land of equal opportunity? Please explain.

6. With the help of a reference librarian, find out whether economists see a connection between the cost of a college education and social mobility (the ability to move from one social class to a higher one). Discuss your findings in a paper.

Income Gains at the Top

Center on Budget and Policy Priorities

In recent years, there has been much talk about the growing disparity between the income of the wealthiest Americans and that of middle-class Americans and poor Americans. This graph represents one attempt to capture the trend visually.

Please note: (1) This graph shows *rates of growth* in income, not *levels* of income — levels of income differ even more dramatically. (2) The middle of the middle class is represented by the second line from the bottom, marked "+25%."

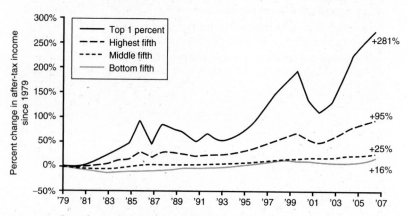

Income Gains at the Top Dwarf Those of Low- and Middle-Income Households
Source: CBPP calculations from Congressional Budget Office data.

Understanding the Text

1. What questions does the graph raise for you?

Reflection and Response

2. Where do you locate your own family on this graph?
3. Should it *matter* to middle-class Americans that the income of their richest fellow citizens goes up at a rate 10 times faster than their own incomes do? Why or why not?

Making Connections

4. Research the Center on Budget and Policy Priorities, the organization that put together this graph, and decide whether the CBPP can be trusted as a source. Report your findings.

5. Run a Web search to find other graphs of income disparity, and compare the CBPP graph with others that you find. Are they all conveying the same story? Discuss the similarities and differences you find.

6. Billionaire investor Warren Buffett is ensconced near the top of the top 1 percent on this graph. Judging from his op-ed piece "Stop Coddling the Super-Rich" (p. 227), what might be Buffett's reactions to a graph like this one?

Inequality and (Un)happiness in America

Arthur C. Brooks

Here, a conservative thinker asks us not to redistribute income (through taxation, for example) until we take a harder look at the connection between income inequality and happiness. He sees inequality as a false issue concealing a real one.

Arthur C. Brooks was the Louis A. Bantle Professor of Business and Government Policy at Syracuse University until 2009. Currently, he serves as president of the American Enterprise Institute. In his younger days, he spent 12 years as a professional musician, playing the French horn with the City Orchestra of Barcelona and other groups.

The United States is a rich nation and is getting richer. According to the U.S. Census Bureau, over the decade ending in 2003 the top quintile of earners in America experienced an average inflation-adjusted income increase of 22 percent. But prosperity didn't end with the top earners. The middle quintile saw an average 17 percent real increase, while the bottom quintile enjoyed a 13 percent rise. In the thirty years leading up to 2003, earners in the top quintile saw their real incomes increase by two-thirds, versus a quarter for those in the middle quintile and a fifth among the bottom earners.[1]

This may seem like reason to celebrate — even if money doesn't buy happiness. Yet, some find within these numbers something to regret: the fact that the rich are getting richer much faster than the poor are getting richer. Income inequality in the United States is rising, according to most responsible estimates. For example, in 1973, the average family in the top quintile earned about ten times what the average bottom-quintile family earned. By 2003, this differential had grown to fifteen times. The U.S. Census Bureau measures economic inequality using what is called a Gini coefficient, in which 0 indicates no inequality (all incomes are the same) and 1 is perfect inequality (one person has all the income). Over the past four decades, the American Gini coefficient has increased by nearly a third, from 0.36 in

---

[1] The figures in this section come from the U.S. Census Historical Income tables. Inflation is neutralized with the chain-weighted price index from the *Statistical Abstract of the United States* (Washington, D.C.: Government Printing Office, various years). While looking at income quintiles is conventional, breaking up income groups using other cut points produces the same conclusions.

1965 to 0.44 in 2005. In European countries, the coefficients generally hover below 0.30, indicating much more economic equality than we see in the United States.[2]

Liberal politicians have placed special emphasis on the fact that economic inequality in America is rising. In particular, North Carolina Senator John Edwards, who rose to prominence when he sought the Democratic nomination for president in 2004 and again in 2008, has based his campaigns almost entirely on the idea that we are "two Americas" — rich America and poor America. In his own words: "Today, under George W. Bush, there are two Americas, not one: One America that does the work, another America that reaps the reward. One America that pays the taxes, another America that gets the tax breaks. One America that will do anything to leave its children a better life, another America that never has to do a thing because its children are already set for life. . . . One America that is struggling to get by, another America that can buy anything it wants, even a Congress and a President."[3]

Edwards must believe that economic inequality is a source of unhappiness to lots of Americans, or he wouldn't use it as his principal campaign theme. Other politicians agree with him. Democratic Senator Barack Obama complained that "the average CEO now earns more in one day than an average worker earns in an entire year." Democratic Senator Hillary Clinton characterized today's economy as "trickle-down economics without the trickle." She declared that a progressive era is at hand because of "rising inequality and rising pessimism in our work force."[4]

But it is not just the Democrats who worry about income inequality in America. Indeed, 2008 Republican presidential contender Mike Huckabee has decried the widening gap as strenuously as any liberal. Conservative populists such as Huckabee are as alarmed as any on the left about the vast fortunes earned by the lucky few in America and the unhappiness it supposedly causes for those who remain behind. 5

---

[2] James A. Davis, Tom W. Smith, and Peter V. Marsden, principal investigators, *General Social Surveys, 1972–2004* [machine-readable data file] (Chicago: National Opinion Research Center [producer]; Storrs, Conn.: The Roper Center for Public Opinion Research, University of Connecticut [distributor], 2004); U.S. Census Bureau, http://www.census.gov/hhes/www/income/histinc/f04.html.

[3] The quote by John Edwards comes from a speech he delivered on December 29, 2003, in Des Moines, Iowa. See http://www.gazetteonline.com/iowacaucus/candidate_news/edwards64.aspx.

[4] Arthur C. Brooks, "The Left's 'Inequality' Obsession," *Wall Street Journal*, July 19, 2007, p. A16.

Many intellectuals and scholars have built whole careers around the subject of income inequality. It is practically an academic article of faith that inequality per se is socially destructive and should be avoided wherever and whenever possible. The prevailing view is that the fairest, least envious societies — that is, the *happiest* societies — are the most economically equal ones. And thus, if we want a happier citizenry, we need less economic inequality.

Perhaps they're right — after all, equality appears side by side with happiness in the U.S. Declaration of Independence: "We hold these truths to be self-evident, that all men are created equal, that they are endowed by their Creator with certain unalienable Rights, that among these are Life, Liberty and the pursuit of Happiness." To be sure, most people understand this sentence as referring to political equality, or equality before the law. But a loose interpretation that includes income equality doesn't necessarily make someone a utopian leftist.

> There are good reasons to question the supposed link between inequality and unhappiness.

But there are good reasons to question the supposed link between inequality and unhappiness. For one thing, the prevailing intellectual view on inequality doesn't seem to match the views expressed by most normal, nonacademic folks. Although some ordinary people of my acquaintance might complain about the enormous compensation of CEOs, I rarely have heard them express any shock or outrage at the great wealth of America's richest people: successful entrepreneurs. On the contrary, they say they hope their *kids* might become the next Bill Gates or Warren Buffett. Most people I know actually admire those successful folks and don't begrudge them their success.

More convincing than my personal experiences are the data showing no link at all between rising inequality and unhappiness. If inequality were so depressing for us, we would expect to see American happiness falling. Yet average happiness has *not* fallen. Remember that, in 1972, 30 percent of the population said they were very happy with their lives. In 1982, 31 percent reported this level of happiness; in 1993, 32 percent; and in 2004, 31 percent. This total lack of significant change in average reported happiness occurred over the same period in which income inequality increased by nearly half. Statistically, income inequality does not explain any of the fluctuations in happiness or unhappiness over the past three decades.[5]

---

[5] GSS 1972–2004; *Statistical Abstract of the United States* (various years).

Nor does income inequality explain happiness differences between 10
American communities. Looking at 30,000 households in forty-nine
American communities in 2000, we see that the variation between
income levels in communities explained nothing about how many
people in each stated that they were very happy. Take two very different communities: the Latino community in Cleveland, Ohio, and the
city of Boulder, Colorado. Boulder is characterized by far higher income
inequality than Cleveland's Hispanic community, yet its citizens are
more than twice as likely — 45 percent versus 18 percent — to say they
are very happy. Income inequality does not lie anywhere behind this
happiness gap.[6]

So is this inequality bad for our nation's happiness, or not? Despite
all the rhetoric from populist politicians and egalitarian academics, a
good hard look at the best available data tells us that, in fact, inequality does *not* cause unhappiness in America. And efforts to diminish
economic inequality — without creating economic opportunity — will
actually lower America's gross national happiness, not raise it.

* * *

If you ask an American whether we have "too much inequality" in our
society, you are about as likely to hear "yes" as "no." In 2005, 55 percent
of U.S. adults believed that income differences in our society were too
large. Forty-nine percent thought income inequality was a "serious
problem." And 53 percent thought the government should "do more to
try to reduce income inequality." Taken on its face, as politicians and
some scholars do, this is a major public concern and one worth addressing, even if these percentages are nowhere near as high as the concern
expressed about other issues such as crime, education, and national
security.[7]

There are several common explanations for the consternation that
many Americans evidently feel about economic inequality. The most
common is a concern for basic *fairness*. No matter how much you may

---

[6] *Social Capital Community Benchmark Survey* (SCCBS) [machine-readable data file]
(Cambridge, Mass.: Saguaro Seminar at the John F. Kennedy School of Government,
Harvard University [producer]; Storrs, Conn.: The Roper Center for Public Opinion
Research, University of Connecticut [distributor], 2000). I regressed the percentage saying
in each family that they were "very happy" on the income variance in each community as
well as on the mean income level in each community. The coefficient on the variance was
insignificant; the mean income level, in contrast, was significant, at the 10 percent level.
[7] Campbell Public Affairs Institute, The Maxwell Poll on Civic Engagement and Inequality
[dataset] (Syracuse, N.Y.: Maxwell School of Citizenship and Public Affairs, 2006).

study or how hard you may work, some believe it is simply unfair for you to be rich while others lack basic health care or worry about making their rent. In fact, even if others don't lack these basics, some say, the obscene income differences in the United States are unfair because they simply *cannot* be attributed to merit differences. Bill Gates has a net worth that is hundreds of thousands of times higher than mine, and millions of times higher than that of many poor Americans. Is Bill Gates really 250,000 times more productive than I am? Is he a million times more productive than the average lower-middle-class fifty-year-old? If he is not, some believe, the income and wealth differences between us are not legitimate. They are immoral. They make us unhappy, if we have any conscience at all.[8]

Perceived unfairness can lead to envy. Envy used to be condemned as a sin; today it is dignified in policy proposals. One prominent British economist — in a book entitled *Happiness* — argued that we should tax higher-earning individuals not just to get their money for public services, or even to redistribute it to those who have less, but because in earning a lot these individuals make others feel bad. This is an extraordinary argument for lowering the incentives for higher earners to work. It runs contrary to millennia of moral teaching that valued hard work and actually compares it instead to a destructive vice like tobacco, which we tax or otherwise penalize in order to curtail an undesirable behavior.[9]

Such arguments may sound dubious to you, but history suggests 15
that too much envy can be a dangerous thing. Plutocrats and oligarchs throughout history have found out the hard way that the envy of the masses can cost you your head. Income inequality during the Industrial Revolution is a conventional explanation for the rise and flourishing of communism. Roman emperors coined the term "bread and circuses" to signify the policy of giving free grain and entertainment to the poor masses in order to avoid social strife, and there is an ancient Chinese saying that states the problem succinctly: "Inequality,

---

[8] According to the U.S. Basic Income Guarantee Network, a group of academics dedicated to achieving greater income equality in America, "equal citizenship is the overriding justification for moving along a path of decreasing income inequality among all persons." U.S. Basic Income Guarantee Network, "Unequal Income Is Unequal Citizenship: The Case against Income Inequality," USBIG Discussion Paper No. 67, 2004.

[9] This economist, Richard Layard, wrote: "If we make taxes commensurate to the damage that an individual does to others when he earns more, then he will only work harder if there is a true net benefit to society as a whole. It is efficient to discourage work effort that makes society worse off." Richard Layard, *Happiness: Lessons from a New Science* (New York: Penguin Press, 2005), p. 228.

rather than want, is the cause of trouble." Some today reach the conclusion that equalizing income a bit would be a smart investment to placate the less fortunate.

Academics argue against income inequality in a slightly more sophisticated way than simply complaining that it isn't fair. They assert, instead, that it is inefficient, advocating income equalization on the belief that transferring money from the rich to poor people hurts the rich less than it helps the poor. This argument relies on what economists call "diminishing marginal utility," which works something like this: Imagine you have two bowls of ice cream and I have none. You eat both and don't share. The first bowl gives you 10 units of happiness, while the second — still tasty but not as delicious as the first, because the first *always* tastes best — gives you 5 units. I get 0 units — or maybe even negative happiness as I sit and watch you enviously. Together, we have 15 units of happiness, at best. Now imagine that you give me your second bowl (or we pass a law taking it away from you). Assuming you and I have the same preferences, our total happiness will be 10 plus 10, or a total of 20 units. According to this logic, equalizing income, like equalizing ice cream, will increase our gross national happiness.

There are lots of problems with this concept as a guide to policy. It might be expensive to redistribute income. If we care about liberty, taking from the earner by force might do disproportionate harm to our society's happiness. And probably most importantly (and in fact a demonstrable truth — more on this later), I might gain far less happiness from getting *your* money than I would from earning money myself. Still, despite these issues, for many, especially political liberals, the concept of diminishing marginal utility justifies income redistribution to rectify income inequality.

Another academic argument against income inequality concerns public health. Some social scientists claim there is an association between bad health outcomes (such as shorter average life spans) and high levels of income inequality. Some have interpreted this association as evidence that inequality *causes* poor health. The implications of this hypothesis can be quite radical. Free markets tend to emphasize the productivity differences between individuals by connecting them to differences in pay. Some believe that the result of this is ill health. In other words, capitalism leads to inequality, inequality makes us sick, and thus unhappy.[10]

---

[10] Vicente Navarro, *The Political Economy of Social Inequalities: Consequences for Health and Quality of Life* (Amityville, N.Y.: Baywood, 2000).

In sum, in an effort to explain why income inequality brings unhappiness, some argue that it is unfair, inefficient, and maybe even unhealthy. Each of these arguments is problematic. But there's one big reason to reject all of them: The evidence shows that it isn't income inequality that leads to unhappiness at all, but something else entirely.

• • •

About half of all American adults think economic inequality is a major   20
problem, and about half of them do not. Do these two groups differ in some way that might explain the contrasting attitudes? As it turns out, their opinions cannot be explained by income, class, race, or education. Instead, what best predicts an individual's views on income inequality is his or her beliefs about income *mobility* — that is, about whether Americans have opportunities to get ahead economically. And it is these beliefs about mobility, not beliefs about income inequality, that lie directly behind much happiness and unhappiness. Those who believe that they and other Americans can get ahead with hard work and perseverance — that America offers paths to success — are generally happy and unfazed by economic inequality. Those who think that economic mobility in the United States is an illusion are relatively unhappy and tend to complain about income inequality.

In other words, some Americans are unhappy because they don't believe they have opportunities to succeed, but they complain about income inequality, as if this were the root cause of their problem. If our leaders focus on getting rid of income inequality, however, the underlying problem — lack of income mobility — will not improve, nor will happiness. (In fact, it will get worse, because the treatment for inequality exacerbates problems with mobility.) They are mistaking a symptom for a root cause.

People mistake symptoms for root causes all the time. If I am an alcoholic, my relationship with my spouse will probably suffer, and that will make me unhappy. I might complain about the bad relationship, even though my drinking is the real problem. I can work on the relationship all I want, but as long as I keep drinking, things probably won't get better. In fact, the longer I ignore the root cause, the worse it will get and the less likely I am to get back the happiness in my relationship.

And so it goes with inequality, immobility, and happiness. Let's look at the evidence.

First, feelings about mobility and inequality go together. Imagine you are asked the following question: "How much upward mobility — children doing better than the family they come from — do you think there is in America: a lot, some, or not much?" If you think there is not much upward mobility in America — you are not a big believer in American opportunity — you will be 46 percent more likely than people who believe there is a lot of mobility to say that income differences in our society are too large. In addition, you will be 63 percent more likely to say that income inequality is a "serious problem," and you will be 71 percent more likely to say that the government should do more to reduce inequality. Perceived immobility is what drives concern about income inequality, pure and simple.[11]

Or take the following statement: "While people may begin with different opportunities, hard work and perseverance can usually overcome those disadvantages." Imagine two people who are identical with respect to income, education, race, sex, religious participation, and family situation. The only difference is that the first person agrees with that statement, while the second disagrees. The optimist about work and perseverance will be 31 percentage points less likely than the pessimist to say inequality in America is too high. He will also be 39 points less likely to say that inequality is a big problem, and 32 points less likely to advocate for more government intervention to lower inequality. Note that this difference is *not* due to the fact that the optimist is more economically successful, better educated, or is of a different race than the pessimist — the two are identical in these ways. This is purely a difference in views about opportunity.[12]

This pessimism about opportunity is clearly linked to unhappiness. In 2004, 700 American adults were presented with a statement about opportunity and asked whether they agreed or disagreed. The statement was: "The way things are in America, people like me and my family have a good chance of improving our standard of living." Those who agreed were 44 percent more likely than those who disagreed to say they were very happy in life. The optimists were also 40 percent less likely than the pessimists to say they felt like they

25

---

[11] Maxwell Poll 2005.
[12] Ibid. These results are based on probit models in which the beliefs about inequality are regressed on beliefs about the importance of work and perseverance, as well as a vector of the demographics listed. The marginal coefficients are estimated at the mean values of the regressors.

were "no good at all" at times, and they were 20 percent less likely to say they felt like a failure.[13]

. . . The fact that Bill Gates is so rich probably raises the happiness of America's optimists, because it demonstrates to them what somebody can do with hard work, good ideas, great luck, and a system that protects free enterprise. Gates is not a duke or a prince; there is no evidence that God especially likes him. He simply had a lot of opportunities and made the most of them.[14]

In contrast, it is depressing to think that no matter how hard you work or how clever you are, you can never get ahead. This is why, when people feel there is a lack of opportunity to advance at their workplace, they often quit their jobs. Indeed, 70 percent of those who say their chances for promotion are good are very satisfied with their jobs, versus just 42 percent who say their chances for promotion are not good. We need clear paths to success, not guarantees of income equality, to be happy. Guarantees of equality actually take us in the wrong direction.[15]

The true relationship between mobility and happiness explains why happiness levels in America have not fallen over time, even though income inequality has risen. Unequal as it is, economically speaking, America is still a happy land of opportunity.

---

[13] 2004 GSS.

[14] Andrew E. Clark, "Inequality-Aversion and Income Mobility: A Direct Test," Centre National de la Recherche Scientifique (CNRS) and Department and Laboratory of Applied and Theoretical Economics (DELTA)–Fédération Jourdan Working Paper 2003–11 (2003); Claudia Senik, "What Can We Learn from Subjective Data? The Case of Income and Well-Being," CNRS and DELTA–Fédération Jourdan Working Paper 2003–06 (2003).

[15] 2002 GSS.

Understanding the Text

1. Why does Arthur Brooks put parentheses around "Un" in the word "Unhappiness" in his title?

2. It takes eight paragraphs to get to the thesis of this piece. Did that seem too long to you, or did Brooks effectively keep you interested through suspense? What methods of suspense does he employ?

   Have you ever written a paper with suspense in mind, or have you left suspense exclusively to fiction writers? What assumptions about fiction and nonfiction are reflected in your answer?

Reflection and Response

3. Brooks includes several types of evidence in his argument: statistics (which he spreads throughout), individual cases (Bill Gates, etc.), comparison (the ice cream analogy), and appeals to authority (like the Chinese saying). Do certain types of evidence carry more weight with you than others do? Explain.

4. Has Brooks succeeded in convincing you? Why or why not?

5. Which forms of equality do you personally think should be guaranteed?
   _____ equal access to the best health care
   _____ equally good housing
   _____ equal pay
   _____ equal say in decisions of the government
   _____ equal access to the best education
   _____ equally effective protection from crime
   _____ equally long vacations
   _____ other:
   _____ none of the above

   What rationale underlies your responses? That is, what's your *philosophical basis* for supporting certain forms of equality and not others?

Making Connections

6. Of the different authors you've encountered in this book, who is most likely to want to take Brooks on and to refute his argument? Explain.

7. About 175 years ago, a French aristocrat named Alexis de Tocqueville wrote a book based on his travels in the U.S. titled *Democracy in America* — perhaps the most insightful book published about our national psyche. In it, he, like Arthur Brooks, remarks how little we Americans seem to care about economic inequality. Look up Tocqueville's book to decide whether he and Brooks explain this American indifference on the subject in the same way.

The Fortune Teller

Georges de la Tour

The most direct means of redistributing wealth is to steal it. It may also be the oldest means. Every society has had to promulgate laws against theft — one of the Ten Commandments is just such a law. And, of course, police blotters around the world attest to the fact that thievery has never ceased, even for a day.

Take a close look at all parts of this painting (c. 1630) by Georges de la Tour, to ascertain everything going on in it. For a color version of this image, do a Web search using both the painting's title and the artist's name.

In 1638, La Tour was named "Painter to the King" in France.

Understanding the Text

1. How many types of theft are depicted in La Tour's painting? Explain.
2. Whose side is the artist on? Which aspects of the scene back up your answer?

Reflection and Response

3. Would the artist's attitude toward this scene have affected you if you hadn't stopped to ponder what it was? That is, would it have affected you subliminally?

   Some thinkers argue that subliminal effects of art and other media — film, TV, music, and the rest — are actually greater than effects we process consciously. Do you agree? What personal experience informs your answer?

4. What sort of fortune is the fortune teller probably dispensing on this occasion? Why would that be her choice?

Making Connections

5. If you are not familiar with the "Robin Hood" legend, research it. Do you imagine that museum goers who notice La Tour's painting enjoy it for much the same reason people have enjoyed the Robin Hood myth? Explain.

6. Are La Tour's sympathies in line with Horatio Alger's (p. 121)? What makes you say so?

The First Tractor
and *Night of the Rich*
Diego Rivera

In *The First Tractor* (undated), Mexican painter and muralist Diego Rivera depicts a farm family contemplating — and perhaps marveling at — the first substantial piece of technology it has been able to afford. In his *Night of the Rich* (1928), by contrast, Rivera portrays two groups: people for whom money is no object and the bullet-laden revolutionaries who take note of their behavior.

Of the well-known artists of the past century, Rivera was among the most political. Famously, he accepted a commission to create a large mural at Rockefeller Center in New York City, only to see it destroyed when the Rockefeller family discovered it included a favorable likeness of the leader of the Russian Revolution of 1917, Vladimir Lenin.

The First Tractor

Night of the Rich

Understanding the Text

1. By what means does Rivera incline us to view the family in *The First Tractor* sympathetically?

   By what means does he assure that we are going to view the figures fore-grounded in *Night of the Rich* unsympathetically?

2. Does Rivera feel that his revolutionaries at the top of *Night of the Rich* would be justified to use their guns to redistribute wealth in Mexico? Explain.

Reflection and Response

3. How do you react to the suggestion that one social class is more virtuous than another? Please elaborate with experiences that you've had or know about, as well as with details from these paintings.

4. Where would you expect to see paintings like Rivera's hanging? What locations would, in your opinion, be inappropriate for them? Why?

Making Connections

5. How does Rivera's depiction of virtue and depravity in the different social strata compare with . . .

   • Georges de la Tour's in the painting *The Fortune Teller* (p. 222)?

   • Toni Cade Bambara's in the story "The Lesson" (p. 195)?

6. Drawing from Rivera's and La Tour's paintings — and from Bambara's story — consider and discuss this question: "Does an artist or writer whose aim is to move others to take political action need to simplify reality, to some degree?"

Stop Coddling the Super-Rich

Warren Buffett

In our society, the most consequential way of spreading wealth around may be taxation. Think, for instance, of Americans' equal access to public education, which is funded by taxes. Think of programs that serve only poor people, like Food Stamps and Medicaid.

On August 14, 2011, in the middle of a national debate on whether to eliminate tax breaks enjoyed by the wealthiest Americans, the *New York Times* published this opinion piece by Warren Buffett.

Legendary as an investor (he was the wealthiest person in the world in 2008), Buffett is known also for his philanthropy. He has pledged to give away 99 percent of his fortune, mainly through the Bill and Melinda Gates Foundation.

Our leaders have asked for "shared sacrifice." But when they did the asking, they spared me. I checked with my mega-rich friends to learn what pain they were expecting. They, too, were left untouched.

> Our leaders have asked for "shared sacrifice." But when they did the asking, they spared me.

While the poor and middle class fight for us in Afghanistan, and while most Americans struggle to make ends meet, we mega-rich continue to get our extraordinary tax breaks. Some of us are investment managers who earn billions from our daily labors but are allowed to classify our income as "carried interest," thereby getting a bargain 15 percent tax rate. Others own stock index futures for 10 minutes and have 60 percent of their gain taxed at 15 percent, as if they'd been long-term investors.

These and other blessings are showered upon us by legislators in Washington who feel compelled to protect us, much as if we were spotted owls or some other endangered species. It's nice to have friends in high places.

Last year my federal tax bill — the income tax I paid, as well as payroll taxes paid by me and on my behalf — was $6,938,744. That sounds like a lot of money. But what I paid was only 17.4 percent of my taxable income — and that's actually a lower percentage than was paid by any of the other 20 people in our office. Their tax burdens ranged from 33 percent to 41 percent and averaged 36 percent.

If you make money with money, as some of my super-rich friends do, your percentage may be a bit lower than mine. But if you earn money from a job, your percentage will surely exceed mine — most likely by a lot.

. . . Back in the 1980s and 1990s, tax rates for the rich were far higher, and my percentage rate was in the middle of the pack. According to a theory I sometimes hear, I should have thrown a fit and refused to invest because of the elevated tax rates on capital gains and dividends.

I didn't refuse, nor did others. I have worked with investors for 60 years and I have yet to see anyone — not even when capital gains rates were 39.9 percent in 1976–77 — shy away from a sensible investment because of the tax rate on the potential gain. People invest to make money, and potential taxes have never scared them off. And to those who argue that higher rates hurt job creation, I would note that a net of nearly 40 million jobs were added between 1980 and 2000. You know what's happened since then: lower tax rates and far lower job creation.

Since 1992, the I.R.S. has compiled data from the returns of the 400 Americans reporting the largest income. In 1992, the top 400 had aggregate taxable income of $16.9 billion and paid federal taxes of 29.2 percent on that sum. In 2008, the aggregate income of the highest 400 had soared to $90.9 billion — a staggering $227.4 million on average — but the rate paid had fallen to 21.5 percent.

. . . I know well many of the mega-rich and, by and large, they are very decent people. They love America and appreciate the opportunity this country has given them. Many have joined the Giving Pledge, promising to give most of their wealth to philanthropy. Most wouldn't mind being told to pay more in taxes as well, particularly when so many of their fellow citizens are truly suffering.

Twelve members of Congress will soon take on the crucial job of 10 rearranging our country's finances. They've been instructed to devise a plan that reduces the 10-year deficit by at least $1.5 trillion. It's vital, however, that they achieve far more than that. Americans are rapidly losing faith in the ability of Congress to deal with our country's fiscal problems. Only action that is immediate, real and very substantial will prevent that doubt from morphing into hopelessness. That feeling can create its own reality.

Job one for the 12 is to pare down some future promises that even a rich America can't fulfill. Big money must be saved here. The 12 should then turn to the issue of revenues. I would leave rates for 99.7 percent of taxpayers unchanged and continue the current 2-percentage-point reduction in the employee contribution to the payroll tax. This cut helps the poor and the middle class, who need every break they can get.

But for those making more than $1 million — there were 236,883 such households in 2009 — I would raise rates immediately on taxable income in excess of $1 million, including, of course, dividends and capital gains. And for those who make $10 million or more — there were 8,274 in 2009 — I would suggest an additional increase in rate.

My friends and I have been coddled long enough by a billionaire-friendly Congress. It's time for our government to get serious about shared sacrifice.

Understanding the Text

1. How would you summarize Buffett's argument?

2. Below are two excerpts from interviews that Buffett has given over the years. Do they help to clarify where he's coming from, philosophically, in "Stop Coddling the Super-Rich"?

> I personally think that society is responsible for a very significant percentage of what I've earned. If you stick me down in the middle of Bangladesh or Peru or someplace, you'll find out how [little] this talent [of mine] is going to produce in the wrong kind of soil. I will be struggling thirty years later.

> I work in a market system that happens to reward what I do very well — disproportionately well. [Heavyweight boxing champion] Mike Tyson, too. If you can knock a guy out in ten seconds . . . this world will pay [you] a lot for that. If you can bat .360, the world will pay a lot for that. If you're a marvelous teacher, this world won't pay a lot for it. If you are a terrific nurse, this world will not pay a lot for it.

> • • •

> If I wanted to, [with the money I have] I could hire ten thousand people to do nothing but paint my picture every day for the rest of my life. And the GNP [the nation's Gross National Product] would go up. But the utility of the product would be zilch, and I would be keeping those ten thousand people from doing AIDS research, or teaching, or nursing.

Write a paper that draws both on "Stop Coddling the Super-Rich" and on the quotes above.

Reflection and Response

3. If you had Buffett's wealth, would you hold his views, as expressed in this selection? Why or why not?

Making Connections

4. Buffett coined the phrase "ovarian lottery." Based on what you've read of him here, what do you imagine it means? Why? Research the phrase to see if you're correct.

5. Running for the U.S. Senate in 2011, Elizabeth Warren (author of "The Vanishing Middle Class," p. 64) said,

> There is nobody in this country who got rich on his own — nobody.

> You built a factory out there? Good for you. But I want to be clear. You moved your goods to market on the roads the rest of us paid for. You hired workers the rest of us paid to educate. You were safe in your factory because of police forces and fire forces that the rest of us paid for. You didn't have to worry that marauding bands would come and seize everything at your factory — and [have to] hire someone to protect against this — because of the work the rest of us did.

> Now look, you built a factory and it turned into something terrific, or a great idea. God bless — keep a big hunk of it. But part of the underlying social contract is, you take a hunk of that and pay forward for the next kid who comes along.

How close a fit are these sentiments with Buffett's?

6. Read Milton Friedman's "The Responsibility of Business Is to Increase Its Profits" (p. 157) — but, as you do so, mark it in the way Warren Buffett might, if he were reading it. Which ideas of Friedman's might Buffett agree with, and which would he object to? Why?

From Mishneh Torah

Maimonides

Still another common means of wealth redistribution is charity. This rank-ordering of all the forms of charity — from the highest kind to the lowest — goes back 800 years. Maimonides, the person who formulated it, is widely regarded as the greatest Jewish thinker of medieval times. He wrote about Jewish law in his 14-volume *Mishneh Torah* and about ways to reconcile secular and sacred knowledge in his *Guide for the Perplexed.*

There are eight degrees in alms-giving, one lower than the other. Supreme above all is to give assistance to a fellowman who has fallen on evil

> There are eight degrees in alms-giving, one lower than the other.

times by presenting him with a gift or loan, or entering into a partnership with him, or procuring him work, thereby helping him to become self-supporting. Next best is giving alms in such a way that the giver and recipient are unknown to each other. This is, indeed, the performance of a commandment from disinterested motives; and it is exemplified, by the Institution of the Chamber of the Silent which existed in the Temple, where the righteous secretly deposited their alms and the respectable poor were secretly assisted.

Next in order is the donation of money to the charity fund of the Community, to which no contribution should be made unless there is confidence that the administration is honest, prudent, and efficient.

Below this degree is the instance where the donor is aware to whom he is giving the alms, but the recipient is unaware from whom he received them. The great Sages, for example, used to go about secretly throwing money through the doors of the poor. This is quite a proper course to adopt and a great virtue where the administrators of a charity fund are not acting fairly.

Inferior to this degree is the case where the recipient knows the identity of the donor, but not vice versa. For example, the great Sages would sometimes tie sums of money in linen bundles and throw them behind their backs for poor men to pick up, so that they should not feel shame.

The next four degrees in their order are: the man who gives money 5 to the poor before he is asked; the man who gives money to the poor after he is asked; the man who gives less than he should, but does it with good grace; and lastly, he who gives grudgingly.

Understanding the Text

1. A question posed by a student: Is Maimonides' rank-ordering based on how the different kinds of charity affect the giver differently, or on how they affect the recipient differently?

2. What unspoken principles lie behind this rank-ordering? That is, what big assumptions about life and human nature does Maimonides seem to be making here? In addressing this question, be sure to account for the placement of all eight "degrees" of charity. The principle that accounts for the placement of some of them may not account for the placement of all of them.

Reflection and Response

3. Can you think of instances, real or hypothetical, in which a person *shouldn't* follow these guidelines? Explain.

4. Maimonides's rank-ordering does not address the issue of amount: How *much* of one's own income should a person give to charity? What might be a reasonable answer to that question? Why?

Making Connections

5. Generate a list of 10 acts of charity (such as giving spare change to a homeless person on the street) and charitable programs (such as the Red Cross, the Special Olympics, or Amnesty International). Where does each act or program fit on Maimonides's spectrum? In each case, explain.

6. In 2006, Muhammad Yunus received the Nobel Peace Prize for pioneering microcredit, a new banking concept that allowed people who had no collateral — very poor people — to obtain small loans and go into business for themselves. Already, millions of the poor in different countries have had their standards of living improved as a result.

   With the help of your librarian or a Web search engine, find a fuller definition of microcredit. Put what you discover about it into your own words. Where does granting microcredit fit on Maimonides' spectrum? Explain.

7. The kind of charity advocated by Peter Singer in "Rich and Poor" (p. 233) is not at the high end of Maimonides's scale. How might Singer defend his position to Maimonides?

Rich and Poor

Peter Singer

Of all the pieces in this book, Peter Singer's "Rich and Poor" may be the one that most unsettles readers. In it, Singer argues that affluent people who don't give sums of money to prevent starvation in the world are committing a sophisticated form of murder. He also tries to explain why most of us refuse to see the situation that way.

Singer has taught bioethics at Princeton University and written on a variety of controversial ethical issues, such as euthanasia. His book *Animal Liberation* is a text of great importance in the animal rights movement.

Some Facts about Poverty

At the end of the twentieth century, the World Bank sent out a team of researchers to record the views of 60,000 women and men living in extreme poverty. Visiting seventy-three countries, the research team heard, over and over, that poverty meant these things:

- You are short of food for all or part of the year, often eating only one meal per day, sometimes having to choose between stilling your child's hunger or your own, and sometimes being able to do neither.

- You can't save money. If a family member falls ill and you need money to see a doctor, or if the crop fails and you have nothing to eat, you have to borrow from a local moneylender; he will charge you so much interest that the debt continues to mount, and you may never be free of it.

- You can't afford to send your children to school; or if they do start school, you have to take them out again if the harvest is poor.

- You live in an unstable house, made with mud or thatch that you need to rebuild every two or three years, or after severe weather.

- You have no close source of safe drinking water. You have to carry it a long way, and even then, it can make you ill unless you boil it.

Along with these material deprivations goes, very often, a humiliating state of powerlessness, vulnerability and a deep sense of shame or failure.

Extreme poverty, as defined by the World Bank, means not having enough income to meet the most basic human needs for adequate food, water, shelter, clothing, sanitation, health care or education. In 2008, the Bank calculated that this requires a daily income that is the purchasing power equivalent of about US$1.25 per day in the United States. This is not the foreign exchange equivalent of US$1.25, which might not be so bad, because as everyone who travels from a rich country to a poor one knows, the currencies of rich countries often have much greater purchasing power in poor countries. The World Bank's definition takes that difference into account: the poor earn only as much as will buy, in their currency, the quantity of necessities that $1.25 will buy in the United States. The bank estimates that 1.4 billion people have less income than this.

In industrialized countries, people are poor by comparison to others in their society. Their poverty is relative — they have enough to meet their basic needs and usually access to free health care as well. The 1.4 billion people living in extreme poverty in developing countries are poor by an absolute standard: they have difficulty meeting their basic needs. Absolute poverty kills. According to UNICEF, the United Nations International Children's Emergency Fund, 8.8 million children under five years old died from avoidable, poverty-related causes in 2008. That comes to 24,000 — think of it as a football stadium full of children — dying unnecessarily every day. (The number of children dying has been falling steadily since the 1960s but still remains far too high.) Millions of adults also die because of absolute poverty. Life expectancy in the rich nations is now seventy-eight years; in developing countries, it is around fifty. When absolute poverty does not cause death, it still causes misery of a kind not often seen in the affluent nations. Malnutrition in young children stunts both physical and mental development. Millions of people on poor diets suffer from deficiency diseases, like goiter, or blindness caused by a lack of vitamin A. The food value of what the poor eat is further reduced by parasites such as hookworm and ringworm, which are endemic in conditions of poor sanitation and health education.

Death and disease apart, absolute poverty remains a miserable con- 5 dition of life, with inadequate food, shelter, clothing, sanitation, health services and education. This is the "normal" situation of our world. At least ten times as many people died from preventable, poverty-related diseases on September 11, 2001, as died in the terrorist attacks on the World Trade Center and the Pentagon on that black day. The terrorist attacks led to trillions of dollars being spent on the "war on terrorism" and on security measures that have inconvenienced every air traveller since then. The deaths caused by poverty were ignored. So whereas very few people have died from terrorism since September 11, 2001, approximately 30,000 people died from poverty-related causes on September 12, 2001, and on every day between then and now, and will die tomorrow. Even when we consider larger events, like the Asian tsunami of 2004, which killed approximately 230,000 people, or the 2010 earthquake in Haiti that killed up to 200,000, we are still talking about numbers that represent just one week's toll for preventable, poverty-related deaths — and that happens fifty-two weeks in every year.

Some Facts about Affluence

We can juxtapose a picture of "absolute affluence" against this picture of absolute poverty. Those who are absolutely affluent are not necessarily affluent by comparison with their neighbors, but they have more income than they need to provide themselves adequately with all the basic necessities of life. After buying (either directly or through their taxes) food, shelter, clothing, basic health services and education, the absolutely affluent still have money to spend on luxuries. The absolutely affluent choose their food for the pleasures of the palate, not to stop hunger; they buy new clothes to look good, not to keep warm; they move house to be in a better neighborhood or have more space for the children to play, not to keep out the rain; and after all this, there is still money to spend on home entertainment centers and exotic holidays.

At this stage, I am making no ethical judgments about absolute affluence; I am merely pointing out that it exists. Its defining characteristic is a significant amount of income above the level necessary to provide for the basic human needs of oneself and one's dependents. By this standard, the majority of citizens of Europe, North America, Japan, Australia, New Zealand and the oil-rich Middle Eastern states are all absolutely affluent. There are also hundreds of millions of affluent people in countries like China, India and Brazil, although there is also extreme poverty in those countries. These affluent people have wealth that they could, without threatening their own basic welfare, transfer to the extremely poor.

At present, very little is being transferred. In 1970, the United Nations General Assembly set a modest target for the amount of foreign aid that the rich nations should give: 0.7 percent of Gross National Income, or 70 cents for every hundred dollars a nation earns. Forty years later, only Denmark, Luxembourg, The Netherlands, Norway and

Sweden have reached that level. In 2008, the United States and Japan, the two largest economies among the affluent nations, gave only 0.19 percent, or 19 cents in every $100 they earned. Australia and Canada did only slightly better, at 0.32 percent, whereas France, Germany and Britain were around the average for affluent nations, giving between 0.38 and 0.43 percent. In comparison to their income, what the rich nations are giving is relatively trivial.

The Moral Equivalent of Murder?

These facts suggest that, by giving far less than they could, rich people are allowing more than a billion people to continue to live in conditions of deprivation and to die prematurely. This conclusion applies not only to governments but to each affluent individual, for each of us has the opportunity to do something about the situation; for instance, to give our time or money to voluntary organizations that are helping to provide health care, safe drinking water, education and better agricultural techniques for the poor. If, then, allowing someone to die is not intrinsically different from killing someone, it would seem that we are all murderers.

Is this verdict too harsh? Many will 10 reject it as self-evidently absurd. They would sooner take it as showing that allowing to die cannot be equivalent to killing than as showing that living in an affluent style without contributing to an aid agency is ethically equivalent to going over to Ethiopia and shooting a few peasants. They point to several significant differences between spending money on luxuries, when we could use it to save lives, and deliberately shooting people. Let us look at some of these differences and then consider which of them really are morally significant.

First, the motivation will normally be different. Those who deliberately shoot others go out of their way to kill. Motivated by malice, sadism or some equally unpleasant motives, they want their victims dead. A person who buys an iPod presumably wants to enhance her enjoyment of music — not in itself a terrible thing. At worst, spending money on luxuries instead of giving it away indicates selfishness and indifference to the sufferings of others, characteristics that may be undesirable but are not comparable to actual malice or similar motives.

Second, it is not difficult for most of us to act in accordance with a rule against killing people: it is, on the other hand, very difficult to obey a rule that commands us to save all the lives we can. To live a comfortable or even luxurious life, it is not necessary to kill anyone, but we do have to allow to die some whom we might have saved, for the money that we need to live comfortably could have been given away. Thus, the duty to avoid killing is much easier to discharge completely than the duty to save. Saving every life we possibly could save would mean cutting our standard of living down to the bare essentials needed to keep us alive.[1] To discharge this duty completely would require a degree of moral heroism utterly different from that required by mere avoidance of killing.

A third difference is the greater certainty of the outcome of shooting when compared with not giving aid. If I point a loaded gun at someone at close range and pull the trigger, it is virtually certain that the person will be killed; whereas the money that I could give might be spent on a project that turns out to be unsuccessful and helps no one.

Fourth, when people are shot, there are identifiable individuals who have been harmed. We can point to them and to their grieving families. When I buy my iPod, I cannot know who my money would have saved if I had given it away.

Fifth, it might be said that the plight of the hungry is not my doing, and so I cannot be held responsible for it. The starving would have been starving if I had never existed. If I kill, however, I am responsible for my victims' deaths, for those people would not have died if I had not killed them.

These differences need not shake our previous conclusion that there is no intrinsic difference between killing and allowing to die. They are extrinsic differences, that is, differences normally but not necessarily associated with the distinction between killing and allowing to die. We can imagine cases in which someone allows another to die for malicious or sadistic reasons. We can imagine a world in which there are so few people needing assistance and they are so easy to assist, that our duty not to allow people to die is as easily discharged as our duty not to kill. We can imagine situations in which the outcome of not helping is as sure as shooting. We can imagine cases in which we can identify the person we allow to die. We can even imagine a

15

---

[1] Strictly, we would need to cut down to the minimum level compatible with earning the income which after providing for our needs, left us most to give away. Thus, if my present position pays me $100,000 a year but requires me to spend $30,000 a year on living in a more expensive location than I otherwise might, I cannot save more people by moving to an inexpensive rural area if that will mean taking a job that pays only $60,000.

case of allowing to die in which, if I had not existed, the person would not have died — for instance, a case in which if I had not been in a position to help (though I didn't help), someone else would have been in my position and would have helped. These imaginary situations aside, however, it is true that the extrinsic differences that *normally* mark off killing and allowing to die help to explain why we *normally* regard killing as much worse than allowing to die. To explain our conventional ethical attitudes, however, is not to justify them. Do the five differences not only explain, but also justify, our attitudes? Let us consider them one by one.

(1) Take the lack of an identifiable victim first. Research has shown that people offered an opportunity to give to a poor child are more likely to give if they are shown a photograph of the child and told her name and age than if they are not given any identifying details. But this may show no more than that, during the millions of years in which our ancestors lived in small face-to-face groups, we developed an instinctive response to help individuals. In contrast, we did not develop any response to giving more anonymous forms of aid, for which there was no opportunity anyway. Should this make any difference to our ethical obligations? Suppose that I am a travelling salesperson, selling tinned food, and I learn that a batch of tins contains a contaminant, the known effect of which, when consumed, is to double the risk that the consumer will die from stomach cancer. Suppose I continue to sell the tins. My decision may have no identifiable victims. Some of those who eat the food will die from stomach cancer. The proportion of consumers dying in this way will be twice that of the community at large, but who among the consumers died because they ate what I sold, and who would have contracted the disease anyway? It is impossible to tell; but surely this impossibility makes my decision no less reprehensible than it would have been had the contaminant had more readily detectable, though equally fatal, effects. Moreover, if this is true for killing an unidentifiable individual, why should it be any different for failing to save one?

(2) The lack of certainty that by giving money I could save a life does reduce the wrongness of not giving, by comparison with deliberate killing; but it is insufficient to show that not giving is acceptable conduct. The motorist who speeds through pedestrian crossings, heedless of anyone who might be on them, is not a murderer. She may never actually hit a pedestrian; yet if she knowingly risks killing an innocent person, what she does is very wrong indeed.

(3) The idea that we are responsible for our acts but not for our omissions is more puzzling. On the one hand, we feel ourselves to be

under a greater obligation to help those whose misfortunes we have caused. (It is for this reason that advocates of increased foreign aid often argue that the rich nations have created the poverty of the poor nations, through forms of economic exploitation that go back to the colonial system.) On the other hand, any consequentialist would insist that we are responsible for all the consequences of our actions; and if a consequence of my spending money on an iPod is that someone dies, I am responsible for that death. It is true that the person would have died even if I had never existed, but what is the relevance of that? The fact is that I do exist, and the consequentialist will say that our responsibilities derive from the world as it is, not as it might have been.

One way of making sense of the non-consequentialist[2] view of responsibility is to base it on a theory of rights of the kind proposed by John Locke and more recently defended by libertarians like Robert Nozick and Jan Narveson.[3] If everyone has a right to life, and this right is a right *against* others who might threaten my life but not a right *to* assistance from others when my life is in danger, then we can understand the feeling that we are responsible for killing but not for omitting to save. The former violates the rights of others, the latter does not.

Should we accept such a theory of rights? If we build up our theory of rights by imagining, as Locke and Nozick do, individuals living independently from one another in a "state of nature," it may seem natural to adopt a conception of rights in which as long as each leaves the other alone, no rights are violated. I might, on this view, quite properly have maintained my independent existence if I had wished to do so. So if I do not make you any worse off than you would have been if I had had nothing at all to do with you, how can I have violated your rights? The factual basis of this theory is doubtful. Thomas Pogge challenges it in *World Poverty and Human Rights*, arguing that several features of the world economic order show that we contribute to the impoverishment of some people to our own benefit. To take just one example, we rely on oil and minerals bought from countries ruled by dictators who use the money to enrich themselves or to strengthen

20

---

[2] Consequentialists decide whether an action is ethical by evaluating its results, while non-consequentialists evaluate only the action itself, regardless of outcomes. For example, a non-consequentialist might say that lying is unethical no matter what, whereas a consequentialist might say that lying is ethically sound if it saves a person from harm or embarrassment. Singer is a consequentialist.

[3] These philosophers propose that humans have a set of "natural rights," generally including rights to life, liberty, and property.

their armies and entrench themselves in power. These dictators have no moral right to the wealth that lies beneath the soil of the countries in which they have seized power. The proceeds should go to the people of the country as a whole. The dictators are robbers and murderers, and we are receivers of stolen goods. Our willingness to hand over billions of dollars to dictators in return for oil and mineral rights also creates a huge incentive for anyone who fancies their chances of overthrowing an existing government, and thus increases instability in these countries, which in turn contributes to poverty.

Even if we put aside such problems with the factual basis of the libertarian argument, we need to ask why we should start from the unhistorical, abstract and ultimately inexplicable idea of a human being living independently. Our ancestors were — like other primates — social beings long before they were human beings, and they could not have developed the abilities and capacities of human beings if they had not been social beings first. We are not, now, isolated individuals, and we never have been. So why should we assume that rights must be restricted to rights against interference? We might, instead, adopt the view that taking rights to life seriously is incompatible with standing by and watching people die when one could easily save them.

(4) What of the difference in motivation? That a person does not positively wish for the death of another lessens the severity of the blame she deserves, but not by as much as is suggested by our present attitudes to giving aid. The behavior of the speeding motorist is again comparable, for such motorists usually have no desire at all to kill anyone. They merely want to get somewhere sooner, or they enjoy speeding and are indifferent to the consequences. Despite their lack of malice, those who kill with cars deserve not only blame but also severe punishment.

(5) The difference I have left for last is the most significant. The fact that to avoid killing people is normally not difficult whereas to save all one possibly could save is heroic must make an important difference to our attitude to failure to do what the respective principles demand. Not to kill is a minimum standard of acceptable conduct we can require of everyone. In contrast, to save all one possibly could is not something that can realistically be required, especially not in societies accustomed to giving as little as ours do. Given the generally accepted standards, people who give, say, 10 percent of what they earn to help the poor are more aptly praised for their above-average generosity than blamed for giving less than they might. The appropriateness of praise and blame is, however, a separate issue from the rightness or wrongness of actions. The former evaluates the agent; the latter

evaluates the action. Perhaps many people who give 10 percent really ought to give 50 percent, but to blame them for not giving more could be counterproductive. It might make them feel that what is required is too demanding, and if one is going to be blamed anyway, one might as well not give anything at all. That an ethic that puts saving all one possibly can on the same footing as not killing would be an ethic for saints or heroes should not lead us to assume that the alternative must be an ethic that makes it obligatory not to kill but puts us under no obligation to save anyone. There are positions in between these extremes, as we shall see.

Let's summarize the five differences that normally exist between killing and allowing to die in the context of extreme poverty and overseas aid. The lack of an identifiable victim is of no moral significance, though it may play an important role in explaining our attitudes. The idea that we are directly responsible for those we kill, but not for those we do not help, depends on a questionable notion of responsibility and may need to be based on a dubious theory of rights. Differences in certainty and motivation are ethically significant and show that not aiding the poor is not to be condemned as murdering them; it could, however, be on a par with killing someone as a result of reckless driving, which is serious enough. Finally, the difficulty of completely discharging the duty of saving all one possibly can makes it inappropriate to blame those who fall short of this target in the same way that we blame those who kill; but this does not show that the act itself is less serious. Nor does it excuse those who make no effort to save anyone.

In any case, whereas failing to save a life may not always be ethically on par with deliberate killing, it is clear that how we respond to the existence of both absolute poverty and absolute affluence is one of the great moral issues of our time. So let us consider afresh whether we have an obligation to assist those whose lives are in danger and, if so, how this obligation applies to the present world situation.

The Obligation to Assist

The Argument for an Obligation to Assist

On my way to give a lecture, I pass a shallow ornamental pond and notice that a small child has fallen in and is in danger of drowning. I look around to see where the parents, or babysitter, are, but to my surprise, I see that there is no one else around. It seems that it is up to me to make sure that the child doesn't drown. Would anyone deny that I ought to wade in and pull the child out? This will mean getting my clothes muddy, ruining my shoes and either cancelling my lecture or delaying it until I can find something dry to change into; but compared with the avoidable death of a child none of these things are significant.

A plausible principle that would support the judgment that I ought to pull the child out is this: if it is in our power to prevent something very bad from happening, without thereby sacrificing anything of comparable moral significance, we ought to do it. This principle seems uncontroversial. It will obviously win the assent of consequentialists; but non-consequentialists should accept it too, because the injunction to prevent what is bad applies only when nothing comparably significant is at stake. Thus, the principle cannot lead to the kinds of actions of which non-consequentialists strongly disapprove — serious violations of individual rights, injustice, broken promises and so on. If non-consequentialists regard any of these as comparable in moral significance to the bad thing that is to be prevented, they will automatically regard the principle as not applying in those cases in which the bad thing can only be prevented by violating rights, doing injustice, breaking promises or whatever else is at stake. Most non-consequentialists hold that we ought to prevent what is bad and promote what is good. Their dispute with consequentialists lies in their insistence that this is not the sole ultimate ethical principle: that it is *an* ethical principle is not denied by any plausible ethical theory.

Nevertheless, the uncontroversial appearance of the principle that we ought to prevent what is bad when we can do so without sacrificing anything of comparable moral significance is deceptive. If it were taken seriously and acted on, our lives and our world would be fundamentally changed. For the principle applies, not just to rare situations in which one can save a child from a pond, but to the everyday situation in which we can assist those living in absolute poverty. In saying this, I assume that absolute poverty, with its hunger and malnutrition, lack of shelter, illiteracy, disease, high infant mortality and low life expectancy, is a bad thing. Additionally, I assume that it is within the power of the affluent to reduce absolute poverty, without sacrificing anything of comparable moral significance. If these two assumptions and the principle we have been discussing are correct, we have an obligation to help those in absolute poverty that is no less strong than our obligation to rescue a drowning child from a pond. Not to help would be wrong, whether or not it is intrinsically equivalent to killing. Helping is not, as conventionally thought, a charitable act that is praiseworthy to do but not wrong to omit. It is something that everyone ought to do.

Set out more formally, this argument would look like this.   30

First premise:	If we can prevent something bad without sacrificing anything of comparable significance, we ought to do it.
Second premise:	Extreme poverty is bad.
Third premise:	There is some extreme poverty we can prevent without sacrificing anything of comparable moral significance.
Conclusion:	We ought to prevent some extreme poverty.

Understanding the Text

1. Would you agree that the author of this reading, Peter Singer, designed his "shallow pond" scenario (paragraphs 27–29) to show all of his readers that he and they share a moral principle in common? What, in your own words, is that principle?

   Did Singer judge correctly that his readers would also subscribe to it?

2. Recap all the reasons why, according to Singer, very few of us apply that moral principle to the problem of premature death in impoverished regions of the world.

Reflection and Response

3. Review Singer's *rebuttals* of the reasons for inaction — his ways of explaining why those reasons are inadequate. Which of his rebuttals do you find compelling? Which, not? Why?

4. A student who became upset with Singer wrote in the margin of this piece, "Are we supposed to dispose of all our income to Third World countries?" How similar to that reaction is your own?

Making Connections

5. Certain readings in this book — in particular, the Roper Center Survey (p. 24) and Charles Murray's "What's So Bad about Being Poor?" (p. 26) — suggest that what we mean by "being poor" changes over time and from one setting to another. In that connection, is the World Bank definition of absolute poverty (paraphrased by Singer in paragraphs 1 and 2 of this reading) helpful? If so, in what sense? If not, why?

6. Research the "categorical imperative," a demanding version of the Golden Rule introduced by philosopher Immanuel Kant. Would you describe Peter Singer's stance as Kantian?

7. A disciple of Singer's named Peter Unger took the ideas in "Rich and Poor" and expanded them into a whole book, which he titled *Living High and Letting Die*. How would you assess that title in terms of aptness? How would you assess it in rhetorical terms — in terms of its effect on prospective readers?

5

Has Money Blinded Us to Higher Values?

The first four sections of this book examine aims we generally profess to hold more dear than wealth: personal contentment, friendship or love, ethical behavior, and equality of well-being throughout humanity. We have seen how money (and the pursuit of money) can either help us to achieve these goals or prevent us from achieving them. However, these four aims are not the only ones money can promote or undermine.

After a preliminary look at some salaries paid for doing different jobs in our society, the items in this final section of the book bring to our attention several "higher values" not discussed in Chapters 1–4.

- In *The Price of Motherhood,* the higher value at stake is good parenting.
- In "Military Service," as well as in the painting *Collaboration (Dollar Sign, Don't Tread on Me),* it's giving back to one's country.
- In "College Sports, Inc.," it's good sportsmanship.
- In "Quitting the Paint Factory: On the Virtues of Idleness," "Does God Want You to Be Rich?," the painting *The Banker and His Wife,* and "Buddhist Economics," it's communion with the world and the world's Creator.

The final question posed to you after the last reading in this anthology is "Has money become a religion in its own right?" (p. 315). It may be thought of as a capstone question. It's an invitation to consider whether money now trumps all other values we espouse.

May 2011 Wage Estimates

U.S. Bureau of Labor Statistics

Whether it's from idle curiosity or envy, Americans display an avid interest in the incomes of their fellow citizens. To satisfy the common appetite for such information, media outlets like *Parade* magazine publish mug shots of people from across the United States with their names, ages, current jobs, and salaries.

A more reliable source of information about salaries is the long list of "wage estimates" compiled by the U.S. Bureau of Labor Statistics. Most of the salaries reported below — all of them, in fact, except those with marks after them — are averages drawn from that source.

Top-paid Hollywood Actor in 2012 (Tom Cruise)	$75,000,000†
Football Players on the List of 100 Top-Paid Players in 2012	$26,000,000†
CEO's of Companies in the S&P 500 Index (500 of the world's largest companies)	$12,940,000*
Anesthesiologists	$234,950
Dentists	$161,750
Lawyers	$130,490
Airline Pilots	$118,070
Advertising and Promotions Managers	$103,350
Economists	$100,270
Computer Programmers	$76,010
Fashion Designers	$73,930
Elevator Installers and Repairers	$73,560
Landscape Architects	$66,520
Historians	$57,610
Postal Service Mail Carriers	$51,390
Events Planners	$49,840
Firefighters	$47,720
Embalmers	$45,060

(continued)

Massage Therapists	$39,920
State and Local Legislators	$38,860
Forest and Conservation Specialists	$37,460
Trash and Recyclable Material Collectors	$34,420
Public Defenders (starting salary)	$32,000–$52,125, depending on state‡
Sewing Machine Operators	$23,080
Home Health Aides	$21,820
Maids and Cleaners	$21,440
Childcare Workers	$21,320
Farmworkers	$20,020
Fast-Food Cooks	$18,720

*aflcio.org
†Forbes.com
‡law.com

Understanding the Text

1. What patterns can you detect here? For example, do blue-collar workers earn less than other people earn?

2. What surprises you about any of these salary amounts? Why?

Response and Reflection

3. Based on the data here and other facts you know, would you say that money incentivizes the pursuits and careers that benefit society the most? (In answering this question, be sure to identify the life-priorities or values you bring with you to this issue. For example, one student wrote, "Without careers such as teachers, doctors, and police, we would be a bunch of uneducated, sick people living in anarchy.")

4. On a scale of 1 to 5 — where 1 means "very little" and 5 means "very much" — what number would indicate how much weight you currently incline to give salary in deciding on a career? Elaborate at length, taking care to address probable objections to your way of thinking.

Making Connections

5. Read Mark Slouka's essay "Quitting the Paint Factory: On the Virtues of Idleness" (p. 278). Adopting Slouka's humorous-but-serious voice, write an open letter to the president about the "May 2011 Wage Estimates."

From The Price of Motherhood

Ann Crittenden

Here, Ann Crittenden argues that our economic system actually penalizes those who perform the work society deems most important: raising children.

A Pulitzer Prize nominee for journalism, Crittenden has written three books and contributed articles on economic topics to a host of outlets, such as the *New York Times, Newsweek,* the *Nation, McCall's,* and *Working Woman.*

> The good mother, the wise mother . . . is more important to the community than even the ablest man; her career is more worthy of honor and is more useful to the community than the career of any man, no matter how successful.
>
> —THEODORE ROOSEVELT

When my son was small, we loved to read *The Giving Tree,* a book about a tree that gave a little boy apples to eat, branches to climb, and shade to sleep under. This made them both happy. As the boy grew into a man, the tree gave him her apples to sell for money, then her branches to build a house, and finally her trunk to make a boat. When the boy became a tired old man, the tree, by now nothing but a stump, offered him all she had left to sit on and rest. I would read the last line, "And the tree was happy," with tears flowing down my cheeks every time.

The very definition of a mother is selfless service to another.[1] We don't owe Mother for her gifts; *she owes us.* And in return for her bounty, Mother receives no lack of veneration. According to an ancient Jewish proverb, "God could not be everywhere, and therefore He made mothers." The Arabs also have a saying: "The mother is a school; if she is well reared, you are sure to build a nation."

In the United States, motherhood is as American as apple pie. No institution is more sacrosanct; no figure is praised more fulsomely.°

---

fulsomely: excessively, insincerely.

[1] "Mother" is often used throughout this book to refer to anyone who is the primary caregiver of another person. Barbara Katz Rothman, in *Recreating Motherhood,* makes the fundamental point that motherhood is based on caregiving and nurturance, and that whoever provides these to a child are its real "mothers," be they men or women, blood relatives, adopted or foster parents, nannies or other paid caregivers, friends, or a combination of the above. Although women still overwhelmingly fill the maternal, nurturing role, men certainly can. The fact that relatively few do surely has something to do with the fact that caregivers are still seriously disadvantaged.

Maternal selflessness has endowed mothers with a unique moral authority, which in the past has been used to promote temperance, maternal and child health, kindergartens, a more lenient juvenile justice system, and most recently, to combat drunk driving and lax gun controls.

If anything, awareness of the importance of mothers' work is increasing. In 1996 Microsoft founder Bill Gates and executive vice president Steve Ballmer gave Harvard University a $29-million state-of-the-art facility for computer science and electrical engineering. The new building was named Maxwell Dworkin, in honor of their mothers' maiden names. This may have been the first such recognition given to mothers' role in the creation of vast fortunes and an entire new industry.

When I was on a radio talk show in 1998, several listeners called in   5 to say that child-rearing is the most important job in the world. A few weeks later, at a party, Lawrence H. Summers, a distinguished economist who subsequently became the secretary of the treasury, used exactly the same phrase. "Raising children," Summers told me in all seriousness, "is the most important job in the world." As Summers well knows, in the modern economy, two-thirds of all wealth is created by human skills, creativity, and enterprise — what is known as "human capital." And that means parents who are conscientiously and effectively rearing children are literally, in the words of economist Shirley Burggraf, "the major wealth producers in our economy."[2]

But this very material contribution is still considered immaterial. All of the lip service to motherhood still floats in the air, as insubstantial as clouds of angel dust. On the ground, where mothers live, the lack of respect and tangible recognition is still part of every mother's experience. Most people, like infants in a crib, take female caregiving utterly for granted.

The job of making a home for a child and developing his or her capabilities is often equated with "doing nothing." Thus the disdainful question frequently asked about mothers at home: "What do they *do* all day?"

. . . Maxine Ross, a stay-at-home mother in Fairfax, Virginia, admitted to me that before she had her child, she too felt nothing but scorn for mothers at home: "We used to live in a four-family co-op, and two of the other women stayed at home with their children. One of them

---

[2] Shirley P. Burggraf, *The Feminine Economy and Economic Man* (Boston: Addison-Wesley, 1997), p. 64.

got a cleaning lady and I thought, 'Do you *believe* that? She has so much time, and she doesn't even clean her own house! What does she do all day, watch soap operas?'"

Even our children have absorbed the cultural message that mothers have no stature. A friend of mine gave up a job she loved as the head of a publishing house in order to raise her daughter. One day, when she corrected the girl, the child snapped, "Why should I listen to you? You're just a housewife!"

In my childless youth I shared these attitudes. In the early 1970s I wrote an article for the very first issue of *MS* magazine on the economic value of a housewife. I added up all the domestic chores, attached dollar values to each, and concluded that the job was seriously underpaid and ought to be included in the Gross National Product. I thought I was being sympathetic, but I realize now that my deeper attitude was one of compassionate contempt, or perhaps contemptuous compassion. Deep down, I had no doubt that I was superior, in my midtown office overlooking Madison Avenue, to those unpaid housewives pushing brooms. "Why aren't they making something of themselves?" I wondered. "What's wrong with them? They're letting our side down." 10

I imagined that domestic drudgery was going to be swept into the dustbin of history as men and women linked arms and marched off to run the world in a new egalitarian alliance. It never occurred to me that women might be at home because there were children there; that housewives might become extinct, but mothers and fathers never would.

• • •

A mother's work is not just invisible; it can become a handicap. Raising children may be the most important job in the world, but you can't put it on a résumé.

A woman from Long Island, New York, with a master's degree in special education was advised repeatedly that when she went job hunting she should not mention her thirteen years of caring for a disabled, chronically ill child. All those years of courageous tenacity and resilience would be held against her or, at best, considered irrelevant. She was warned that she had better pad her résumé with descriptions of volunteer work and occasional freelance writing.

The idea that time spent with one's child is time wasted is embedded in traditional economic thinking. People who are not formally employed may create human capital, but they themselves are said to suffer a deterioration of the stuff, as if they were so many pieces of equipment left out to rust. The extraordinary talents required to do the long-term work of building human character and instilling in young children the ability and desire to learn have no place in the economists' calculations. Economic theory has nothing to say about the acquisition of skills by those who work with children; presumably there are none.

Here is how economists have summed up the adverse effects of child-rearing on a person's qualifications: "As a woman does not work [*sic*] during certain periods, less working experience is accumulated. [Moreover] during periods of non-participation, the human capital stock suffers from additional depreciation due to a lack of mainte-nance. This effect is known as atrophy."[3] In fact, the only things that atrophy when a woman has children are her income and her leisure.

The devaluation of mothers' work permeates virtually every major institution. Not only is caregiving not rewarded, it is penalized. These stories illustrate the point:

• Joanna Upton, a single mother working as a store manager in Massachusetts, sued the company for wrongful dismissal after it fired her for refusing to work overtime — until nine or ten at night and all day Saturday. Upton had been hired to work 8:15 A.M. until 5:30 P.M.; she could not adequately care for or barely even see her son if she had to work overtime. Yet she lost her suit. The Massachusetts Su-preme Judicial Court ruled that under state contract law, an at-will employee may be fired "for any reason or for no reason at all" unless the firing violates a "clearly established" public policy. Massachusetts had no public policy dealing with a parent's responsibility to care for his or her child.[4]

• A woman in Texas gave up a fifteen-year career in banking to raise two children. Her husband worked extremely long hours and spent much of his time on the road. She realized that only if she left her own demanding job would the children have the parental time and attention they needed. For almost two decades she worked part-time as a consultant from her home, and for several years she had little or no income. Recently the Social Security Administration sent her an estimate of her retirement income — a statement that was full of zeroes for the years spent caregiving. Social Security confirmed that

[3] L. F. M. Groot, J. J. Schippers, and J. J. Siegers, "The Effect of Interruptions and Part-Time Work on Women's Wage Rate," *De Economist* 136, no. 2 (1988): 220.

[4] This case is described in detail in Mona Harrington, *Care and Equality*, pp. 51–52, 153.

her decision to be the responsible, primary parent had reduced the government pension by hundreds of dollars a month in retirement income.

• A mother in Maryland had a son who had been a problem child ever since kindergarten. At junior high, the boy was suspended several times; he was finally caught with a gun in his backpack and expelled. The boy's father sued for custody, and the mother countered with a request for more child support, to help pay the $10,000 tuition for a special private school. She also quit her full-time job to have more time for her family. At his new school, the boy showed dramatic improvement both in his academic work and in his behavior. When the case came to court, the father was denied custody, but the judge refused to require him to pay half the costs of the boy's rehabilitation, including therapy and tutoring, despite evidence that the father could afford to do so. A mother who did not work full-time was, in the judge's view, a luxury that "our world does not permit." So the mother was in effect penalized for having tried to be a more attentive mother, and the boy was forced to leave the only school in which he had enjoyed any success.[5]

As these examples reveal the United States is a society at war with itself. The policies of American business, government, and the law do not reflect Americans' stated values. Across the board, individuals who assume the role of nurturer are punished and discouraged from performing the very tasks that everyone agrees are essential. We talk endlessly about the importance of family, yet the work it takes to make a family is utterly disregarded. This contradiction can be found in every corner of our society.

First, inflexible workplaces guarantee that many women will have to cut back on, if not quit, their employment once they have children. The result is a loss of income that produces a bigger wage gap between mothers and childless women than the wage gap between young men and women. This forgone income, the equivalent of a huge "mommy tax," is typically more than $1 million for a college-educated American woman.

Second, marriage is still not an equal financial partnership. Mothers in forty-seven of the fifty states — California, Louisiana, and New Mexico are the exceptions — do not have an unequivocal legal right to

---

[5] This 1999 Maryland case was brought to my attention by Laura Morgan, a national authority on child support at the National Legal Research Group in Charlottesville, Virginia. The case is *Dunlap v. Fiorenza*, 128 Md. App. 357, 738 A. 2d 312 (1999).

half of the family's assets. Nor does a mother's unpaid work entitle her to any ownership of the primary breadwinner's income — either during marriage or after a divorce. Family income belongs solely to "he who earns it," in the phrase coined by legal scholar Joan Williams. A married mother is a "dependent," and a divorced mother is "given" what a judge decides she and the children "need" of the father's future income. As a result, the spouse who principally cares for the children — and the children — are almost invariably worse off financially after divorce than the spouse who devotes all his energies to a career.

Third, government social policies don't even define unpaid care of 20 family dependents as work. A family's primary caregiver is not considered a full productive citizen, eligible in her own right for the major social insurance programs. Nannies earn Social Security credits; mothers at home do not. Unless she is otherwise "employed," the primary parent is not entitled to unemployment insurance or workman's compensation. The only safety net for a caregiver who loses her source of support is welfare, and even that is no longer assured.

> As the twenty-first century begins, women may be approaching equality, but mothers are still far behind.

For all these reasons, motherhood is the single biggest risk factor for poverty in old age. American mothers have smaller pensions than either men or childless women, and American women over sixty-five are more than twice as likely to be poor as men of the same age.

The devaluation of a mother's work extends to those who do similar work for pay. Even college-educated teachers of infants are often characterized as "baby-sitters," and wages for child care are so low that the field is hemorrhaging its best-trained people. Increasingly, day care is being provided by an inexperienced workforce — what one expert calls "Kentucky Fried Day Care" — while highly trained Mary Poppins–style nannies are officially classified as "unskilled labor," and as such largely barred from entry into the United States.

The cumulative effect of these policies is a heavy financial penalty on anyone who chooses to spend any serious amount of time with children. This is the hard truth that lies beneath all of the flowery tributes to Mom. American mothers may have their day, but for the rest of the year their values, their preferences, and their devotion to their children are short-changed. As the twenty-first century begins, women may be approaching equality, but mothers are still far behind. Changing the status of mothers, by gaining real recognition for their work, is the great unfinished business of the women's movement.

But revaluing motherhood will not be easy. Even feminists are often reluctant to admit that many women's lives revolve around their children. They measure progress by the distance women have traveled from *Kinder* and *Küche,* and worry that if child-rearing is made a more tempting choice, many women — those natural nurturers — will drift back into domestic subservience. They fear that if women are seen to be mothers first, the very real gains that women have made in the workplace could be jeopardized.

Thus the standard feminist response to the fact that child-rearing   25
marginalizes women is not to raise its status but to urge men to do more of it. Though this has been the cry for more than thirty years, almost 100 percent of the primary caregivers of young children are still women. This suggests that feminism needs a fresh strategy.

Conservatives, for their part, are not willing to put their money where their mouths are. Their eyes grow moist over family values, but they are loath to put any tangible value on the work that a family entails. They cling to the conviction that the only "good" mother is the self-sacrificing, saintly figure who performs the moral, caring work of society at the expense of her own equality and aspirations.

Social conservatives often expect daughters but not sons to renounce ambition and serve their families without compensation. They preach early marriage and childbearing, without warning young women that this increases their chances of divorce and lowers their lifetime income. They embrace an economy that relies on free or badly paid female labor, and then wonder why women express frustration with their lot. As Burggraf has so perceptively noted, "Getting 'women's work' done when women are no longer volunteering their unpaid or underpaid labor is what much of the public discussion of family values is really about."[6]

---

[6] Economist Shirley P. Burggraf uses the term "feminine economy" to describe all the work of caring for dependents, from infants to the sick and the elderly. By far the greatest portion of the feminine economy involves caring for children, but elder care is rapidly increasing. A survey released in 1997 found that 22 million elderly people are being cared for by a relative, three times as many as only ten years earlier. Nearly one out of four households is engaged in caring for an aged relative. These caregivers, the great majority of whom are women, spend on average about eighteen hours a week at this often stressful task. One-quarter of them provide at least forty hours a week of unpaid service to an elderly family member. (1997 Caregiving Survey, sponsored by the National Alliance for Caregiving, American Association of Retired Persons, and Glaxo Wellcome.)

It is true, of course, that caring for one's child is not a job that anyone does for the sake of remuneration. As *The Giving Tree* implies, raising a child is much more like a gift; a gift motivated by maternal love, the most unselfish emotion in the human repertoire. How can one be paid for a labor of love? The very idea seems emotionally askew, foreign to the essence of care. But just because caring work is not self-seeking doesn't mean a person should be penalized for doing it. Just because giving to one's child is altruistic doesn't mean that it isn't also a difficult, time-consuming obligation that is expected of one sex and not the other. The gift of care can be both selfless and exploited.[7] As Balzac so memorably put it, "Maternal love makes of every woman a slave."

Every now and then, someone calculates what a family would have to pay for a mother's services. In one such exercise, a mother's worth was estimated at $508,700 per year in wages alone, not counting retirement, health, and other benefits. This astronomical sum was arrived at by adding up the median annual salaries of the seventeen occupations a mother is expected to perform, from child-rearing, cooking, and cleaning to managing household finances and resolving family emotional problems.[8] A more realistic assessment would probably value a mother's work at the level of a middle manager, plus the additional occasional services of a psychologist, a financial planner, a chauffeur, and so on. This package could easily add up to $100,000 a year — or $100,000 a year more than a mother is paid.

"No one's crazy enough to work for free but moms," says Ric Edel- 30
man, whose firm, Edelman Financial Services, made the $500,000 calculation. "And no one has enough money to hire a good mom. . . . From that perspective our mothers are indeed priceless."

Unpaid female caregiving is not only the life blood of families, it is the very heart of the economy. A spate of new studies reveals that the amount of work involved in unpaid child care is far greater than economists ever imagined. Indeed, it rivals in size the largest industries of the visible economy. By some estimates, even in the most industrialized countries the total hours spent on unpaid household work — much of it associated with child-rearing — amount to at least

---

[7] For a discussion of these contradictions, see Nancy Folbre, "Holding Hands at Midnight: The Paradox of Caring Labor," *Feminist Economics* 1, no. 1 (spring 1995); and "Children as Public Goods," *American Economic Review Papers and Proceedings* 84, no. 2 (May 1994).

[8] "Mothers Are Worth $508,700!" Press release put out by Edelman Financial Services of Fairfax, Virginia, May 1997.

half of the hours of paid work in the market.[9] Up to 80 percent of this unpaid labor is contributed by women.

This huge gift of unreimbursed time and labor explains, in a nutshell, why adult women are so much poorer than men — even though they work longer hours than men in almost every country in the world.[10] One popular economics textbook devotes four pages to problems of poverty without once mentioning the fact that the majority of poor people are women and children. The author never considers that this poverty might be related to the fact that half the human race isn't paid for most of the work it does.

In economics, a "free rider" is someone who benefits from a good without contributing to its provision: in other words, someone who gets something for nothing. By that definition, both the family and the global economy are classic examples of free riding. Both are dependent on female caregivers who offer their labor in return for little or no compensation. . . .

---

[9] *Human Development Report, 1995,* published by the United Nations Development Programme (UNDP) (New York and Oxford: Oxford University Press, 1995), pp. 96–97. Luisella Goldschmidt-Clermont and Elisabetta Pagnossin-Aligisakis, "Measures of Unrecorded Economic Activities in Fourteen Countries," UNDP Occasional Papers 20, New York, 1995, pp. 25–26. Also Robin A. Douthitt, "The Value of Unpaid Work in the System of National Income Accounts: A Satellite Account Approach," *Consumer Interest Annual* 42 (1996): 5. Douthitt calculated that in 1985 American women spent more time in home child care than was spent by all people working in retail, the third largest paid industry. In Australia, where the data on nonmarket activity are particularly good, unpaid child care at home in 1992 absorbed more hours of labor than any other industry, with the exception of wholesale and retail trade.

[10] Women perform on average 51 percent of the total work done in industrialized countries and 53 percent in developing countries. These data are based on time-use studies collected for fourteen industrial countries, nine developing countries, and eight countries in eastern Europe. *Human Development Report 1995,* p. 88.

Understanding the Text

1. In paragraph 20, Ann Crittenden calls the United States "a society at war with itself" and contends, "The policies of American business, government, and the law do not reflect Americans' stated values." To what is she referring? What does she offer as evidence?

2. What does the economist whom Crittenden quotes in paragraph 5 mean by calling mothers "major wealth producers"? Is that mothers' most significant role to Crittenden?

3. In paragraph 32, Crittenden presents two calculations of what a mother's work is worth in dollars, but at no point does she propose that mothers actually be paid for mothering. What does she want then?

Reflection and Response

4. Do you *agree* with Crittenden that in the United States there is a disconnect between the value placed on good parenting and the support provided for it? Why or why not? Write a paper on the subject, drawing both on the examples Crittenden provides and on examples you have observed in your own life.

Making Connections

5. Replace Crittenden's opening with one that focuses on the mother and children in the story "Twenty Grand," by Rebecca Curtis (p. 42).

6. Where in her piece could Crittenden have plausibly referred to "shaken baby syndrome" (p. 104)? Write the paragraph she could have inserted there.

7. How does legal and financial support for mothering in the United States compare with that in France, for example?

   Should the United States adopt French policies? Are there other countries we should try to emulate instead? Is there no country with policies better than ours at this time?

Military Service

Michael Sandel

The military draft during the Vietnam War had been such a big contributing factor in political dissent that the U.S. Congress soon eliminated it. However, the pay-based system that replaced it worries thinkers like Michael Sandel.

A popular professor of government at Harvard University, Sandel has authored such books as *Justice: What's the Right Thing to Do?* and *The Case against Perfection: Ethics in the Age of Genetic Engineering.*

M ilitary service can be allocated° in different ways, some involving the market, others not. Conscription° allocates service without the use of markets. In its simplest version, it fills places according to a lottery of eligible citizens. A second way of allocating places in the military was employed by the Union during the American Civil War. It introduced market principles, but only to a point. In the first American draft, enacted in 1863, those who were called but who did not want to serve could hire a substitute to take their place. Many draftees advertised for substitutes in the newspapers, offering amounts from a few hundred dollars up to fifteen hundred dollars. The system was less than a resounding success. There were widespread protests. In the New York draft riots a thousand people died. Congress tried to quell the protest by amending the policy by setting a flat fee for exemption. If you were drafted and didn't want to serve, you could pay a three-hundred-dollar fee to the government. You didn't have to bother finding someone else. Three hundred dollars in those days was equivalent to one year's wages for a laborer.[1]

A third way of filling the ranks of the military carries market principles one step further. Rather than draft people and then allow the market to operate, the present-day American all-volunteer army uses market principles from the start. The term "volunteer" is something of a misnomer.° Soldiers do not volunteer in the way that people volunteer to work in the local soup kitchen on Thanksgiving — that is, to serve without pay. The volunteer army is a professional army, in which soldiers work for pay. It is voluntary only in the sense that all

---

allocated: distributed, assigned.
conscription: compulsory enrollment, especially for the military.
misnomer: a wrong or misleading name for something.

---

[1] On the Civil War draft, see James M. McPherson, *Battle Cry of Freedom* (New York: Oxford University Press, 1988), pp. 600–611; and Guide Calabresi and Philip Bobbitt, *Tragic Choices* (New York: W. W. Norton, 1978), pp. 158–67.

paid labor is voluntary. No one is conscripted, and the job is performed by those who agree to do so in exchange for money and other benefits.

Compare these three ways of allocating military service — conscription, conscription with a buy-out provision (the Civil War system), and the market system. Which is most desirable? From the standpoint of market reasoning, the Civil War system is preferable to a system of pure conscription because it increases the range of choice. Those who are conscripted but who do not want to serve have the option of buying their way out, and those who are not conscripted but who want the job can buy their way in. From the standpoint of market reasoning, however, the volunteer army is better still. Like the Civil War system, it enables people to buy their way into or out of military service. But it is preferable to the Civil War system because it places the cost of hiring soldiers on the society as a whole, not just on the unlucky few who happen to be drafted and must therefore serve or hire a substitute to take their place.

So from the standpoint of market reasoning, the volunteer army is best, the Civil War system second best, and conscription the least desirable way of allocating military service. But there are at least two objections to this line of argument. One is that we cannot prefer the volunteer army without knowing more about the background conditions that prevail in the society. The volunteer army seems attractive because it avoids the coercion of conscription. It makes military service a matter of consent. But some of those who serve in the all-volunteer army may be as averse to military service as those who stay away. If poverty and economic disadvantage is widespread, the choice to serve may simply reflect the lack of alternatives. This is the problem of the poor persons' army. According to this objection (an instance of the objection from coercion), those who buy their way in, or fail to buy their way out, are conscripted by the lottery of economic necessity.

The difference between conscription and the volunteer army is not ₅ that one is compulsory, whereas the other is not; it is rather that each employs a different form of compulsion — the state in the first case, economic necessity in the second. Only if people are similarly situated to begin with can it be said that the choice to serve for pay reflects people's preferences, rather than their limited alternatives.

The actual composition of the American all-volunteer army seems to bear out this objection. Thirty percent of the U.S. army troops who were sent to fight the Gulf War were African Americans, almost three times the percent of African Americans in the population as a whole. The enlistment rates for children of the richest fifteen percent of the population are one-fifth of the national average.[2] So it is easy to appreciate the force of the objection that the volunteer army is not as voluntary as it seems.

It is worth pointing out that this objection can in principle be met without doing away with the all-volunteer army. It can be met by making the background conditions of the society sufficiently equal so that people's choice of work reflects meaningful consent rather than dire economic necessity. In this case as in others, the argument from coercion is not an objection to the commodification of military service as such, only to commodification that takes place under certain unfair background conditions.

A second objection to letting people buy their way into and out of military service is independent of the first. It holds that, even in a society where the choice of work did not reflect deep inequalities in life circumstances, military service should not be allocated by the labor market, as if it were just another job. According to this argument, all citizens have an obligation to serve their country. Whether this obligation is best discharged through military or other national service, it is not the sort of thing that people should be free to buy or sell. To turn such service into a commodity — a job for pay — is to corrupt or degrade the sense of civic virtue that properly attends it. A familiar instance of this argument is offered by Jean-Jacques Rousseau: "As soon as public service ceases to be the chief business of the citizens and they would rather serve with their money than with their persons, the state is not far from its fall. When it is necessary to march out to war, they pay troops and stay at home. . . . In a country that is truly free, the citizens do everything with their own arms and nothing by means of money; so far from paying to be exempted from their duties, they would even pay for the privilege of fulfilling them themselves. . . . I hold enforced labor to be less opposed to liberty than taxes."[3]

Rousseau's argument against commodifying military service is an instance of the argument from corruption. It invokes the republican°

> If military service is just another job . . . is there any principled distinction between the volunteer army and the mercenary forces . . . ?

---

republican: related to or favoring the form of government known as a republic.

[2] Larry Tye, "All-Volunteer Force No Minor of Society," *Boston Globe*, February 2, 1991, pp. 1, 3.

[3] Jean-Jacques Rousseau, *The Social Contract* (1762), trans. G. D. H. Cole, book 3, ch. 15 (London: J. M. Dent & Sons, 1973), p. 265.

conception of citizenship. Market advocates might defend the volunteer army by rejecting the republican conception of citizenship, or by denying its relevance to military service. But doesn't the volunteer army as currently practiced implicitly acknowledge certain limits to market principles, limits that derive from a residual commitment to the ideal of republican citizenship?

Consider the difference between the contemporary volunteer army 10 and an army of mercenaries. Both pay soldiers to fight. Both entice people to enlist by the promise of pay and other benefits. The U.S. army runs television commercials that make the job seem as attractive as possible. But if the market is an appropriate way of allocating military service, what is wrong with mercenaries? It might be replied that mercenaries are foreign nationals who fight only for pay, whereas the American volunteer army hires only Americans. But if military service is just another job, why should the employer discriminate in hiring on the basis of nationality? Why shouldn't the U.S. military be open to citizens of any country who want the work and possess the relevant qualifications?

The logic of the market could be extended to challenge the notion that armies should be run by the government. Why not subcontract military functions to private enterprise? In fact, the privatization of war, like the privatization of prisons, is a growing trend. Private corporations that hire mercenary forces play an increasing role in conflicts around the world. Sandline International is a London-based company registered in the Bahamas. It was hired by Papua New Guinea last year to put down a secessionist rebellion. Papua New Guinea's prime minister hired Sandline for $32 million to crush rebels his own army was unable to defeat. "I am sick and tired of our boys coming back in body bags," he said.[4]

Sandline, in turn, subcontracted with a South African–based company euphemistically named Executive Outcomes, which supplies and trains the soldiers. "Executive Outcomes has racked up an impressive record of military victories for its customers," reports the *Boston Globe.* "Equipped with Russian attack helicopters, heavy artillery, and battle-hardened veterans recruited from the troops that defended South Africa's former white supremacist government, Executive Outcomes

---

[4] Colum Lynch, "Soldiers for Hire Tempt War-Weary," *Boston Globe,* March 8, 1997, pp. A1, A12. See also Raymond Bonner, "U.S. Reportedly Backed British Mercenary Group in Africa," *New York Times,* May 13, 1998; and David Shearer, "Outsourcing War," *Foreign Policy* (Fall 1998): 68–80.

has waged war on behalf of the governments of Angola and Sierra Leone."[5]

In 1989, the United Nations proposed the International Convention against the Recruitment, Use, Financing, and Training of Mercenaries. But only ten nations have signed it, and two of them, Angola and Zaire, have already violated it. The United States did pressure the South African government to restrain the role of Executive Outcomes in Angola. But the American principled position was complicated by the fact that the United States then lobbied the Angolan government to hire a competing U.S. firm, Military Professional Resources Inc., to train the Angolan armed forces.[6]

The cases we have considered pose the following challenge to the commodification of military service represented by the all-volunteer army: If the Civil War system is objectionable on the grounds that it allows people to buy their way out of a civic obligation, isn't the volunteer army objectionable on similar grounds? And if military service is just another job to be allocated by the labor market, is there any principled distinction between the volunteer army and the mercenary forces recruited by Sandline, Executive Outcomes, and other firms? All three policies — the Civil War system, the volunteer army, and the mercenary forces — offend the republican conception of citizenship. Our unease in each case is best articulated and justified by the argument from corruption, which presupposes in turn the republican ideal of citizenship.

---

[5] Lynch, "Soldiers for Hire."
[6] Ibid.

Understanding the Text

1. Why does Sandel say that the current American army "carries market principles one step further" than the federal government did in providing for an army during the Civil War?

2. What two problems does Sandel see with a system where the ranks of a nation's armed forces are filled largely by people who want or need the pay offered for enlisting?

3. In 2010, the Opinion Research Corporation reported that 78 percent of men and women in the American military intended to remain enlisted longer than they first had planned because of worries about income stemming from the ongoing economic downturn of that year. Where in Sandel's essay could he have inserted this fact, if he had known it?

Reflection and Response

4. To what extent do personal economic circumstances explain your own interest — or disinterest — in military service?

5. Do you share Sandel's qualms about today's American army? Why or why not?

Making Connections

6. As Sandel says, the word "volunteer" in the phrase "the American all-volunteer army" is somewhat misleading. Why? Using a thesaurus and dictionary, try to come up with a more accurate word or phrase to replace "all-volunteer." In a short paper, either defend your choice or explain why none of the alternatives to "all-volunteer" does a better job of describing the reality.

7. Would the military service of the husband in Rebecca Curtis's story "Twenty Grand" (p. 42) make a good case in point for Sandel's argument? Explain.

Collaboration (Dollar Sign, Don't Tread on Me)

Andy Warhol and
Jean-Michel Basquiat

In *Collaboration (Dollar Sign, Don't Tread on Me)* (1984–1985), artists Andy Warhol and Jean-Michel Basquiat seem to have created a statement on the value attached to money in the United States.

The elder of the two, Warhol, was the celebrated innovator in pop art who coined the expression "fifteen minutes of fame." Basquiat, who would die at age 27 in 1988, had come to people's attention for the distinctive, politically charged graffiti art he sprayed on buildings in Manhattan in the 1970s.

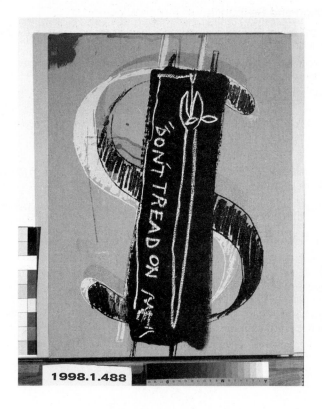

1998.1.488

Understanding the Text

1. "Don't tread on me" is a motto of the American Revolution emblazoned on a flag of that era with the image of a coiled snake — a warning to the British not to mistreat their colonies if they wanted to avoid being "bitten." (To *tread* means to step.)

   With that in mind, what, exactly, do Warhol and Basquiat seem to be saying in this work of art? What details of the painting lend support to your interpretation?

2. How, if at all, would it change the painting's meaning to replace the phrase "Don't tread on me" with one that didn't have as much historic resonance, such as "Don't step on me"?

Reflection and Response

3. Choose one of the following sentences to open a short paper on the Warhol/Basquiat painting:

   Collaboration (Dollar Sign, Don't Tread on Me) gives beautiful expression to the prevailing attitude toward money in America.

or

   In their *Collaboration (Dollar Sign, Don't Tread on Me)*, Andy Warhol and Jean-Michel Basquiat make too simple a statement to do justice to the place of money in American consciousness.

or

   The statement made in *Collaboration (Dollar Sign, Don't Tread on Me)* is too ambiguous to evaluate.

   Support whichever sentence you choose with evidence from the painting.

Making Connections

4. Would *Collaboration (Dollar Sign, Don't Tread on Me)* make a good illustration to accompany the Michael Sandel excerpt "Military Service" (p. 259)? Explain.

5. Stylistically, what sets the Warhol/Basquiat painting apart from all the other paintings reproduced in this book (pp. 90, 222, 224, and 305)? Does the style "work" as well for you as the styles of the others? Why or why not?

College Sports, Inc.
Murray Sperber

For many athletes, good sportsmanship and fairness are sacred ideals, but when the enticements and pressures of money make themselves felt in a sports event, those high standards are severely tested and all too often compromised. Here, Murray Sperber tells the history of money's influence in sports at the college level in the United States. The first excerpt deals with the earliest signs of it; the second, with a single, famous modern case of it — the influence of Nike sportswear.

A professor emeritus in English and American studies at Indiana University, Sperber has spoken out for many years on the issues he addresses in "College Sports, Inc." He is a former chair of the Drake Group, which seeks reform in this area.

History

Almost every sports historian agrees that the first intercollegiate athletic event in American history was a boat race between Harvard and Yale in 1852 on Lake Winnepesaukee in New Hampshire. Crew was becoming popular as a club sport in the United States, in both gentlemen's clubs and student clubs. Because of the fame of the Oxford-Cambridge boat race in England and the anglophilia of schools like Harvard and Yale, it was inevitable that a boat race between the two would occur. But why at this time and place?

The superintendent of the Boston, Concord, and Montreal Railroad, James M. Elkins, who had invested capital in land, tracks, and equipment at the New Hampshire lake, wanted to develop the area as a summer resort. He had the bright idea that a boat race on the lake between the two most famous schools in the nation would attract newspaper coverage and publicity for his resort area. He wrote to the crew people at the schools: "If you will get up a regatta on the lake between Yale and Harvard, I will pay all the bills" (Smith and Lucas 1978, 197). Apparently, for the owner of the railroad, "the first intercollegiate contest was entirely a commercial venture" (197).

Historians have examined the student records at Yale and Harvard for this period and have determined that a number of members of both crews were not registered students at the schools; probably they were professional rowers who hired themselves out to gentlemen's clubs in Boston and New York. On this day they were ringers hired to help their employers (Yale or Harvard) win the race (Smith 1988, Rader 1983). Thus, in the very first college sports

In the very first sports contest in American history the event was totally commercial, and the participants were cheating. The history of intercollegiate athletics has gone downhill from there.

contest in American history, even before the starting gun went off or an oar hit the water, two elements were at play: the event was totally commercial, and the participants were cheating. The history of intercollegiate athletics has gone downhill from there.

Crew remained the most popular college sport for a number of decades and was always highly commercial. Then football replaced it as the number-one sport in American collegiate athletics. Again commercialism reigned, as did ringers and tramp athletes — men who went from school to school selling their services for a football season or a game or two. Professional football did not exist, and the colleges provided tramp athletes with a nice income. One famous athlete was James Hogan, considered the best player at the turn of the twentieth century, employed by no less a luminary than Yale's legendary Walter Camp, the man who wrote the basic rules of football and invented such elements as the All-America team.

Hogan was already twenty-seven years old when he started play- 5
ing at Yale. He lived in luxurious accommodations provided by Yale alumni; never attended classes; and (most profitably for him) was given the American Tobacco Company concession for New Haven, receiving a commission from every cigarette pack sold in the city. Of course, the company also used his name and picture to promote its products. In addition, Hogan was in charge of the game programs for all Yale home football contests and took a cut of the advertising sold for them, much of it from the tobacco companies. In this way, the American Tobacco Company identified itself with one of the most prestigious universities in the country.

American Tobacco and Yale was not a singular tie-in. Looking through football game programs and student publications from the first decades of the twentieth century, the reader can see the omnipresence of tobacco companies, which promoted an abundance of cigarette brands and tied most of the ads to images of the healthiest young men on campus: the athletes who endorsed the products. The Carnegie Foundation issued a famous report in 1929 on intercollegiate athletics, noting: "The advertiser [particularly the cigarette manufacturers but also other companies] has been among the most persistent exploiter of college athletics" and college athletes (Savage et al. 1929, 276).

Thus, the first corporations to consistently use colleges and universities for their own ends were tobacco companies. Throughout the first half of the twentieth century, cigarette company advertising emphasized youth and healthiness; and their advertising agencies purchased key locations in college football programs and other student publications, everything from the student newspaper and yearbook to playbills for the drama club's productions. Even though scientific studies on the lethality of smoking came much later, Americans have long known about its dangers; "coffin nails" and "death sticks" were popular early twentieth-century nicknames for cigarettes. But the tobacco industry countered this awareness with ads featuring handsome, fit young men and women smoking its products. College athletes were featured often because in the 1920s college football had exploded in popularity, becoming the second most popular sport in the United States, just behind professional baseball.

Cigarette advertising gained momentum in the 1930s at a time when economic depression made smoking a cheap pleasure. During World War II, the tobacco industry tied much of its advertising to both sports and patriotism. In a typical wartime advertising campaign, which appeared in a full season of football programs, Liggett and Myers showed a male collegian in an Army Reserve uniform bicycling across the middle pages of the program, his left hand gripping both the handlebar and a cigarette. The logo "Chesterfield," in large type, occupies the upper half of the page; the team rosters appear in tiny print within the bike wheels. Not just the uniform indicated patriotism; because of the gas shortage, so did the bicycle (Sperber 1998).

The volume and slickness of cigarette advertising, as well as its ubiquity, help explain college students' increasing consumption of and, for many, addiction to nicotine from the 1920s on. Moreover, cigarette companies urged female students to smoke, with the goal of making smoking acceptable for all women; previously, females who smoked were considered déclassé. Significantly, neither the college sports establishment nor any individual school objected to the cigarette ads or even the prominence of brand logos compared with school logos. The amount of money generated by the tobacco industry was already so large and its support of college sports so important, especially during the Depression and World War II, that higher education authorities not only failed to question the ethics of tobacco industry advertising but actively solicited it for game programs and other campus publications. Student newspapers and magazines, traditionally underwritten by the school, were willingly shifted to commercial advertisers.

Meanwhile, university researchers had started to study the effects 10 of smoking; and scientific journals as well as some national magazines relayed the early, generally negative, findings. Thus, in the 1940s and 1950s, university personnel, even more than most Americans, knew about the dangers of smoking. Nevertheless, partly because of the tobacco industry's financial support of college sports and student publications, they did not act on their knowledge.

More than a half-century later, why should we care about these historic tobacco ads in campus publications? Wasn't it a good thing that cigarette advertising sustained various student periodicals? Wouldn't many of them have gone under without the support of advertisers? Without these publications, wouldn't many budding journalists or authors have had their careers aborted? These same arguments continue today: schools need money, so why not accept corporate sponsorship? For answers, let's begin with the Carnegie Report of 1929 and its condemnation of commercialism in college sports and college life. The report summed up the sins of college sports in the 1920s, noting an increasing number of large stadiums, the media hype that surrounded football games, and the increase in importance of coaches like Knute Rockne: "Commercialism has made possible the erection of fine academic buildings and the increase of equipment from the profits of college athletics, but those profits have been gained because colleges have permitted the youths entrusted to their care to be openly exploited. At such colleges and universities, the primary emphasis has been transferred from the things of the spirit or the mind to the material" (Savage et al. 1929, 306–7).

The authors of the report came from private liberal arts colleges and lacked sympathy for large land-grant institutions with their mandate for public service. Nevertheless, they did believe that colleges and universities were special places separated from the ordinary commerce of society. The authors did not deny that profits from college sports had made many campus buildings possible. They did, however, question the entire commercial sports enterprise, wondering whether colleges and universities had departed too far from their educational missions by providing entertainment for the public. The report authors argued:

It is the undergraduates who have suffered most, and will continue to suffer most, from commercialism, and its results. More than any other force, it has tended to distort the values of college life and to increase its emphasis upon the material and the monetary. Indeed, at no point in the educational process has commercialism in college athletics wrought more mischief than

*in its effect upon the American undergraduate. And the distressing fact is
that the college, the Fostering Mother, has permitted and even encouraged
it to do these things in the name of education. (306–7)*

In other words, the university proponents of college sports, particularly university presidents and boards of trustees, claimed that the
function of sports is educational. Disputing that claim, the report
also attempted to refute an argument still put forth today:

*The argument that commercialism in college athletics is merely a reflec-
tion of the commercialism of modern life is specious. It is not the affair of
the college or the university to reflect [absolutely contemporary] modern
life. If the university is to be a socializing agency worthy of the name, it
must endeavor to ameliorate the conditions of existence, spiritual as well
as physical, and to train men and women who shall lead the nations out
of bondage to those conditions. To neither of these missions does commercialism in college athletics soundly contribute [nor do other elements of
commercialism on campus]. (306–7)*

We could not write these words today; in the postmodern era we
have become more cynical. Yet for all of the antique phrases and sentiments in the Carnegie Report, its vision of colleges and universities
as special and unique places unsullied by commercialism, its view of
undergraduates as different from other cohorts of the population,
and its assertion of the special meaning of a college education are
still meaningful. For that reason, the report remains a central document in the history of American higher education. . . .

Nike Schools

. . . In the late 1970s, a Las Vegas promoter named Sonny Vaccaro, who   15
had a passion for college basketball, wanted to promote basketball
tournaments and approached Nike to sponsor them. At the time,
Nike was a small company in Beaverton, Oregon, that manufactured
mainly track shoes but was interested in the basketball shoe market.
Vaccaro asked Nike to provide free shoes for the players as a way of
promoting the company's shoes and to give money to the coaches to
ensure that the players on their teams wore the free Nikes. The company was skeptical but agreed to try Vaccaro's scheme. In March 1979,
when *Sports Illustrated* featured a cover photograph of Larry Bird, then
a college player, with his Nike shoes clearly visible, the company realized the value of Vaccaro's concept. Sales exploded after the Bird

photos, and Nike became a major sponsor of college athletics. Its competitors, particularly Reebok and Adidas, quickly followed, vying with Nike to sign coaches, especially those in charge of teams that frequently appeared on television (Strasser and Becklund 1993).

In the early 1990s, the shoe endorsement money for a top coach reached a half-million dollars a year; and even lesser known coaches received six figures, causing a number of schools to step in and work out direct deals with corporate sponsors. Although the coach would still receive his or her money, the school would sign an exclusive contract with the corporation, the latter supplying all of the school's teams with equipment and paying the university for the privilege. The schools even claimed that this was a major college sports reform: they now had control of their coaches because the latter could not independently sign contracts with shoe companies but had to exist under the school's umbrella contract with corporate sponsors. The coaches liked the new arrangement — almost always a sign of non-reform — because they continued to receive the big bucks from the companies and now avoided the hassle of dealing with them directly.

The University of North Carolina at Chapel Hill was one of the first institutions to become a "Nike school." In 1993, it signed a five-year deal with Nike worth an estimated $11 million to the university, and Nike placed its swoosh logo on all UNC Chapel Hill team uniforms and shoes as well as on all coaches' jackets, hats, and other apparel — in short, on any UNC item that might appear on a telecast of a Tarheel game in any sport (*http://gazette.unc.edu/archives/01Oct24/file.5.html*). Television executives estimated that if UNC played another Nike-outfitted school such as the University of Michigan in a late-round National College Athletic Association (NCAA) men's basketball tournament game or a major bowl game, viewers would see the swoosh for about twenty minutes during the broadcast. At 1990s ad rates, that exposure was worth about $20 million. Considering that the sale of collegiate goods and apparel averaged $2.5 billion a year in the United States in the 1990s, Nike and its competitors were benefiting nicely from the university tie-ins.

Nike's director of college sports marketing, Kit Morris, commented, "The college market is one of our key target audiences. Outfitting college sports teams gives Nike authenticity and sends a strong message to consumers" (*Raleigh [N.C.] News and Observer*, 9 November 1997). The key word is *authenticity*. How could Nike translate the image of sneakers, sweatshirts, and warm-up suits, all of them inexpensive to make, into products for which young people will pay sizable sums of money? Nike's solution was to associate the company with an institution that represents authenticity, to mingle Nike's name with that of a prestigious university such as UNC Chapel Hill. In the *News and Observer,* Morris proudly explained that the company liked "the association with one of the premier universities in this country, a university that distinguishes itself in the classroom, on the playing field and court, and in the production of leaders. That's a very enviable association that's attractive for us."

After the company had signed up a number of distinguished universities as Nike schools, the law of unintended consequences caught up with Nike. Students at these institutions, better informed and more politically inclined than collegians at other big-time college sports schools, became concerned about how the shoes were made — specifically, about Nike's labor practices in Asia. The students learned that women in Nike's Asian factories usually worked very long hours for very little pay to produce the shoes. UNC Chapel Hill students organized campus rallies protesting Nike's labor practices; and the media picked up the story, giving Nike reams of unwanted negative publicity. Students at other Nike schools joined the protest movement. The *News and Observer* summed up the situation: "Having lent their athletic teams to Nike, dignified universities are finding themselves identified with an unpleasant image, that of poor Asians earning a few dollars a day working overtime to sew $100 sneakers."

Officials at UNC Chapel Hill and other schools answered students 20 and the media with a very old argument, essentially saying that the schools needed Nike money and could not support their athletic departments without the company's sponsorship. A coach at North Carolina State University explained that college sports is a business that must generate money in any way it can. The coach was correct. He failed, however, to state that college athletics is one of the most dysfunctional businesses in the United States. No matter how much revenue it generates, it spends more, often because of waste and mismanagement as well as its "athletics arms race": the habit of building new and often unnecessary multimillion-dollar facilities because rivals are constructing them. In the *Albany [N.Y.] Times Union,* 24 December 2000, the marketing director of Syracuse University's athletic department summed up the financial situation honestly: "Only 7 percent of NCAA Division I programs operate in the black . . . this is a multi-million dollar business. The reality is that the expenses are such that only a rare number of schools actually turn a profit. So it's either eliminate sports or try to enhance revenue with marketing and sales."

The truth is that schools do not need all the intercollegiate sports they play. For instance, twenty-six intercollegiate sports are played at the University of Michigan at a time of very tight educational budgets. It's difficult to understand why college administrators are willing to cut academic programs, even whole departments, yet rarely rein in athletic department growth and expenditures, even though they know that athletic department budgets are frequently in the red. In the *News and Observer* article, the chancellor of UNC Chapel Hill, Michael Hooker, offered a typical response to questions about Nike's tie-in with his university and athletic department: "I have misgivings about the propriety of a university being in the entertainment business, but that's what college athletics have become, and it's too late to turn back. The Nike contract falls within the context of the operation of the modern athletic department." This argument — accept the inevitability of affliction — has never carried much weight, but for a university president to make it is sad.

The most interesting aspect of the Nike case is its ethical dimension and what that says about the commercialization of the university. UNC Chapel Hill and other prestigious schools, including the University of Michigan, allied themselves with a corporation engaged in questionable labor practices. In the *News and Observer* piece, a student critic put the case succinctly: "college sports teams have been walking billboards for a company which is synonymous with the exploitation of young female workers." Obviously, this view casts an unfavorable light on the Nike schools; and as a UNC Chapel Hill faculty member said in the same article, "To the extent that we [this university] remain silent, we open ourselves to moral censure, if not ridicule." Universities should stand for positive values and ideals, not the exploitation of young Asian women and a corporation's manufacturing, marketing strategies, and bottom line. In a final irony, North Carolina was willing to tarnish its good name for a paltry sum of money. Considering the size of the school and its annual budget, Nike's $11 million over five years amounted to "chump change," and UNC played the role of the chump.

The Nike contract with these schools raises other important issues, including the nature of corporate sponsorship and the impact of the alliance with corporate America on the traditional independence of the university. The standard sporting-goods company contract contains clauses whereby universities agree to take reasonable steps necessary to address any remark by any university employee that disparages the company or its products. Obviously, this requirement runs counter to the university tradition of free speech.

One of academia's most cherished traditions is freedom of speech and research; indeed, tenure guarantees those freedoms. But corporate America has never valued those freedoms and sees little point in upholding them when it signs a contract with a university. Not surprisingly, during the Nike labor practice protests, Nike invoked the gag rule clause whenever possible, even asking St. John's University in New York, a Nike school, to fire an assistant soccer coach because he spoke out against Nike's Asian labor practices and refused to wear Nike apparel on the job. The university complied, and the coach filed a lawsuit that is now in litigation (Sperber 1990, 2000).

Aware of the prestige of a tie-in with an Ivy League institution, 25 Nike signed a deal with Brown University. Brown's students, however, were particularly active in protesting the company's Asian labor practices; so the company pulled out of the deal. Observers in higher education saw Nike's move as a clear warning to other Nike schools: end campus protests, or lose their Nike contract.

Other clauses in the standard Nike contract with schools bear close examination. Not only must athletes and coaches wear Nike equipment and apparel at all times, even if they prefer products sold by other sporting-goods companies, but they must also appear at various functions to promote Nike merchandise. Sporting-goods companies are not the only ones who make such stipulations. For example, the football players at Ohio State University are not allowed to celebrate an important victory by dousing their head coach with Gatorade, as professional football teams do. The players must use PowerAde because Coca-Cola, the company that makes PowerAde, has exclusive contracts with Ohio State (Sperber 1990, 2000). In essence, the athletes become part of the company's marketing strategy, losing independence of action in the bargain.

Even the incentive clauses in the standard contracts have a negative aspect. In addition to making an annual payout to the school, sporting-goods companies promise universities six-figure bonuses if their teams make the final rounds of the NCAA Division I basketball tournaments or play in major bowl games. At one level, the companies are simply rewarding schools for providing them with additional television and print exposure for their products. These clauses, however, like similar ones in coaches' contracts, also increase the importance of winning. Not surprisingly, some coaches and athletic departments respond to these inducements by placing student athletes in less rigorous courses to allow more time for sports training.

Nike's contracts with various universities, as well as the labor practice issue, illustrate the perils of corporate sponsorship in higher education. However, the Nike controversy did not discourage schools from pursuing corporate sponsors. After Nike made improvements in its Asian factories, the labor practice issue died down; and athletic departments pursued corporate sponsorships with increasing zeal, seemingly without concern for the nature of the corporation or the tie-in's impact on the school's educational mission. In the *Columbus [Ohio] Dispatch*, 6 December 1998, a long-time observer of higher education noted, "If you go back to the mid-1980s, the mind-set in the collegiate world was to go out and negotiate a deal with corporate America only when there was a serious financial need. Now the college decision-makers hustle every deal that they can." . . .

References

Quotations from the *Raleigh [N.C.] News and Observer* can be found at http://www
.uta.edu/depken/ugrad/sports/readings/athletes-as-billboards.pdf. Quotations
from all other cited newspapers can be found at http://web.lexis-nexis.com.

Rader, Benjamin. 1983. *American Sports: From the Age of Folk Games to the Age of Spectators.* Englewood Cliffs, N.J.: Prentice Hall.

Savage, Howard, et al. 1929. "American College Athletics." Bulletin no. 23. New York: Carnegie Foundation.

Smith, Ronald A. 1988. *Sports and Freedom: The Rise of Big-Time College Athletics.* Oxford: Oxford University Press.

Smith, Ronald A., and John A. Lucas. 1978. *Saga of American Sport.* Philadelphia: Lea and Febiger.

Sperber, Murray. 1990. *College Sports, Inc.: The Athletic Department vs. the University.* New York: Holt.

———. 1998. *Onward to Victory: The Crises That Shaped College Sports.* New York: Holt.

———. 2000. *Beer and Circus: How Big-Time College Sports Is Crippling Undergraduate Education.* New York: Holt.

Strasser, J. B., and Laurie Becklund. 1993. *Swoosh: The Unauthorized Story of Nike and the Men Who Played There.* New York: HarperBusiness.

Understanding the Text

1. Which of the following issues in the commercialization of college sports does Sperber address? For each that he takes up, use no more than two or three sentences to summarize what he has to say on the subject.

   school priorities

   sportsmanship and fairness

   the physical and mental well-being of student athletes

   academic freedom of speech

2. Which of these issues come up in the case of Nike sportswear? Explain.

Reflection and Response

3. Here is an actual entry from one student's "money journal":

> In August, I experienced two concussions playing on [the school's] varsity football team, and I am still feeling the effects of them today—"post-concussion syndrome," as doctors call it. Since then, I've spent months with headaches and have lost thirty-five pounds because I haven't been able to work out. Although I dreamed my whole life of becoming a college football player, I know it is time to walk away from the game for my own safety and well-being. Yesterday, I called my aunt to tell her I was going to tell the coaches I could no longer play, and she freaked out. "Don't tell them anything yet! I don't want them to take away your scholarship!" I explained to her that I wanted to be open and honest with my coaches, and maybe ask them for a position as team manager, in order to earn some of my $5,000 scholarship back. She told me not to do anything yet, and I listened, because I am not the one who will be paying that money out of my own pocket. . . .
>
> I'm sure there are plenty of young athletes, just like me, who are playing a sport they wish they could stop playing, but are forced to stick with it for financial reasons. Heck, even pro athletes hold out until they can negotiate better, larger contracts. I thought sports were played for the love of the game. It never occurred to me what a huge role money plays in them.

   How would Sperber probably react to this true account? Drawing from Sperber's own piece, say what makes you think so.

4. Look again at the journal entry quoted in question 3 — this time, homing in on the phrase "for the love of the game," in the second-to-last sentence. As fully as you can, spell out what this phrase means to you.

   What sports or other activities have you pursued "for the love of it"? Have monetary incentives ever been present? If so, what effect did they have? If not, what effect can you *imagine* such incentives having?

5. Are you as upset by the effects of commercialization in sports as Sperber is? Why or why not?

6. Of the situations Sperber laments, are there ones that might have existed even if big money weren't a factor on the college sports scene? Elaborate.

Making Connections

7. Read Arianna Huffington's "CSI USA: Who Killed the American Dream?" (p. 169). Could she just as easily have written a piece titled "CSI NCAA: Who Killed the Ideals of Good Sportsmanship in College Athletics?" To what extent do Huffington's and Sperber's analyses parallel each other?

8. Did it surprise you to learn that college sports in America were, in part, commercial spectacles from the beginning? Why or why not?

   Can the same be said of college sports in other countries? With help online or from a librarian, find out.

   What, if any, questions about the culture of America do your findings raise?

Quitting the Paint Factory: On the Virtues of Idleness

Mark Slouka

Just as promised in the subtitle of this essay, Mark Slouka uses it to champion "down time," time set apart from the life of money-making.

Slouka has been a contributing editor at *Harper's Magazine* and the director of the University of Chicago's writing program. He has garnered recognition not just for his essays, but also for his works of fiction, such as the novel *God's Fool*.

> Love yields to business. If you seek a way out of love, be busy; you'll be safe, then.
>
> —OVID, *REMEDIA AMORIS*

I distrust the perpetually busy; always have. The frenetic ones, spinning in tight little circles like poisoned rats. The slower ones, grinding away their fourscore and ten in righteousness and pain. They are the soul-eaters.

When I was young, my parents read me Aesop's fable of "The Ant and the Grasshopper," wherein, as everyone knows, the grasshopper spends the summer making music in the sun while the ant toils with his fellow *formicidae*. Inevitably, winter comes, as winters will, and the grasshopper, who hasn't planned ahead and who doesn't know what a 401K is, has run out of luck. When he shows up at the ant's door, carrying his fiddle, the ant asks him what he was doing all year. "I was singing, if you please," the grasshopper replies, or something to that effect. "You were singing?" says the ant. "Well, then, go and sing." And perhaps because I sensed, even then, that fate would someday find me holding a violin or a manuscript at the door of the ants, my antennae frozen and my bills overdue, I confounded both Aesop and my well-meaning parents, and bore away the wrong moral. That summer, many a wind-blown grasshopper was saved from the pond, and many an anthill inundated under the golden rain of my pee.

I was right.

In the lifetime that has passed since Calvin Coolidge gave his speech to the American Society of Newspaper Editors in which he famously proclaimed that "the chief business of the American people is business," the dominion of the ants has grown enormously. Look about: The business of business is everywhere and inescapable; the song of the buyers and the sellers never stops; the term "workaholic" has been folded up and put away. We have no time for our friends or our families, no time to think or to make a meal. We're moving product, while the soul drowns like a cat in a well.[1]

* * *

A resuscitated orthodoxy, so pervasive as to be nearly invisible, rules the land. Like any religion worth its salt, it shapes our world in its image, demonizing if necessary, absorbing when possible. Thus has the great sovereign territory of what Nabokov called "unreal estate," the continent of invisible possessions from time to talent to contentment, been either infantilized, rendered unclean, or translated into the grammar of dollars and cents. Thus has the great wilderness of the inner life been compressed into a median strip by the demands of the "real world," which of course is anything but. Thus have we succeeded in transforming even ourselves into bipedal products, paying richly for seminars that teach us how to market the self so it may be sold to the highest bidder. Or perhaps "down the river" is the phrase.

Ah, but here's the rub: Idleness is not just a psychological necessity, requisite to the construction of a complete human being; it constitutes as well a kind of political space, a space as necessary to the workings of an actual democracy as, say, a free press. How does it do this? By allowing us time to figure out who we are, and what we believe; by allowing us time to consider what is unjust, and what we might do about it. By giving the inner life (in whose precincts we are most ourselves) its due. Which is precisely what makes idleness dangerous. All manner of things can grow out of that fallow soil. Not for nothing did our mothers grow suspicious when we had "too much time on our hands." They knew we might be

> Idleness is not just a psychological necessity . . . it constitutes as well a kind of political space, a space as necessary to the workings of an actual democracy as, say, a free press.

---

[1] "I think that there is far too much work done in the world," Bertrand Russell observed in his famous 1932 essay "In Praise of Idleness," adding that he hoped to "start a campaign to induce good young men to do nothing." He failed. A year later, National Socialism, with its cult of work (think of all those bronzed young men in Leni Riefenstahl's *Triumph of the Will* throwing cordwood to each other in the sun), flared in Germany.

up to something. And not for nothing did we whisper to each other, when we *were* up to something, "Quick, look busy."

Mother knew instinctively what the keepers of the castles have always known: that trouble — the kind that might threaten the symmetry of a well-ordered garden — needs time to take root. Take away the time, therefore, and you choke off the problem before it begins. Obedience reigns, the plow stays in the furrow; things proceed as they must. Which raises an uncomfortable question: Could the Church of Work — which today has Americans aspiring to sleep deprivation the way they once aspired to a personal knowledge of God — be, at base, an anti-democratic force? Well, yes. James Russell Lowell, that nineteenth-century workhorse, summed it all up quite neatly: "There is no better ballast for keeping the mind steady on its keel, and saving it from all risk of crankiness, than business."

Quite so. The mind, however, particularly the mind of a citizen in a democratic society, is not a boat. Ballast is not what it needs, and steadiness, alas, can be a synonym for stupidity, as our current administration has so amply demonstrated. No, what the democratic mind requires, above all, is time; time to consider its options. Time to develop the democratic virtues of independence, orneriness, objectivity, and fairness. Time, perhaps (to sail along with Lowell's leaky metaphor for a moment), to ponder the course our unelected captains have so generously set for us, and to consider mutiny when the iceberg looms.

Which is precisely why we need to be kept busy. If we have no time to think, to mull, if we have no time to piece together the sudden associations and unexpected, mid-shower insights that are the stuff of independent opinion, then we are less citizens than cursors, easily manipulated, vulnerable to the currents of power.

● ● ●

But I have to be careful here. Having worked all of my adult life, I   10
recognize that work of one sort or another is as essential to survival as protein, and that much of it, in today's highly bureaucratized, economically diversified societies, will of necessity be neither pleasant nor challenging nor particularly meaningful. I have compassion for those making the most of their commute and their cubicle; I just wish they could be a little less cheerful about it. In short, this isn't about us so much as it is about the *Zeitgeist* we live and labor in, which, like a cuckoo taking over a thrush's nest, has systematically shoved all the

other eggs of our life, one by one, onto the pavement. It's about illuminating the losses.

We're enthralled. I want to dis-enchant us a bit; draw a mustache on the boss.

Infinite Bustle

I'm a student of the narrowing margins. And their victim, to some extent, though my capacity for sloth, my belief in it, may yet save me. Like some stubborn heretic in fifth-century Rome, still offering gifts to the spirit of the fields even as the priests sniff about the *tempa* for sin, I daily sacrifice my bit of time. The pagan gods may yet return. Constantine and Theodosius may die. But the prospects are bad.

In Riverside Park in New York City, where I walk these days, the legions of "weekend nannies" are growing, setting up a play date for a ten-year-old requires a feat of near-Olympic coordination, and the few, vestigial, late-afternoon parents one sees, dragging their wailing progeny by the hand or frantically kicking a soccer ball in the fading light, have a gleam in their eyes I find frightening. No outstretched legs crossed at the ankles, no arms draped over the back of the bench. No lovers. No be-hatted old men, arguing. Between the slide and the sandbox, a very fit young man in his early thirties is talking on his cell phone while a two-year-old with a trail of snot running from his nose tugs on the seam of his corduroy pants. "There's no way I can pick it up. Because we're still at the park. Because we just got here, that's why."

It's been one hundred and forty years since Thoreau, who itched a full century before everyone else began to scratch, complained that the world was increasingly just "a place of business. What an infinite bustle!" he groused. "I am awaked almost every night by the panting of the locomotive. It interrupts my dreams. There is no Sabbath. It would be glorious to see mankind at leisure for once. It is nothing but work, work, work." Little did he know. Today the roads of commerce, paved and smoothed, reach into every nook and cranny of the republic; there is no place apart, no place where we would be shut of the drone of that damnable traffic. Today we, quite literally, live to work. And it hardly matters what kind of work we do; the process justifies the ends. Indeed, at times it seems there is hardly an occupation, however useless or humiliating or downright despicable, that cannot at least in part be redeemed by our obsessive dedication to it: "Yes, Ted sold shoulder-held Stingers to folks with no surname, but he worked so *hard!*"

Not long ago, at the kind of dinner party I rarely attend, I made the   15
mistake of admitting that I not only liked to sleep but liked to get at
least eight hours a night whenever possible, and that nine would be
better still. The reaction — a complex Pinot Noir of nervous laughter
displaced by expressions of disbelief and condescension — suggested
that my transgression had been, on some level, a political one. I was
reminded of the time I'd confessed to Roger Angell that I did not
much care for baseball.

My comment was immediately rebutted by testimonials to sleep-
lessness: two of the nine guests confessed to being insomniacs; a
member of the Academy of Arts and Letters claimed indignantly that
she couldn't remember when she had *ever* gotten eight hours of sleep;
two other guests declared themselves grateful for five or six. It mattered little that I'd arranged my life differently, and accepted the
sacrifices that arrangement entailed. Eight hours! There was something willful about it. Arrogant, even. Suitably chastened, I held my
tongue, and escaped alone to tell Thee.

• • •

Increasingly, it seems to me, our world is dividing into two kinds of
things: those that aid work, or at least represent a path to it, and those
that don't. Things in the first category are good and noble; things
in the second aren't. Thus, for example, education is good (as long as
we don't have to listen to any of that "end in itself" nonsense) because
it will presumably lead to work. Thus playing the piano or swimming
the 100-yard backstroke are good things for a fifteen-year-old to do
not because they might give her some pleasure but because rumor
has it that Princeton is interested in students who can play Chopin or
swim quickly on their backs (and a degree from Princeton, as any
fool knows, can be readily converted to work).

Point the beam anywhere, and there's the God of Work, busily tram-
pling out the vintage. Blizzards are bemoaned because they keep us
from getting to work. Hobbies are seen as either ridiculous or self-
indulgent because they interfere with work. Longer school days are
all the rage (even as our children grow demonstrably stupider), not
because they make educational or psychological or any other kind of
sense but because keeping kids in school longer makes it easier for us
to work. Meanwhile, the time grows short, the margin narrows; the
white spaces on our calendars have been inked in for months. We're
angry about this, upset about that, but who has the time to do any-

thing anymore? There are those reports to report on, memos to remember, emails to deflect or delete. They bury us like snow.

The alarm rings and we're off, running so hard that by the time we stop we're too tired to do much of anything except nod in front of the TV, which, like virtually all the other voices in our culture, endorses our exhaustion, fetishizes and romanticizes it and, by daily adding its little trowelful of lies and omissions, helps cement the conviction that not only is this how our three score and ten must be spent but that the transaction is both noble and necessary.

Ka-chink!

Time may be money (though I've always resisted that loathsome platitude, the alchemy by which the very gold of our lives is transformed into the base lead of commerce), but one thing seems certain: Money eats time. Forget the visions of sanctioned leisure: the view from the deck in St. Moritz, the wafer-thin TV. Consider the price. 20

Sometimes, I want to say, money costs too much. And at the beginning of the millennium, in this country, the cost of money is well on the way to bankrupting us. We're impoverishing ourselves, our families, our communities — and yet we can't stop ourselves. Worse, we don't want to.

Seen from the right vantage point, there's something wonderfully animistic about it. The god must be fed; he's hungry for our hours, craves our days and years. And we oblige. Every morning (unlike the good citizens of Tenochtitlán, who at least had the good sense to sacrifice others on the slab) we rush up the steps of the ziggurat to lay ourselves down. It's not a pretty sight.

Then again, we've been well trained. And the training never stops. In a recent ad in *The New York Times Magazine*, paid for by an outfit named Wealth and Tax Advisory Services, Inc., an attractive young woman in a dark business suit is shown working at her desk. (She may be at home, though these days the distinction is moot.) On the desk is a cup, a cell phone, and an adding machine. Above her right shoulder, just over the blurred sofa and the blurred landscape on the wall, are the words, "Successful entrepreneurs work continuously." The text below explains: "The challenge to building wealth is that your finances grow in complexity as your time demands increase."

The ad is worth disarticulating, it seems to me, if only because some version of it is beamed into our cerebral cortex a thousand times a day. What's interesting about it is not only what it says but what it so blithely assumes. What it says, crudely enough, is that in order to be successful, we must not only work but work *continuously;* what it assumes is that time is inversely proportional to wealth: our time demands *will* increase the harder we work and the more successful we become. It's an organic thing; a law, almost. Fish gotta swim and birds gotta fly, you gotta work like a dog till you die.

Am I suggesting then that Wealth and Tax Advisory Services, Inc.   25 spend $60,000 for a full-page ad in *The New York Times Magazine* to show us a young woman at her desk writing poetry? Or playing with her kids? Or sharing a glass of wine with a friend, attractively thumbing her nose at the acquisition of wealth? No. For one thing, the folks at Wealth and Tax, etc. are simply doing what's in their best interest. For another, it would hardly matter if they did show the woman writing poetry, or laughing with her children, because these things, by virtue of their placement in the ad, would immediately take on the color of their host; they would simply be the rewards of working *almost* continuously.

What I am suggesting is that just as the marketplace has co-opted rebellion by subordinating politics to fashion, by making anger chic so it has quietly underwritten the idea of leisure, in part by separating it from idleness. Open almost any magazine in America today and there they are: The ubiquitous tanned-and-toned twenty-somethings driving the $70,000 fruits of their labor; the moneyed-looking men and women in their healthy sixties (to give the young something to aspire to) tossing Frisbees to Irish setters or tying on flies in midstream or watching sunsets from their Adirondack chairs.

Leisure is permissible, we understand, because it costs money; idleness is not, because it doesn't. Leisure is focused; whatever thinking it requires is absorbed by a certain task: sinking that putt, making that cast, watching that flat-screen TV. Idleness is unconstrained, anarchic. Leisure — particularly if it involves some kind of high-priced technology — is as American as a Fourth of July barbecue. Idleness, on the other hand, has a bad attitude. It doesn't shave; it's not a member of the team; it doesn't play well with others. It thinks too much, as my high school coach used to say. So it has to be ostracized.[2]

---

[2] Or put to good use. The wilderness of association we enter when we read, for example, is one of the world's great domains of imaginative diversity: a seedbed of individualism. What better reason to pave it then, to make it an accessory, like a personal organizer, a sure-fire way of raising your SAT score, or improving your communication skills for that next interview. You say you like to read? Then don't waste your time; put it to work. Order *Shakespeare in Charge: The Bard's Guide to Leading and Succeeding on the Business Stage,* with its picture of the bard in a business suit on the cover.

With idleness safely on the reservation, the notion that leisure is necessarily a function of money is free to grow into a truism. "Money isn't the goal. Your goals, that's the goal," reads a recent ad for Citibank. At first glance, there's something appealingly subversive about it. Apply a little skepticism though, and the implicit message floats to the surface: And how else are you going to reach those goals than by investing wisely with us? Which suggests that, um, money is the goal, after all.

The Church of Work

There's something un-American about singing the virtues of idleness. It is a form of blasphemy, a secular sin. More precisely, it is a kind of latter-day antinomianism, as much a threat to the orthodoxy of our day as Anne Hutchinson's desire 350 years ago to circumvent the Puritan ministers and dial God direct. Hutchinson, we recall, got into trouble because she accused the Puritan elders of backsliding from the rigors of their theology and giving in to a Covenant of Works, whereby the individual could earn his all-expenses-paid trip to the pearly gates through the labor of his hands rather than solely through the grace of God. Think of it as a kind of frequent-flier plan for the soul.

The analogy to today is instructive. Like the New England clergy, the Religion of Business — literalized, painfully, in books like *Jesus, C.E.O.* — holds a monopoly on interpretation; it sets the terms, dictates value.[3] Although today's version of the Covenant of Works has substituted a host of secular pleasures for the idea of heaven, it too seeks to corner the market on what we most desire, to suggest that the work of our hands will save us. And we believe. We believe across all the boundaries of class and race and ethnicity that normally divide us; we believe in numbers that dwarf those of the more conventionally faithful. We repeat the daily catechism, we sing in the choir. And we tithe, and keep on tithing, until we are spent.

It is this willingness to hand over our lives that fascinates and appalls me. There's such a lovely perversity to it; it's so wonderfully counterintuitive, so very Christian: You must empty your pockets, turn them inside out, and spill out your wife and your son, the pets you hardly knew, and the days you simply missed altogether watching

---

[3] In this new lexicon, for example, "work" is defined as the means to wealth, "success," as a synonym for it.

the sunlight fade on the bricks across the way. You must hand over the rainy afternoons, the light on the grass, the moments of play and of simply being. You must give it up, all of it, and by your example teach your children to do the same, and then — because even this is not enough — you must train yourself to believe that this outsourcing of your life is both natural and good. But even so, your soul will not be saved.

The young, for a time, know better. They balk at the harness. They do not go easy. For a time they are able to see the utter sadness of subordinating all that matters to all that doesn't. Eventually, of course, sitting in their cubicle lined with *New Yorker* cartoons, selling whatever it is they've been asked to sell, most come to see the advantage of enthusiasm. They join the choir and are duly forgiven for their illusions. It's a rite of passage we are all familiar with. The generations before us clear the path; Augustine stands to the left, Freud to the right. We are born into death, and die into life, they murmur; civilization will have its discontents. The sign in front of the Church of Our Lady of Perpetual Work confirms it. And we believe.

• • •

All of which leaves only the task of explaining away those few miscreants who out of some inner weakness or perversity either refuse to convert or who go along and then, in their thirty-sixth year in the choir, say, abruptly abandon the faith. Those in the first category are relatively easy to contend with; they are simply losers. Those in the second are a bit more difficult; their apostasy requires something more . . . dramatic. They are considered mad.

In one of my favorite anecdotes from American literary history (which my children know by heart, and which in turn bodes poorly for their futures as captains of industry), the writer Sherwood Anderson found himself, at the age of thirty-six, the chief owner and general manager of a paint factory in Elyria, Ohio. Having made something of a reputation for himself as a copywriter in a Chicago advertising agency, he'd moved up a rung. He was on his way, as they say, a businessman in the making, perhaps even a tycoon in embryo. There was only one problem: he couldn't seem to shake the notion that the work he was doing (writing circulars extolling the virtues of his line of paints) was patently absurd, undignified; that it amounted to a kind of prison sentence. Lacking the rationalizing gene, incapable of numbing himself sufficiently to make the days and the years pass without pain, he suffered and flailed. Eventually he snapped.

It was a scene he would revisit time and again in his memoirs and 35
fiction. On November 27, 1912, in the middle of dictating a letter to his
secretary ("The goods about which you have inquired are the best of
their kind made in the . . ."), he simply stopped. According to the story,
the two supposedly stared at each other for a long time, after which
Anderson said: "I have been wading in a long river and my feet are
wet," and walked out. Outside the building he turned east toward
Cleveland and kept going. Four days later he was recognized and
taken to a hospital, suffering from exhaustion.

Anderson claimed afterward that he had encouraged the impression that he might be cracking up in order to facilitate his exit,
to make it comprehensible. "The thought occurred to me that if
men thought me a little insane they would forgive me if I lit out,"
he wrote, and though we will never know for sure if he suffered a
nervous breakdown that day or only pretended to one (his biogra-
phers have concluded that he did), the point of the anecdote is elsewhere: Real or imagined, nothing short of madness would do for an
excuse.

Anderson himself, of course, was smart enough to recognize the
absurdity in all this, and to use it for his own ends; over the years that
followed, he worked his escape from the paint factory into a kind of
parable of liberation, an exemplar for the young men of his age. It became the cornerstone of his critique of the emerging business culture:
To stay was to suffocate, slowly; to escape was to take a stab at "alive-
ness." What America needed, Anderson argued, was a new class of
individuals who "at any physical cost to themselves and others" would
"agree to quit working, to loaf, to refuse to be hurried or try to get on
in the world."

"To refuse to be hurried or try to get on in the world." It sounds quite
mad. What would we do if we followed that advice? And who would we
be? No, better to pull down the blinds, finish that sentence. We're all in
the paint factory now.

Clearing Brush

At times you can almost see it, this flypaper we're attached to, this
mechanism we labor in, this delusion we inhabit. A thing of such
magnitude can be hard to make out, of course, but you can rough out
its shape and mark its progress, like Lon Chaney's Invisible Man, by
its effects: by the things it renders quaint or obsolete, by the trail of
discarded notions it leaves behind. What we're leaving behind today,
at record pace, is whatever belief we might once have had in the

value of unstructured time: in the privilege of contemplating our lives before they are gone, in the importance of uninterrupted conversation, in the beauty of play. In the thing in itself — unmediated, leading nowhere. In the present moment.

Admittedly, the present — in its ontological, rather than consumerist, sense — has never been too popular on this side of the Atlantic; we've always been a finger-drumming, restless bunch, suspicious of jawboning, less likely to sit at the table than to grab a quick one at the bar. Whitman might have exhorted us to loaf and invite our souls, but that was not an invitation we cared to extend, not unless the soul played poker, ha, ha. No sir, a Frenchman might invite his soul. One expected such things. But an American? An American would be out the swinging doors and halfway to tomorrow before his silver dollar had stopped ringing on the counter.

• • •

I was put in mind of all this last June while sitting on a bench in London's Hampstead Heath. My bench, like many others, was almost entirely hidden; well off the path, delightfully overgrown, it sat at the top of a long-grassed meadow. It had a view. There was whimsy in its placement, and joy. It was thoroughly impractical. It had clearly been placed there to encourage one thing — solitary contemplation.

And sitting there, listening to the summer drone of the bees, I suddenly imagined George W. Bush on my bench. I can't tell you why this happened, or what in particular brought the image to my mind. Possibly it was the sheer incongruity of it that appealed to me, the turtle-on-a-lamppost illogic of it; earlier that summer, intrigued by images of Kafka's face on posters advertising the Prague Marathon, I'd entertained myself with pictures of Franz looking fit for the big race. In any case, my vision of Dubya sitting on a bench, reading a book on his lap — smiling or nodding in agreement, wetting a finger to turn a page — was so discordant, so absurd, that I realized I'd accidentally stumbled upon one of those visual oxymorons that, by its very dissonance, illuminates something essential.

What the picture of George W. Bush flushed into the open for me was the classically American and increasingly Republican cult of movement, of busy-ness; of doing, not thinking. One could imagine Kennedy reading on that bench in Hampstead Heath. Or Carter, maybe. Or even Clinton (though given the bucolic setting, one could also imagine him in other, more Dionysian scenarios). But Bush? Bush would be

40

clearing brush. He'd be stomping it into submission with his pointy boots. He'd be making the world a better place.

Now, something about all that brush clearing had always bothered me. It wasn't the work itself, though I'd never fully understood where all that brush was being cleared from, or why, or how it was possible that there was any brush still left between Dallas and Austin. No, it was the frenetic, anti-thinking element of it I disliked. This wasn't simply outdoor work, which I had done my share of and knew well. This was brush clearing as a statement, a gesture of impatience. It captured the man, his disdain for the inner life, for the virtues of slowness and contemplation. This was movement as an answer to all those equivocating intellectuals and Gallic pontificators who would rather talk than do, think than act. Who could always be counted on to complicate what was simple with long-winded discussions of complexity and consequences. Who were weak.

And then I had it, the thing I'd been trying to place, the thing that 45 had always made me bristle — instinctively — whenever I saw our fidgety, unelected President in action. I recalled reading about an Italian art movement called Futurism, which had flourished in the first decades of the twentieth century. Its practitioners had advocated a cult of restlessness, of speed, of dynamism; had rejected the past in all its forms; had glorified business and war and patriotism. They had also, at least in theory, supported the growth of fascism.

The link seemed tenuous at best, even facile. Was I seriously linking Bush — his shallowness, his bustle, his obvious suspicion of nuance — to the spirit of fascism? As much as I loathed the man, it made me uneasy. I'd always argued with people who applied the word carelessly. Having been called a fascist myself for suggesting that an ill-tempered rottweiler be put on a leash, I had no wish to align myself with those who had downgraded the word to a kind of generalized epithet, roughly synonymous with "asshole," to be applied to whoever disagreed with them. I had too much respect for the real thing. And yet there was no getting around it; what I'd been picking up like a bad smell whenever I observed the Bush team in action was the faint but unmistakable whiff of fascism; a democratically diluted fascism, true, and masked by the perfume of down-home cookin', but fascism nonetheless.

Still, it was not until I'd returned to the States and had forced myself to wade through the reams of Futurist manifestos — a form that obviously spoke to their hearts — that the details of the connection began to come clear. The linkage had nothing to do with the Futurists' art, which was notable only for its sustained mediocrity, nor with their writing, which at times achieved an almost sublime level of badness.

It had to do, rather, with their ant-like energy, their busy-ness, their utter disdain of all the manifestations of the inner life, and with the way these traits seemed so organically linked in their thinking to aggression and war. "We intend to exalt aggressive action, a feverish insomnia," wrote Filippo Marinetti, perhaps the Futurists' most breathless spokesman. "We will glorify war — the world's only hygiene — militarism, patriotism, the destructive gesture of freedombringers. . . . We will destroy the museums, libraries, academies of every kind. . . . We will sing of great crowds excited by work."

"Militarism, patriotism, the destructive gesture of freedombringers," "a feverish insomnia," "great crowds excited by work" . . . I knew that song. And yet still, almost perversely, I resisted the recognition. It was too easy, somehow. Wasn't much of the Futurist rant ("Take up your pickaxes, your axes and hammers and wreck, wreck the venerable cities, pitilessly") simply a gesture of adolescent rebellion, a FUCK YOU scrawled on Dad's garage door? I had just about decided to scrap the whole thing when I came across Marinetti's later and more extended version of the Futurist creed. And this time the connection was impossible to deny.

In the piece, published in June of 1913 (roughly six months after Anderson walked out of the paint factory), Marinetti explained that Futurism was about the "acceleration of life to today's swift pace." It was about the "dread of the old and the known . . . of quiet living." The new age, he wrote, would require the "negation of distances and nostalgic solitudes." It would "ridicule . . . the 'holy green silence' and the ineffable landscape." It would be, instead, an age enamored of "the passion, art, and idealism of Business."

This shift from slowness to speed, from the solitary individual to   50
the crowd excited by work, would in turn force other adjustments. The worship of speed and business would require a new patriotism, "a heroic idealization of the commercial, industrial, and artistic solidarity of a people"; it would require "a modification in the idea of war," in order to make it "the necessary and bloody test of a people's force."

As if this weren't enough, as if the parallel were not yet sufficiently clear, there was this: The new man, Marinetti wrote — and this deserves my italics — would communicate by *"brutally destroying the syntax of his speech. He wastes no time in building sentences. Punctuation and the right adjectives will mean nothing to him. He will despise subtleties and nuances of language."* All of his thinking, moreover, would be marked by a *"dread of slowness, pettiness, analysis, and detailed explanations. Love of speed, abbreviation, and the summary. 'Quick, give me the whole thing in two words!'"*

Short of telling us that he would have a ranch in Crawford, Texas, and be given to clearing brush, nothing Marinetti wrote could have made the resemblance clearer. From his notorious mangling of the English language to his well-documented impatience with detail and analysis to his chuckling disregard for human life (which enabled him to crack jokes about Aileen Wuornos's execution as well as mug for the cameras minutes before announcing that the nation was going to war), Dubya was Marinetti's "New Man": impatient, almost pathologically unreflective, unburdened by the past. A man untroubled by the imagination, or by an awareness of human frailty. A leader wonderfully attuned (though one doubted he could ever articulate it) to "today's swift pace"; to the necessity of forging a new patriotism; to the idea of war as "the necessary and bloody test of a people's force"; to the all-conquering beauty of Business.

Understanding the Text

1. Would you agree that for an essay that extols idleness, this essay has a very high energy, or mental speed, to it? Explain.

   What are the ingredients of such a prose style? What might account for Mark Slouka's decision to employ such a style?

2. What does Slouka *mean* by "idleness"? How does he distinguish it from "leisure"?

3. Why is idleness important to him?

Reflection and Response

4. The epigraph Slouka chose for this essay is a quote from the Roman poet Ovid: "Love yields to business. If you seek a way out of love, be busy; you'll be safe, then." Does that seem an apt choice for introducing Slouka's piece? Why or why not?

5. A question posed by a student: What might Slouka say about people who work at jobs they love?

Making Connections

6. From Slouka's paragraph 14, we can tell that Henry David Thoreau is a thinker of importance to him. Thoreau once said, "Wealth is the ability to fully experience life." He also said, "If a man walks in the woods for love of them half of each day, he is in danger of being regarded as a loafer. But if he spends his days as a speculator, shearing off those woods and making the earth bald before her time, he is deemed an industrious and enterprising citizen."

   Ten years after graduating from Harvard in 1837, Thoreau and his classmates were asked to submit accounts of the progress they had made in life so far. Here is the letter Thoreau submitted:

I confess that I have very little class spirit, and have almost forgotten that I ever spent four years at Cambridge. That must have been in a former state of existence. . . . However, I will undertake at last to answer your questions as well as I can in spite of a poor memory and a defect of information. . . .

I am not married.

I don't know whether mine is a profession, or a trade, or what not. It is not yet learned, and in every instance has been practised before being studied. . . .

It is not one but legion, I will give you some of the monster's heads. I am a Schoolmaster — a private Tutor, a Surveyor — a Gardener, a Farmer — a Painter, I mean a House Painter, a Carpenter, a Mason, a Day-Laborer, a Pencil-Maker, a Glass-paper Maker, a Writer, and sometimes a Poetaster. If you will act the part of Iolas, and apply a hot iron to any of these heads, I shall be greatly obliged to you.

My present employment is to answer such orders as may be expected from so general an advertisement as the above — that is, if I see fit, which is not always the case, for I have found out a way to live without what is commonly called employment or industry attractive or otherwise. Indeed my steadiest employment, if such it can be called, is to keep myself at the top of my condition, and ready for whatever may turn up in heaven or on earth. For the last two or three years I have lived in Concord woods alone, something more than a mile from any neighbor, in a house built entirely by myself. . . .

P.S. I beg that the Class will not consider me an object of charity, and if any of them are in want of pecuniary assistance, and will make known their case to me, I will engage to give them some advice of more worth than money.

Write a paper in which you describe Thoreau's tone here. What things that he says should be taken literally? What things should not? How can you tell the difference?

From there, go on to say how similar to Thoreau's sentiments you would hope your own to be, ten years after graduation. Elaborate. What seems right or wrong to you in Thoreau's thinking? Why?

7. Read E. F. Schumacher's "Buddhist Economics" (p. 307). Would Mark Slouka's sensibility qualify as Buddhist to Schumacher? Elaborate.

Does God Want You to Be Rich?

David Van Biema
and Jeff Chu

What guidance does organized religion provide regarding the desire to make money? The answer isn't clear, at least in the Judeo-Christian tradition.

Co-author David Van Biema has worked both as a senior writer and as an associate editor at *Time* magazine. Co-author Jeff Chu has been a reporter at *Time* magazine and *Conde Nast Portfolio,* as well as an editor at *Fast Company.*

When George Adams lost his job at an Ohio tile factory last October, the most practical thing he did, he thinks, was go to a new church, even though he had to move his wife and four preteen boys to Conroe, a suburb of Houston, to do it. Conroe, you see, is not far from Lakewood, the home church of megapastor and best-selling author Joel Osteen.

Osteen's relentlessly upbeat television sermons had helped Adams, 49, get through the hard times, and now Adams was expecting the smiling, Texas-twanged 43-year-old to help boost him back toward success. And Osteen did. Inspired by the preacher's insistence that one of God's top priorities is to shower blessings on Christians in this lifetime — and by the corollary assumption that one of the worst things a person can do is to expect anything less — Adams marched into Gullo Ford in Conroe looking for work. He didn't have entry-level aspirations: "God has showed me that he doesn't want me to be a run-of-the-mill person," he explains. He demanded to know what the dealership's top salesmen made — and got the job. Banishing all doubt — "You can't sell a $40,000-to-$50,000 car with menial thoughts" — Adams took four days to retail his first vehicle, a Ford F-150 Lariat with leather interior. He knew that many fellow salesmen don't notch their first score until their second week. "Right now, I'm above average!" he exclaims. "It's a new day God has given me! I'm on my way to a six-figure income!" The sales commission will help with this month's rent, but Adams hates renting. Once that six-figure income has been rolling in for a while, he will buy his dream house: "Twenty-five acres," he says. "And three bedrooms. We're going to have a school-house (his children are home schooled). We want horses and ponies for the boys, so a horse barn. And a pond. And maybe some cattle."

"I'm dreaming big — because all of heaven is dreaming big," Adams continues. "Jesus died for our sins. That was the best gift God could

give us," he says. "But we have something else. Because I want to fol-
low Jesus and do what he ordained, God wants to support us. It's Joel
Osteen's ministry that told me. Why would an awesome and mighty
God want anything less for his children?"

In three of the Gospels, Jesus warns that each of his disciples may
have to "deny himself" and even "take up his Cross." In support of
this alarming prediction, he forcefully contrasts the fleeting pleasures of today with the promise of eternity: "For what profit is it to
a man," he asks, "if he gains the whole world, and loses his own soul?"
It is one of the New Testament's hardest teachings, yet generations of
churchgoers have understood that being Christian, on some level,
means being ready to sacrifice — money, autonomy or even their lives.

But for a growing number of Christians like George Adams, the   5
question is better restated, "Why not gain the whole world plus my
soul?" For several decades, a philosophy has been percolating in the
10 million–strong Pentecostal wing of Christianity that seems to
turn the Gospels' passage on its head: certainly, it allows, Christians should keep one eye on heaven. But the new good news is that
God doesn't want us to wait. Known (or vilified) under a variety of
names — Word of Faith, Health and Wealth, Name It and Claim It, Prosperity Theology — its emphasis is on God's promised generosity in this
life and the ability of believers to claim
it for themselves. In a nutshell, it suggests that a God who loves you does
not want you to be broke. Its signature
verse could be John 10: 10: "I have
come that they may have life, and that
they may have it more abundantly." In a TIME poll, 17% of Christians
surveyed said they considered themselves part of such a movement,
while a full 61% believed that God wants people to be prosperous.
And 31% — a far higher percentage than there are Pentecostals in
America — agreed that if you give your money to God, God will bless
you with more money.

In a nutshell, it suggests that a
God who loves you does not
want you to be broke.

"Prosperity" first blazed to public attention as the driveshaft in
the moneymaking machine that was 1980s televangelism and faded
from mainstream view with the Jim Bakker and Jimmy Swaggart
scandals. But now, after some key modifications (which have inspired some to redub it Prosperity Lite), it has not only recovered
but is booming. Of the four biggest megachurches in the country,
three — Osteen's Lakewood in Houston; T. D. Jakes' Potter's House
in south Dallas; and Creflo Dollar's World Changers near Atlanta — are
Prosperity or Prosperity Lite pulpits (although Jakes' ministry has

many more facets). While they don't exclusively teach that God's riches want to be in believers' wallets, it is a key part of their doctrine. And propelled by Osteen's 4 million-selling book, *Your Best Life Now,* the belief has swept beyond its Pentecostal base into more buttoned-down evangelical churches, and even into congregations in the more liberal Mainline. It is taught in hundreds of non-Pentecostal Bible studies. One Pennsylvania Lutheran pastor even made it the basis for a sermon series for Lent, when Christians usually meditate on why Jesus was having His Worst Life Then. Says the Rev. Chappell Temple, a Methodist minister with the dubious distinction of pastoring Houston's other Lakewood Church (Lakewood United Methodist), an hour north of Osteen's: "Prosperity Lite is everywhere in Christian culture. Go into any Christian bookstore, and see what they're offering."

The movement's renaissance has infuriated a number of prominent pastors, theologians and commentators. Fellow megapastor Rick Warren, whose book *The Purpose Driven Life* has outsold Osteen's by a ratio of 7 to 1, finds the very basis of Prosperity laughable. "This idea that God wants everybody to be wealthy?", he snorts. "There is a word for that: baloney. It's creating a false idol. You don't measure your self-worth by your net worth. I can show you millions of faithful followers of Christ who live in poverty. Why isn't everyone in the church a millionaire?"

The brickbats — both theological and practical (who really gets rich from this?) — come especially thick from Evangelicals like Warren. Evangelicalism is more prominent and influential than ever before. Yet the movement, which has never had a robust theology of money, finds an aggressive philosophy advancing within its ranks that many of its leaders regard as simplistic, possibly heretical and certainly embarrassing.

Prosperity's defenders claim to be able to match their critics chapter and verse. They caution against broad-brushing a wide spectrum that ranges from pastors who crassly solicit sky's-the-limit financial offerings from their congregations to those whose services tend more toward God-fueled self-help. Advocates note Prosperity's racial diversity — a welcome exception to the American norm — and point out that some Prosperity churches engage in significant charity. And they see in it a happy corrective for Christians who are more used to being chastened for their sins than celebrated as God's children. "Who would want to get in on something where you're miserable, poor, broke and ugly and you just have to muddle through until you get to heaven?" asks Joyce Meyer, a popular television preacher and author often lumped in the Prosperity Lite camp. "I believe God wants to give us nice things." If nothing else, Meyer and other new-breed preachers broach a neglected topic that should really be a staple of Sunday messages: Does God want you to be rich?

As with almost any important religious question, the first response of most Christians (especially Protestants) is to ask how Scripture treats the topic. But Scripture is not definitive when it comes to faith and income. Deuteronomy commands believers to "remember the Lord your God, for it is He who gives you power to get wealth," and the rest of the Old Testament is dotted with celebrations of God's bestowal of the good life. On at least one occasion — the so-called parable of the talents (a type of coin) — Jesus holds up savvy business practice (investing rather than saving) as a metaphor for spiritual practice. Yet he spent far more time among the poor than the rich, and a majority of scholars quote two of his most direct comments on wealth: the passage in the Sermon on the Mount in which he warns, "Do not lay up for yourselves treasures on earth . . . but lay up for yourselves treasures in heaven"; and his encounter with the "rich young ruler" who cannot bring himself to part with his money, after which Jesus famously comments, "It is easier for a camel to go through the eye of a needle than for a rich man to enter the kingdom of God."

Both statements can be read as more nuanced than they at first may seem. In each case it is not wealth itself that disqualifies but the inability to understand its relative worthlessness compared with the riches of heaven. The same thing applies to Paul's famous line, "Money is the root of all evil," in his first letter to Timothy. The actual quote is, "The love of money is a root of all kinds of evil."

So the Bible leaves plenty of room for a discussion on the role, positive or negative, that money should play in the lives of believers. But it's not a discussion that many pastors are willing to have. "Jesus' words about money don't make us very comfortable, and people don't want to hear about it," notes Collin Hansen, an editor at the evangelical monthly Christianity Today. Pastors are happy to discuss from the pulpit hot-button topics like sex and even politics. But the relative absence of sermons about money — which the Bible mentions several thousand times — is one of the more stunning omissions in American religion, especially among its white middle-class precincts. Princeton University sociologist Robert Wuthnow says much of the U.S. church "talks about giving but does not talk about the broader financial concerns people have, or the pressures at work. There has long been a taboo on talking candidly about money."

In addition to personal finances, a lot of evangelical churches have also avoided any pulpit talk about social inequality. When conservative Christianity split from the Mainline in the early 20th century, the latter pursued their commitment to the "social gospel" by working on poverty and other causes such as civil rights and the Vietnam-era peace movement. Evangelicals went the other way: they largely concentrated on issues of individual piety. "We took on personal salvation — we need our sins redeemed, and we need our Saviour," says Warren. But "some people tended to go too individualistic, and justice and righteousness issues were overlooked."

A recent Sunday at Lakewood gives some idea of the emphasis on worldly gain that disturbs Warren. Several hundred stage lights flash on, and Osteen, his gigawatt smile matching them, strides onto the stage of what used to be the Compaq Center sports arena but is now his church. "Let's just celebrate the goodness of the Lord!" Osteen yells. His wife Victoria says, "Our Daddy God is the strongest! He's the mightiest!"

And so it goes, before 14,000 attendees, a nonstop declaration of God's love and his intent to show it in the here and now, sometimes verging on the language of an annual report. During prayer, Osteen thanks God for "your unprecedented favor. We believe that 2006 will be our best year so far. We declare it by faith." Today's sermon is about how gratitude can "save a marriage, save your job [and] get you a promotion." 15

"I don't think I've ever preached a sermon about money," he says a few hours later. He and Victoria meet with *Time* in their pastoral suite, once the Houston Rockets' locker and shower area but now a zone of overstuffed sofas and imposing oak bookcases. "Does God want us to be rich?" he asks. "When I hear that word rich, I think people say, 'Well, he's preaching that everybody's going to be a millionaire.' I don't think that's it." Rather, he explains, "I preach that anybody can improve their lives. I think God wants us to be prosperous. I think he wants us to be happy. To me, you need to have money to pay your bills. I think God wants us to send our kids to college. I think he wants us to be a blessing to other people. But I don't think I'd say God wants us to be rich. It's all relative, isn't it?" The room's warm lamplight reflects softly off his crocodile shoes.

Osteen is a second-generation Prosperity teacher. His father John Osteen started out Baptist but in 1959 withdrew from that fellowship to found a church in one of Houston's poorer neighborhoods and explore a new philosophy developing among Pentecostals. If the rest of Protestantism ignored finances, Prosperity placed them center stage, marrying Pentecostalism's ebullient notion of God's gifts with an older tradition that stressed the power of positive thinking. Practically, it emphasized hard work and good home economics. But the real heat was in its spiritual premise: that if a believer could establish, through word and deed (usually donation), that he or she was "in Jesus Christ," then Jesus' father would respond with paternal gifts of health and wealth in this life. A favorite verse is from Malachi: "'Bring all the tithes into the storehouse . . . and try Me now in this,' says the Lord of hosts. 'If I will not for you open the windows of heaven and pour out for you such blessing that there will not be room enough to receive it.'"

It is a peculiarly American theology but turbocharged. If Puritanism valued wealth and Benjamin Franklin wrote about doing well by doing good, hard-core Prosperity doctrine, still extremely popular in the hands of pastors like Atlanta megachurch minister Creflo Dollar, reads those Bible verses as a spiritual contract. God will pay back a multiple (often a hundredfold) on offerings by the congregation. "Poor people like Prosperity," says Stephen Prothero, chairman of the religion department at Boston University. "They hear it as aspirant. They hear, 'You can make it too — buy a car, get a job, get wealthy.' It can function as a form of liberation." It can also be exploitative. Outsiders, observes Milmon Harrison of the University of California at Davis, author of the book *Righteous Riches,* often see it as "another form of the church abusing people so ministers could make money."

In the past decade, however, the new generation of preachers, like Osteen, Meyer and Houston's Methodist megapastor Kirbyjon Caldwell, who gave the benediction at both of George W. Bush's inaugurals, have repackaged the doctrine. Gone are the divine profit-to-earnings ratios, the requests for offerings far above a normal 10% tithe (although many of the new breed continue to insist that congregants tithe on their pretax rather than their net income). What remains is a materialism framed in a kind of Tony Robbins positivism. No one exemplifies this better than Osteen, who ran his father's television-production department until John died in 1999. "Joel has learned from his dad, but he has toned it back and tapped into basic, everyday folks' ways of talking," says Ben Phillips, a theology professor at the Southwestern Baptist Theological Seminary. That language is reflected in *Your Best Life Now,* an extraordinarily accessible exhortation to this-world empowerment through God. "To live your best life now," it opens, to see "your business taking off. See your marriage restored. See your family prospering. See your dreams come to pass . . ." you must "start looking at life through eyes of faith." Jesus is front and center but not his Crucifixion, Resurrection or Atonement. There are chapters on overcoming trauma and a late chapter on emulating God's generosity. (And indeed, Osteen's church gave more than $1 million in relief money after Hurricane Katrina.) But there are many more illustrations of how the Prosperity doctrine has produced personal gain, most memorably, perhaps, for the Osteen family: how Victoria's "speaking words of faith and victory" eventually brought the couple their dream house; how Joel discerned God's favor in being bumped from economy to business class.

Confronting such stories, certain more doctrinally traditional 20 Christians go ballistic. Last March, Ben Witherington, an influential evangelical theologian at Asbury Seminary in Kentucky, thundered that "we need to renounce the false gospel of wealth and health — it is a disease of our American culture; it is not a solution or answer to life's problems." Respected blogger Michael Spencer — known as the Internet Monk — asked, "How many young people are going to be pointed to Osteen as a true shepherd of Jesus Christ? He's not. He's not one of us." Osteen is an irresistible target for experts from right to left on the Christian spectrum who — beyond worrying that he is living too high or inflating the hopes of people with real money problems — think he is dragging people down with a heavy interlocked chain of theological and ethical errors that could amount to heresy.

Most start out by saying that Osteen and his ilk have it "half right": that God's goodness is biblical, as is the idea that he means us to enjoy the material world. But while Prosperity claims to be celebrating that goodness, the critics see it as treating God as a celestial ATM. "God becomes a means to an end, not the end in himself," says Southwestern Baptist's Phillips. Others are more upset about what it de-emphasizes. "[Prosperity] wants the positive but not the negative," says another Southern Baptist, Alan Branch of Midwestern Baptist Theological Seminary in Kansas City, Mo. "Problem is, we live on this side of Eden. We're fallen." That is, Prosperity soft-pedals the consequences of Adam's fall — sin, pain and death — and their New Testament antidote: Jesus' atoning sacrifice and the importance of repentance. And social liberals express a related frustration that preachers like Osteen show little interest in battling the ills of society at large. Perhaps appropriately so, since, as Prosperity scholar Harrison explains, "philosophically, their main way of helping the poor is encouraging people not to be one of them."

Most unnerving for Osteen's critics is the suspicion that they are fighting not just one idiosyncratic misreading of the gospel but something more daunting: the latest lurch in Protestantism's ongoing descent into full-blown American materialism. After the eclipse of Calvinist Puritanism, whose respect for money was counterbalanced by a horror of worldliness, much of Protestantism quietly adopted the idea that "you don't have to give up the American Dream. You just see it as a sign of God's blessing," says Edith Blumhofer, director of Wheaton College's Center for the Study of American Evangelicals. Indeed, a last-gasp resistance to this embrace of wealth and comfort can be observed in the current evangelical brawl over whether comfortable megachurches (like Osteen's and Warren's) with pumped-up day-care centers and high-tech amenities represent a slide from glorifying an all-powerful God to asking what custom color you would prefer he paint your pews. "The tragedy is that Christianity has become a yes-man for the culture," says Boston University's Prothero.

Non-prosperity parties from both conservative and more progressive evangelical camps recently have been trying to reverse the trend. Eastern University professor Ron Sider's book *Rich Christians in an Age of Hunger,* a fringe classic after its publication in 1977, is selling far more copies now, and some young people are even acting on its rather radical prescriptions: a sprinkling of Protestant groups known loosely as the New Monastics is experimenting with the kind of communal living among the poor that had previously been the province of Catholic orders. Jim Wallis, longtime leader of one such community in Washington and the editor of *Sojourners* magazine, has achieved immense exposure lately with his pleas that Evangelicals engage in more political activism on behalf of the poor.

And then there is Warren himself, who by virtue of his energy, hypereloquence and example (he's working in Rwanda with government, business and church sectors) has become a spokesman for church activism. "The church is the largest network in the world," he says. "If you have 2.3 billion people who claim to be followers of Christ, that's bigger than China."

And despite Warren's disdain for Prosperity's theological claims, 25 some Prosperity churches have become players in the very faith-based antipoverty world he inhabits, even while maintaining their distinctive theology. Kirbyjon Caldwell, who pastors Windsor Village, the largest (15,000) United Methodist church in the country, can sound as Prosperity as the next pastor: "Jesus did not die and get up off the Cross so we could live lives full of despair and disappointment," he says. He quotes the "abundant life" verse with all earnestness, even giving it a real estate gloss: "It is unscriptural not to own land," he announces. But he's doing more than talk about it. He recently oversaw the building of Corinthian Pointe, a 452-unit affordable-housing project that he claims is the largest residential subdivision ever built by a nonprofit. Most of its inhabitants, he says, are not members of his church.

Caldwell knows that prosperity is a loaded term in evangelical circles. But he insists that "it depends on how you define prosperity. I am not a proponent of saying the Lord's name three times, clicking your heels and then you get what you ask for. But you cannot give what you do not have. We are fighting what we call the social demons. If I am going to help someone, I am going to have to have something with which to help."

Caldwell knows that the theology behind this preacherly rhetoric will never be acceptable to Warren or Sider or Witherington. But the man they all follow said, "By their fruits you will know them," and for some, Corinthian Pointe is a very convincing sort of fruit. Hard-line Prosperity theology may always seem alien to those with enough money to imagine making more without engaging God in a kind of spiritual quid pro quo. And Osteen's version, while it abandons part of that magical thinking, may strike some as self-centered rather than God centered. But American Protestantism is a dynamic faith. Caldwell's version reminds us that there is no reason a giving God could not invest even an awkward and needy creed with a mature and generous heart. If God does want us to be rich in this life, no doubt it's this richness in spirit that he is most eager for us to acquire.

Verses vs. Verses

The Bible spends a lot of time talking about money. And both sides of the Prosperity camp point to passages that support their view.

It's God's Gift

Then you say in your heart, "My power and the might of my hand have gained me this wealth." And you shall remember the Lord your God, for it is He who gives you power to get wealth, that He may establish His covenant which He swore to your fathers, as it is this day. Deuteronomy 8: 17–18

. . .

Here is what I have seen: It is good and fitting for one to eat and 30 drink, and to enjoy the good of all his labor in which he toils under the sun all the days of his life which God gives him; for it is his heritage.

As for every man to whom God has given riches and wealth, and given him power to eat of it, to receive his heritage and rejoice in his labor — this is the gift of God. Ecclesiastes 5: 18–19

• • •

"Bring all the tithes into the storehouse, that there may be food in my house, and try Me now in this," says the Lord of hosts. "If I will not open for you the windows of heaven, and pour out for you such blessing that there will not be room enough to receive it." Malachi 3: 10

• • •

Give, and it will be given to you: good measure, pressed down, shaken together, and running over will be put into your bosom. For with the same measure that you use, it will be measured back to you. Luke 6: 38

• • •

Then Jesus said . . . "I have come that they may have life, and have it more abundantly. John 10: 10

No, It's Not

Do not be afraid when one becomes rich, when the glory of his house is increased; For when he dies he shall carry nothing away; His glory shall not descend after him. Though while he lives he blesses himself — For men will praise you when you do well for yourself — He shall go to the generation of his fathers; They shall never see light. A man who is in honor, yet does not understand is like the beasts that perish. Psalm 49: 16–20

• • •

Do not lay up for yourselves treasures on earth, where moth and rust 35 destroy and where thieves break in and steal; but lay up for yourselves treasures in heaven, where neither moth nor rust destroys and where thieves do not break in and steal. For where your treasure is, there your heart will be also. Matthew 6: 19–21

• • •

It is easier for a camel to go through the eye of a needle than for a rich man to enter the kingdom of God. Mark 10: 24–26

• • •

Sell what you have and give alms; provide yourselves money bags which do not grow old, a treasure in the heavens that does not fail, where no thief approaches nor moth destroys. Luke 12: 33

• • •

Come now, you rich, weep and howl for your miseries that are coming upon you! Your riches are corrupted, and your garments are moth-eaten. Your gold and silver are corroded, and their corrosion will be a witness against you and will eat your flesh like fire. James 5: 1–3

Understanding the Text

1. Take a sheet of paper and fold it in half vertically. On the left, list Joel Osteen's views on God and money. On the right, do the same for Rick Warren's views. Are the differences as big as the authors of this article make them out to be? Not as big? Bigger?

Reflection and Response

2. If you believe there is a God, with which of these two preachers' views — the wealth-promoting Joel Osteen's or his fellow "megapastor" Rick Warren's — do you tend to agree? Why?

   If you are an agnostic or atheist, which of these two men are you happier to see influence public attitudes about wealth? Why?

3. In paragraph 16, Osteen objects that he has never told people to amass riches. Are you persuaded by the distinction he makes?

   Do you think it fair of the reporter to point out that Osteen is wearing crocodile shoes?

4. Is there a good way to reconcile the Biblical quotations in the section of this article headed "Verses vs. Verses"? (There may or may not be.) Spell out your thinking through a close reading of the quoted texts.

Making Connections

5. As Christians, are both Osteen and Warren equally far in outlook from E. F. Schumacher ("Buddhist Economics," p. 307)? Explain.

6. In 1904, sociologist Max Weber set out to explain why so many European and American capitalists — merchants, investors, etc. — were also pious members of a church. He didn't see a similar merging of commerce with religion throughout most of the world. He believed that in most places, business and spiritual life didn't mix.

   In his classic work, *The Protestant Ethic and the Spirit of Capitalism,* Weber concludes that modern free enterprise sprang from a strand of Christianity known as Calvinism, essentially the same tradition out of which the American Pilgrims and Puritans came. He makes Benjamin Franklin his main case in point.

   Read *The Protestant Ethic and the Spirit of Capitalism.* How good an argument does Weber advance for the link between a person's theology and his/her participation in commerce?

7. Interview a friend or family member who is wealthy — or find a wide-ranging interview with a wealthy person, and read it. Does that individual attribute his/her status in life partly to unseen forces at work? Fate? Luck? A protective deity?

The Banker and His Wife

Quentin Massys

A banker weighs the coins that someone has deposited with him. (Maybe they're the coins of the man visible in the small mirror on his desk.) Next to the banker sits his wife, who has been reading — or at least browsing in — a holy book. The creator of this famous painting (1514) seems to have both money and the higher values on his mind.

Straddling the fifteenth and sixteenth centuries, the Flemish painter Quentin Massys belonged to a family of artists. He was celebrated for his religious works.

For a color version of this, do a Web search using both the painting's title and the artist's name.

Understanding the Text

1. What, if anything, is the painter of this scene telling us about the incompatibility — or compatibility — of money and religion?

   In pondering this question, consider:

   • where the banker's wife's eyes are directed

   • which of the two main items on the table — the money or the holy book — is being handled more reverentially

   • what colors the two figures wear (This and the next bullet require that you find an image of the painting online, to see it in full color.)

   • their complexions

   • what the banker's wife's facial expression reveals (Is it longing? Could it be lament? Could it be both?)

Reflection and Response

2. Do the banker and his wife seem "modern" to you? That is, if you replaced their apparel with contemporary clothes, would you have any difficulty believing that such people are alive today? Why or why not?

3. Reportedly, the frame around this painting — which may or may not have been chosen by the painter — once bore a Biblical inscription: "Just balances, just weights, . . . shall ye have" (Leviticus 19: 36 — the word "just" here means "exact and fair"). Should that line be borne in mind in interpreting the work?

Making Connections

4. Read the article "Does God Want You to Be Rich" (p. 293). What might Joel Osteen want to believe about the banker and his wife? What might Rick Warren want to believe about them? What makes you say so?

5. What might E. F. Schumacher ("Buddhist Economics," p. 307) want to believe about these two people?

Buddhist Economics

E. F. Schumacher

The title of this author's bestselling book of 1966, *Small Is Beautiful,* is practically synonymous with the saying "Less is more" — a slogan of people who advocate living more simply on smaller incomes. The reading below was excerpted from that book.

E. F. Schumacher fled his native Germany before World War II to escape Hitler's Nazi regime and, after the war, worked for the British commission responsible for helping to rebuild Germany's economy. As an economic consultant to Burma beginning in 1955, he developed the ideas that led to publication of *Small Is Beautiful.*

Note: Schumacher wrote his book before the Feminist movement of the late 1960s and 1970s. Today, he might not have referred to childcare as women's work.

"Right livelihood" is one of the requirements of the Buddha's Noble Eightfold Path. It is clear, therefore, that there must be such a thing as Buddhist economics.

Buddhist countries have often stated that they wish to remain faithful to their heritage. So Burma: "The New Burma sees no conflict between religious values and economic progress. Spiritual health and material well-being are not enemies: they are natural allies." Or: "We can blend successfully the religious and spiritual values of our heritage with the benefits of modern technology."[1] Or: "We Burmans have a sacred duty to conform both our dreams and our acts to our faith. This we shall ever do."[2]

All the same, such countries invariably assume that they can model their economic development plans in accordance with modern economics, and they call upon modern economists from so-called advanced countries to advise them, to formulate the policies to be pursued, and to construct the grand design for development, the Five-Year Plan or whatever it may be called. No one seems to think that a Buddhist way of life would call for Buddhist economics, just as the modern materialist way of life has brought forth modern economics.

Economists themselves, like most specialists, normally suffer from a kind of metaphysical blindness, assuming that theirs is a science of

---

[1] *The New Burma* (Economic and Social Board, Government of the Union of Burma, 1954).
[2] Ibid.

absolute and invariable truths, without any presuppositions. Some go as far as to claim that economic laws are as free from "metaphysics" or "values" as the law of gravitation. We need not, however, get involved in arguments of methodology. Instead, let us take some fundamentals and see what they look like when viewed by a modern economist and a Buddhist economist.

There is universal agreement that a fundamental source of wealth 5 is human labor. Now, the modern economist has been brought up to consider "labor" or work as little more than a necessary evil. From the point of view of the employer, it is in any case simply an item of cost, to be reduced to a minimum if it cannot be eliminated altogether, say, by automation. From the point of view of the workman, it is a "disutility"; to work is to make a sacrifice of one's leisure and comfort, and wages are a kind of compensation for the sacrifice. Hence the ideal from the point of view of the employer is to have output without employees, and the ideal from the point of view of the employee is to have income without employment.

The consequences of these attitudes both in theory and in practice are, of course, extremely far-reaching. If the ideal with regard to work is to get rid of it, every method that "reduces the work load" is a good thing. The most potent method, short of automation, is the so-called "division of labor" and the classical example is the pin factory eulogized in Adam Smith's *Wealth of Nations*.[3] Here it is not a matter of ordinary specialization, which mankind has practiced from time immemorial, but of dividing up every complete process of production into minute parts, so that the final product can be produced at great speed without anyone having had to contribute more than a totally insignificant and, in most cases, unskilled movement of his limbs.

The Buddhist point of view takes the function of work to be at least threefold: to give a man a chance to utilize and develop his faculties; to enable him to overcome his ego-centeredness by joining with other people in a common task; and to bring forth the goods and services needed for a becoming existence. Again, the consequences that flow from this view are endless. To organize work in such a manner that it becomes meaningless, boring, stultifying, or nerve-racking for the worker would be little short of criminal; it would indicate a greater concern with goods than with people, an evil lack of compassion and a soul-destroying degree of attachment to the most primitive side of this worldly existence. Equally, to strive for leisure as an alternative

---

[3] Ibid.

to work would be considered a complete misunderstanding of one of the basic truths of human existence, namely that work and leisure are complementary parts of the same living process and cannot be separated without destroying the joy of work and the bliss of leisure.

From the Buddhist point of view, there are therefore two types of mechanization which must be clearly distinguished: one that enhances a man's skill and power and one that turns the work of man over to a mechanical slave, leaving man in a position of having to serve the slave. How to tell the one from the other? "The craftsman himself," says Ananda Coomaraswamy, a man equally competent to talk about the modern West as the ancient East, "can always, if allowed to, draw the delicate distinction between the machine and the tool. The carpet loom is a tool, a contrivance for holding warp threads at a stretch for the pile to be woven round them by the craftsmen's fingers; but the power loom is a machine, and its significance as a destroyer of culture lies in the fact that it does the essentially human part of the work."[4] It is clear, therefore, that Buddhist economics must be very different from the economics of modern materialism, since the Buddhist sees the essence of civilisation not in a multiplication of wants but in the purification of human character. Character, at the same time, is formed primarily by a man's work.

> The Buddhist sees the essence of civilization not in a multiplication of wants but in the purification of human character.

And work, properly conducted in conditions of human dignity and freedom, blesses those who do it and equally their products. The Indian philosopher and economist J. C. Kumarappa sums the matter up as follows:

If the nature of the work is properly appreciated and applied, it will stand in the same relation to the higher faculties as food is to the physical body. It nourishes and enlivens the higher man and urges him to produce the best he is capable of. It directs his free will along the proper course and disciplines the animal in him into progressive channels. It furnishes an excellent background for man to display his scale of values and develop his personality.[5]

---

[4] *Art and Swadeshi* by Ananda K. Coomaraswamy (Ganesh & Co., Madras).
[5] *Economy of Permanence* by J. C. Kumarappa (Sarva-Seva Sangh Publication, Rajghat, Kashi, 4th edn., 1958).

If a man has no chance of obtaining work he is in a desperate position, not simply because he lacks an income but because he lacks this nourishing and enlivening factor of disciplined work which nothing can replace. A modern economist may engage in highly sophisticated calculations on whether full employment "pays" or whether it might be more "economic" to run an economy at less than full employment so as to ensure a greater mobility of labor, a better stability of wages, and so forth. His fundamental criterion of success is simply the total quantity of goods produced during a given period of time. "If the marginal urgency of goods is low," says Professor Galbraith in *The Affluent Society*, "then so is the urgency of employing the last man or the last million men in the labour force."[6] And again: "If . . . we can afford some unemployment in the interest of stability — a proposition, incidentally, of impeccably conservative antecedents — then we can afford to give those who are unemployed the goods that enable them to sustain their accustomed standard of living."

From a Buddhist point of view, this is standing the truth on its head 10 by considering goods as more important than people and consumption as more important than creative activity. It means shifting the emphasis from the worker to the product of work, that is, from the human to the subhuman, a surrender to the forces of evil. The very start of Buddhist economic planning would be a planning for full employment, and the primary purpose of this would in fact be employment for everyone who needs an "outside" job: it would not be the maximization of employment nor the maximization of production. Women, on the whole, do not need an "outside" job, and the large-scale employment of women in offices or factories would be considered a sign of serious economic failure. In particular, to let mothers of young children work in factories while the children run wild would be as uneconomic in the eyes of a Buddhist economist as the employment of a skilled worker as a soldier in the eyes of a modern economist.

While the materialist is mainly interested in goods, the Buddhist is mainly interested in liberation. But Buddhism is "The Middle Way" and therefore in no way antagonistic to physical well-being. It is not wealth that stands in the way of liberation but the attachment to wealth; not the enjoyment of pleasurable things but the craving for them. The keynote of Buddhist economics, therefore, is simplicity and non-violence. From an economist's point of view, the marvel of the

---

[6] *The Affluent Society* by John Kenneth Galbraith (Penguin Books Ltd., 1962).

Buddhist way of life is the utter rationality of its pattern — amazingly small means leading to extraordinarily satisfactory results.

For the modern economist this is very difficult to understand. He is used to measuring the "standard of living" by the amount of annual consumption, assuming all the time that a man who consumes more is "better off" than a man who consumes less. A Buddhist economist would consider this approach excessively irrational: since consumption is merely a means to human well-being, the aim should be to obtain the maximum of well-being with the minimum of consumption. Thus, if the purpose of clothing is a certain amount of temperature comfort and an attractive appearance, the task is to attain this purpose with the smallest possible effort, that is, with the smallest annual destruction of cloth and with the help of designs that involve the smallest possible input of toil. The less toil there is, the more time and strength is left for artistic creativity. It would be highly uneconomic, for instance, to go in for complicated tailoring, like the modern West, when a much more beautiful effect can be achieved by the skillful draping of uncut material. It would be the height of folly to make material so that it should wear out quickly and the height of barbarity to make anything ugly, shabby, or mean. What has just been said about clothing applies equally to all other human requirements. The ownership and the consumption of goods is a means to an end, and Buddhist economics is the systematic study of how to attain given ends with the minimum means.

Modern economics, on the other hand, considers consumption to be the sole end and purpose of all economic activity, taking the factors of production — land, labor, and capital — as the means. The former, in short, tries to maximize human satisfactions by the optimal pattern of consumption, while the latter tries to maximize consumption by the optimal pattern of productive effort. It is easy to see that the effort needed to sustain a way of life which seeks to attain the optimal pattern of consumption is likely to be much smaller than the effort needed to sustain a drive for maximum consumption. We need not be surprised, therefore, that the pressure and strain of living is very much less in, say, Burma than it is in the United States, in spite of the fact that the amount of labor-saving machinery used in the former country is only a minute fraction of the amount used in the latter.

Simplicity and non-violence are obviously closely related. The optimal pattern of consumption, producing a high degree of human satisfaction by means of a relatively low rate of consumption, allows people to live without great pressure and strain and to fulfill the primary injunction of Buddhist teaching: "Cease to do evil; try to do good." As physical resources are everywhere limited, people satisfying their needs by means of a modest use of resources are obviously less likely to be at each other's throats than people depending upon a high rate of use. Equally, people who live in highly self-sufficient local communities are less likely to get involved in large-scale violence than people whose existence depends on worldwide systems of trade.

From the point of view of Buddhist economics, therefore, produc-   15
tion from local resources for local needs is the most rational way of economic life, while dependence on imports from afar and the consequent need to produce for export to unknown and distant peoples is highly uneconomic and justifiable only in exceptional cases and on a small scale. Just as the modern economist would admit that a high rate of consumption of transport services between a man's home and his place of work signifies a misfortune and not a high standard of life, so the Buddhist economist would hold that to satisfy human wants from faraway sources rather than from sources nearby signifies failure rather than success. The former tends to take statistics showing an increase in the number of ton/miles per head of the population carried by a country's transport system as proof of economic progress, while to the latter — the Buddhist economist — the same statistics would indicate a highly undesirable deterioration in the *pattern* of consumption.

Another striking difference between modern economics and Buddhist economics arises over the use of natural resources. Bertrand de Jouvenel, the eminent French political philosopher, has characterized "Western man" in words which may be taken as a fair description of the modern economist:

He tends to count nothing as an expenditure, other than human effort; he does not seem to mind how much mineral matter he wastes and, far worse, how much living matter he destroys. He does not seem to realise at all that human life is a dependent part of an ecosystem of many different forms of life. As the world is ruled from towns where men are cut off from any form of life other than human, the feeling of belonging to an ecosystem is not revived. This results in a harsh and improvident treatment of things upon which we ultimately depend, such as water and trees.[7]

The teaching of the Buddha, on the other hand, enjoins a reverent and non-violent attitude not only to all sentient beings but also, with

---

[7] *A Philosophy of Indian Economic Development* by Richard B. Gregg (Navajivan Publishing House, Ahmedabad, India, 1958).

great emphasis, to trees. Every follower of the Buddha ought to plant a tree every few years and look after it until it is safely established, and the Buddhist economist can demonstrate without difficulty that the universal observation of this rule would result in a high rate of genuine economic development independent of any foreign aid. Much of the economic decay of southeast Asia (as of many other parts of the world) is undoubtedly due to a heedless and shameful neglect of trees.

Modern economics does not distinguish between renewable and non-renewable materials, as its very method is to equalize and quantify everything by means of a money price. Thus, taking various alternative fuels, like coal, oil, wood, or water-power: the only difference between them recognized by modern economics is relative cost per equivalent unit. The cheapest is automatically the one to be preferred, as to do otherwise would be irrational and "uneconomic." From a Buddhist point of view, of course, this will not do; the essential difference between non-renewable fuels like coal and oil on the one hand and renewable fuels like wood and water-power on the other cannot be simply overlooked. Non-renewable goods must be used only if they are indispensable, and then only with the greatest care and the most meticulous concern for conservation. To use them heedlessly or extravagantly is an act of violence, and while complete non-violence may not be attainable on this earth, there is nonetheless an ineluctable duty on man to aim at the ideal of nonviolence in all he does.

Just as a modern European economist would not consider it a great economic achievement if all European art treasures were sold to America at attractive prices, so the Buddhist economist would insist that a population basing its economic life on non-renewable fuels is living parasitically, on capital instead of income. Such a way of life could have no permanence and could therefore be justified only as a purely temporary expedient. As the world's resources of non-renewable fuels — coal, oil, and natural gas — are exceedingly unevenly distributed over the globe and undoubtedly limited in quantity, it is clear that their exploitation at an ever-increasing rate is an act of violence against nature which must almost inevitably lead to violence between men.

This fact alone might give food for thought even to those people in 20 Buddhist countries who care nothing for the religious and spiritual values of their heritage and ardently desire to embrace the materialism of modern economics at the fastest possible speed. Before they dismiss Buddhist economics as nothing better than a nostalgic dream, they might wish to consider whether the path of economic development outlined by modern economics is likely to lead them to places where they really want to be. Towards the end of his courageous book *The Challenge of Man's Future*, Professor Harrison Brown of the California Institute of Technology gives the following appraisal:

Thus we see that, just as industrial society is fundamentally unstable and subject to reversion to agrarian existence, so within it the conditions which offer individual freedom are unstable in their ability to avoid the conditions which impose rigid organisation and totalitarian control. Indeed, when we examine all of the foreseeable difficulties which threaten the survival of industrial civilisation, it is difficult to see how the achievement of stability and the maintenance of individual liberty can be made compatible.[8]

Even if this were dismissed as a long-term view there is the immediate question of whether "modernization," as currently practiced without regard to religious and spiritual values, is actually producing agreeable results. As far as the masses are concerned, the results appear to be disastrous — a collapse of the rural economy, a rising tide of unemployment in town and country, and the growth of a city proletariat without nourishment for either body or soul.

It is in the light of both immediate experience and long-term prospects that the study of Buddhist economics could be recommended even to those who believe that economic growth is more important than any spiritual or religious values. For it is not a question of choosing between "modern growth" and "traditional stagnation." It is a question of finding the right path of development, the Middle Way between materialist heedlessness and traditionalist immobility, in short, of finding "Right Livelihood."

---

[8] *The Challenge of Man's Future* by Harrison Brown (The Viking Press, New York, 1954).

Understanding the Text

1. How many of the differences between "modern economics" and "Buddhist economics" can you recall from your reading of Schumacher's essay? Scan the piece again. Did you forget any differences or distort any? Which ones?

2. Schumacher once said, "Economics without Buddhism, i.e., without spiritual, human, and ecological values, is like sex without love." Is that thought consistent with his essay? Why or why not?

Reflection and Response

3. What, if any, aspects of Buddhist economics do you find attractive? Why?
   What aspects, if any, repel you?

Making Connections

4. At the end of "Does God Want You to Be Rich?" (p. 293), a list of contradictory
   quotations from the Bible demonstrates that Jews and Christians can find
   scriptural support both for and against pursuing wealth. Is the same true of
   Buddhists and their sacred writings? Find out.

5. How do other religions, such as Hinduism and Islam, deal with money-
   making? Name a religion that intrigues you, and find out what you can about
   its view of money. (For example, in the case of Islam, you might want to focus
   on the concept of *riba* — money, such as interest on loans, that is forbidden
   because it is begotten by money itself, rather than by labor.)

6. Theologian Paul Tillich has defined religious faith as ". . . the state of being
   grasped by an ultimate concern, a concern which makes all other concerns
   secondary and which itself contains the answer to the question of the
   meaning of life."

   Some authors represented in this book might say that, by that definition,
   money has gone from being a subject religions address to becoming a religion
   in its own right. Would you agree?

   While pondering the matter, be sure to consult not only your assigned
   readings in the last section of this book, but also any readings that appear in
   other sections but may be relevant. (See, for example, "Lethal Consumption,"
   p. 75.) In addition, draw on personal experience and observations.

Acknowledgments (*continued from page iv*)

Text Credits

Briallen and Johanna Hopper. "Should Working-Class People Get B.A.'s and Ph.D.'s?" from *Chronicle of Higher Education*, March 29, 2012. Copyright © 2012 Briallen Hopper and Johanna Hopper. Reprinted with permission of the authors.

Arianna Huffington. "CSI USA: Who Killed the American Dream?" from *Third World America: How Our Politicians Are Abandoning the Middle Class and Betraying the American Dream* by Arianna Huffington. Copyright © 2010, 2011 by Arianna Huffington. Used by permission of Crown Publishers, a division of Random House, Inc. Any third party use of this material, outside of this publication, is prohibited. Interested parties must apply directly to Random House, Inc. for permission.

Georges de la Tour. *The Fortune Teller*. Courtesy of the Bridgeman Art Library.

Mary Loftus. Excerpts from "Till Debt Do Us Part" from *Psychology Today*, November 1, 2004. Copyright © 2004 Psychology Today. Reprinted by permission of Sussex Publishers, LLC. www.Psychologytoday.com.

Maimonides. *Mishneh Torah*. Twelfth century.

Mary Kay, Inc. "Truth about Abuse Survey" from National Findings from Third Survey of Domestic Violence Shelters in the United States, Released April 2011. Reprinted by permission of Mary Kay, Inc.

Quentin Massys. *The Banker and His Wife*. Courtesy of Giraudon/The Bridgeman Art Library.

MasterCard "Priceless" TV Ads. "There are some things money can't buy. For everything else, there's MasterCard." Copyright © MasterCard. Reprinted by permission of MasterCard.

Charles Murray. "What's So Bad about Being Poor?" from *National Review*, October 28, 1988. Copyright © 1988 by National Review, Inc. Reprinted by permission.

David G. Myers. Excerpts from "The Funds, Friends, and Faith of Happy People" from *American Psychologist*, Vol. 55 (1), January 2000. Copyright © 2000 by the American Psychological Association. Reprinted with permission. The use of this information does not imply endorsement by the publisher.

Meera Nair. Excerpt from "My Inheritance" from *Money Changes Everything: Twenty-two Writers Tackle the Last Taboo with Tales of Sudden Windfalls, Staggering Debts, and Other Surprising Turns of Fortune*, edited by Jenny Offill and Elissa Schappell. Copyright © 2007 by Jenny Offill and Elissa Schappell. Used by permission of Doubleday, a division of Random House, Inc. Any third party use of this material, outside of this publication, is prohibited. Interested parties must apply directly to Random House, Inc. for permission.

Occupy Wall Street. "You Can't Evict an Idea Whose Time Has Come." Reprinted by permission of Occupy Solidarity Network.

Michael Powell. "Wealth, Race, and the Great Recession" from *The New York Times*, May 17, 2010. Copyright © 2010 The New York Times. All rights reserved. Used by permission and protected by the Copyright Laws of the United States. The printing, copying, redistribution, or retransmission of this Content without express written permission is prohibited.

Diego Rivera. *The First Tractor* and *Night of the Rich* courtesy of Schalkwijk/Art Resource, NY.

Norman Rockwell. *New Kids in the Neighborhood*. Norman Rockwell Museum Collections. Printed by permission of the Norman Rockwell Family Agency. Copyright © 1967 the Norman Rockwell Family Entities.

Michael Sandel. "Military Service" from *What Money Can't Buy: The Moral Limits of Markets* (pp. 109–114). The Tanner Lectures on Human Values, Vol. 21, edited by Grethe B. Peterson. Copyright © 2000 Salt Lake City: University of Utah Press. Reprinted by permission of The University of Utah Press.

Melanie Scheller. "On the Meaning of Plumbing and Poverty" by Melanie Scheller. Originally published in *The Independently Weekly.* Copyright © 1990 Melanie Scheller. Reprinted by permission of the author.

Juliet B. Schor. "When Spending Becomes You" (pp. 67–68) from *The Overspent American* by Juliet B. Schor. Copyright © 1998 Juliet B. Schor. Reprinted by permission of HarperCollins Publishers.

E. F. Schumacher. "Buddhist Economics" (pp. 56–66) from *Small Is Beautiful: Economics as if People Mattered* by E. F. Schumacher. Copyright © 1973 by E. F. Schumacher. Published by Hutchinson. Reprinted by permission of HarperCollins Publishers and The Random House Group Limited.

Peter Singer. "Rich and Poor," (pp. 191–200) from *Practical Ethics 3/e.* Copyright © 1980, 1993, 2011 Peter Singer. Reprinted with the permission of Cambridge University Press.

Mark Slouka. "Quitting the Paint Factory: On the Virtues of Idleness" by Mark Slouka from *Harper's Magazine,* November 2004. Copyright © 2004 by Harper's Magazine. All rights reserved. Reproduced from the November issue by special permission.

Bradley A. Smith. Excerpt from *Unfree Speech.* Copyright © 2001 Princeton University Press, 2003 paperback edition. Reprinted by permission of Princeton University Press.

Sheldon Solomon, Jeff Greenberg, and Thomas A. Pyszczynski. Excerpts from "Lethal Consumption: Death-Denying Materialism" from *Psychology and Consumer Culture: The Struggle for a Good Life in a Materialistic World.* Edited by Tim Kasser and Allen D. Kanner. Copyright © 2003 by the American Psychological Association. Reprinted with permission. The use of this information does not imply endorsement by the publisher.

Murray A. Sperber. Excerpt from "College Sports, Inc: How Big-Time Athletic Departments Run Interference for College, Inc." from *Buying In or Selling Out? The Commercialization of the American Research University.* Edited by Donald G. Stein, Rutgers University Press, Piscataway, NJ, 2004. Copyright © 2004 Murray A. Sperber. Reprinted by permission of Murray A. Sperber.

David Van Biema and Jeff Chu. "Does God Want You to Be Rich?" from *Time,* September 10, 2006. Copyright © TIME INC. Reprinted by permission. TIME is a registered trademark of Time Inc. All rights reserved.

Andy Warhol and Jean-Michel Basquiat. *Collaboration (Dollar Sign, Don't Tread on Me),* 1984–1985 Collection of The Andy Warhol Museum, Pittsburgh. Copyright © 2013 The Andy Warhol Foundation for the Visual Arts, Inc./Artist Rights Society, New York. Copyright © The Estate of Jean-Michel Basquiat/ADAGP, Paris/ARS, New York 2013.

Elizabeth Warren. Excerpt from *Ending Poverty in America.* Copyright © 2007 by the University of North Carolina at Chapel Hill on behalf of the Center on Poverty, Work and Opportunity. "The Vanishing Middle Class," copyright © 2007 Elizabeth Warren. Reprinted by permission of The New Press. www.thenewpress.com.

Image Credits

Pages 13, **14**, **83**, **84**, **119**, **120**, **193**, **194**, **245**, and **246**, © Steven Puetzer/Getty Images. **90**, Norman Rockwell Museum Collections. Printed by permission of the Norman Rockwell Family Agency, © 1967 the Norman Rockwell Family Entities. **222**, The Bridgeman Art Library. **224**, © 2013 Banco de México Diego Rivera Frida Kahlo Museums Trust, Mexico, D. F./Artists Rights Society (ARS), New York. Schalkwijk/Art Resource, New York. **225**, © 2013 Banco de México Diego Rivera Frida Kahlo Museums Trust, Mexico, D. F./Artists Rights Society (ARS), New York. Schalkwijk/Art Resource, New York. **265**, *Collaboration (Dollar Sign, Don't Tread on Me),* 1984–1985 Collection of The Andy Warhol Museum, Pittsburgh, © 2013 The Andy Warhol Foundation for the Visual Arts, Inc./Artist Rights Society, New York, © 2013 The Estate of Jean-Michel Basquiat/ADAGP, Paris/ARS, New York. **305**, Giraudon/The Bridgeman Art Library.

Index of Authors and Titles